You're
Still
Away

You're Still Away

Golfing with Tiger and Ernie and Emeril and Clint

Golfing in Scotland and Singapore and Cork and Clare

Golfing well and poorly, in illness and in health, for richer and for poorer

Golfing for fun

Golfing for all of us

by Robert Sullivan

MAPLE STREET PRESS
HINGHAM, MA

The pieces in this book were previously published, sometimes in slightly different form or with different titles, in *Attache*, *Sports Illustrated* and *Travel + Leisure Golf*—reprinted by permission. Chapter XXII, "Fine Feathered Friends," first appeared in the United States Golf Association's Golf Journal, which no longer publishes. It is herein reprinted by permission of the USGA.

Front cover photo © 2007 SXC. Reprinted with permission.
Author jacket photo: Wendy Speake
Jacket design: Garrett Cullen
Interior design: Bryan Davidson

Robert Sullivan. *You're Still Away*
ISBN 978-1-934186-04-6

Library of Congress Control Number: 2007926993

Maple Street Press LLC
11 Leavitt Street
Hingham, MA 02043
www.maplestreetpress.com

Printed in the United States of America
07 7 6 5 4 3 2 First Printing

For Luci,
sometimes on Sundays a golf-writer widow,
with love

Table of Contents

Listening, Remembering, Telling the Tale

A Foreword by Brad Faxon

Back in the mid 1970s, I was fortunate enough to spend much of my time at a golf course called Eastward Ho! in Chatham, Massachusetts. My dad, who was a scratch golfer with a handicap of six (that is supposed to be funny), would take me with him on weekends to caddy for his group. Eastward Ho! was a magnificent, undulating course saddled next to Cape Cod's Pleasant Bay. It was the hilliest course you could imagine; only the most fit dared to walk it. Being a caddy at Eastward Ho! wasn't unlike serving as a Sherpa guide in the Himalayas.

To hazard another metaphor, the golf bags we lugged felt like washing machines. They were filled with golf balls, umbrellas, ball retrievers, suntan lotions, old gloves, extra socks, caps and rain gear. Some of the guys were experimenting with weighted devices that attached to the shaft of a club to help them warm up; after a few morning practice swings, these were relegated to a bottom pocket of the bag—extra ballast. Those were enormous, colorful, Rodney Dangerfield bags, bedecked with tags from all the dozens of courses "your man" had ever played. Did I say "man"? I meant men. Though the notion of carrying even one of those bags around and up and down Eastward Ho! for six miles was ridiculous, most of us would carry two. And as I remember it, your pair of players would very likely hit a hook and slice on the same hole—happened all the time—doubling the difficulty of your job. Our Sherpa trek was seldom a straight line but almost always side to side. Then, of course, there were the left-behind headcovers, and the mad sprints back down the fairway in the hundred-degree midsummer heat.

At Eastward Ho! I discovered for a certainty that the golf course was where I wanted to be.

My dad was a good enough player with good enough friends, and I looked forward to those weekends with keen anticipation. There was Jack Bailey, who had infinite wisdom, and Malcolm Fletcher, who never was without a smile (even if he always looked like he was recovering from the previous night). Dave MacNaughton was slender and quiet, with an elegant swing for such a tall man. Dan Keefe, the head golf professional and former Brown University hockey player, gave me my first lesson. There was, also, Congressman Tip O'Neill, the Speaker of the House, who never walked the course, never was without his cigar, and never hit an iron. He liked to have a fore caddy and he liked my dad, so I got to spend a few rounds with him, learning a little more about the Kennedys and about Watergate than a young man should.

It was during those impressionistic years that I realized the sport of golf was not only an athletic endeavor, but had a social side that was equally important. My dad's foursomes never played at the crack of dawn but would leisurely show up around 10 and finish in mid-afternoon. After playing, they repaired to the outdoor porch, which overlooked Eastward Ho!'s demanding 466-yard par-4 18th. This was headquarters for the next few hours as lunch was served and Miller Lites were consumed. (Many days, it seemed, lunch *was* Miller Lites!) I would get a club sandwich and a Coke and listen as the men replayed their rounds and opined about everything that had to do with anything.

I came to believe during those lazy late afternoons that there was nothing quite as entertaining—even exciting—as golf stories. Jack Bailey was the elder of my dad's gang, and he was well traveled. He had known great players, and told stories about Hogan and Palmer. He taught me terms like "Texas wedge" (just by the way, that's a putter when used from off the green) and could paint a picture of a golf course with his marvelous words. One day, after a "quick shrimp" on the last hole ended up out of play and on the beach, Mr. Bailey coined a mellifluous phrase that became semi-famous at the club: "End the day in Pleasant Bay."

My quest for golf was on at this point, and I started reading anything I could about the game. I wanted to pile up stories—stories like Mr. Bailey's, stories about the great players, stories of fact and fiction, lore and legend. I began with bios of Nicklaus and Palmer, and loved reading anything by Dan Jenkins. The humor and eloquence of P. G. Wodehouse and the imagery and eloquence of Herbert Warren Wind captured my mind.

I'm sure that Robert Sullivan has been influenced by those writers, and I've got to believe he has spent time on a veranda that was just like the magical porch at Eastward Ho! I've always felt that we New Englanders are an observant bunch. We can be matter-of-fact or blunt, crass or terse (which is exactly what the writer Michael Bamberger labeled me in the second chapter of *The Green Road Home* [Thunder's Mouth Press, 2006]; I took it as a compliment, sort of, figuring he meant I was not afraid to express whatever I was thinking about). Yes, we can be various things, but we tend to be observant. Sullivan's New England upbringing and his recollection of detail reminds me of my teenage days when I was straining to hear every word or phrase—and to remember them. His subject matter is diverse (the Walrus, Craig Stadler, is in these pages, as is the chef Emeril Lagasse; there's a mystical journey through Ireland and a whimsical inquiry into Bill Clinton's mulliganitus) but the attention paid to the small notes that make a story sing is always the same. These chapters will keep you smiling and may, occasionally, as with the stories about Harry Bane and Chi Chi's Kids, bring you close to tears. That's because there's passion here, too, and wisdom. As with all of us who grew up loving the game, Sullivan has an obsession about golf, one he is able to share through his writing. As you read *You're Still Away,* you'll feel like you're holding the club in your hands (lightly of course).

Sullivan freely admits he is an average golfer at best. But as a writer, he's scratch.

And I don't mean scratch with a handicap of six.

Introduction

Finding the Range

There have been a lot of golf books by golfers and now there is this one.

Oh, it's not that I don't play. I do play. I play at it, like you do. I love it like I love few other things in life. Just like you do.

But I don't play often enough, and I don't play well. Of the many jokes around our house, one of them is that Daddy spends about as much time being a golf writer as Daddy's friends spend being golfers. As Henry Kissinger was wont to observe (biffing from Plato vis-à-vis Atlantis, by the way): This particular jape has the very great advantage of being true. So little time, that's the problem, the whole problem. Daughter Caroline is young yet, and the twins are younger still. Golf's a hard game to fit into the schedule with wee ones scuttling about, needful of things like milk and food and stories and toys and "log me on for Club Penguin" and each and every minute of your weekend time.

Ahhh, but: Even before the advent of Caroline, I didn't play all that much, now that I think about it. I was a self-taught golfer, and golf is not a game in which one should be self-taught. As boys, my brother and I tried the game with bent and chipped clubs that my mother had bought us, but we gave it up. Tennis was my game as much as anything was, and my summer job during college was to be the tennis pro—loosely used term, *pro*—at a peculiar little country club in Franconia, New Hampshire. Franconia, a village in the White Mountains, is a high-country alpine Shangri La of rare serenity and beauty, and although the club's bumpy clay tennis courts and rustic nine-hole golf course were not what you'd call five-star sporting venues, playing upon them was still a special treat. All around you were mountains and big-pine forest. In the evenings after work, my friend Ron, the club's short-order cook, and I would take some of the rusted golf sticks from the barn and play five or six holes before sundown, teaching ourselves the game. Did we do it to learn golf, or because there was always a splendid pink sunset, and often as not a moose browsing at the dogleg of the fifth fairway? We did it for all reasons, and that's the way I've approached golf ever since.

I like sunsets and Sunday bags, walking the course and playing in shorts. I play most poorly at corporate outings and during a six-hour round. If my golfing future were to be made up of corporate outings and six-hour rounds, I would quit the game altogether. These statements are made merely by way of introduction. If they offend, close this book—do not buy it. (Well, maybe buy it, and then skip the first section, "Teeing Off," which is where I get my opinions out of the way—where I vent my spleen, where I air out whatever my personal 'tude might be.)

I came away from Franconia with a hesitant swing that could place the ball in the fairway. I am, as a golfer, God's waste of six feet and two inches, 190 pounds. I could eat Sergio Garcia's weight in pancakes for breakfast, yet I seldom drive the ball more than 220 yards. I am reticent of swing because I don't play enough, but even if I played more, I wouldn't be a big hitter. You know how I play.

Which brings me to a question that needs to be asked: Am I then, as a golf writer, a poseur? A phony? A fraud? A fakeroo?

Beats me. I am a student of the game, I will say that—a student if not in swing mechanics then in lore, legend, literature, fact, fiction, and tradition. I love the game like I love baseball, a game I haven't actually played in . . . oh, lots and lots of years. And when I am out on a golf course, walking, playing as well as I can, playing with family or friends—well, I'm about as happy as I can be.

Anyway, it's not a question for me to answer, this business about whether I'm a fraud. Kindly editors including Jim Kelly, Steve Koepp, Bill Saporito, and Jane Wulf at *Time;* Rick Stengel and Mark Coatney at *Time.com;* Jim Gaines, John Atwood, Jon Rizzi, and Kate Meyers at *Travel + Leisure Golf;* Bill Colson and Jim Herre at *Sports Illustrated;* Cathy Wolf at the United States Golf Association (USGA)'s late, lamented *Golf Journal;* Jay Heinrichs and Lance Elko at *Attaché;*

and, now, James T. Walsh and his marvelous Maple Street Press have encouraged me through the years, and so I scribble away. If I'm a poseur, I'm their poseur. Blame them.

For my part, I thank them.

I thank them because I enjoy writing about golf as much as my friends who get to play seem to enjoy playing. And I thank them in this season because I have a feeling that this is my season of heavy writing, to be followed—I hope, I dream—by a season of heavier playing. Daughter Caroline will not always be young, twins Mary Grace and Jack will not always be younger-still, and the day will come when they will ask *wuzzat?* in reference to a golf club. That will be a happy day for them and for their old man. *Honey,* Daddy will announce to Mommy, *the kids want to try golf.*

Sure they do, Mommy will answer, but by then the screen door will have slammed shut, and Daddy and Kids will be in the back yard, swiping at Wiffles. The writing will suffer at that point, I have little doubt. The words will be fewer as the play grows greater.

And so, in anticipation of that happy day, I present this modest volume as a souvenir for my children. I want them to think well of Daddy in re Golf, despite what they'll see when we play together. At least with this book they will know that, although Daddy isn't long, and isn't bold with his putts, nor consistent with his chips, once upon a time . . .

He sure could spell.

—R.S., December, 2006

Teeing Off

Chapter I

I Am the Walrus

The Aesthetic Appeal of Craig Stadler
(and All That This Implies)

The Backswing:

I had written only occasionally on golf before the spring of 1997 when I received a phone call from the editor of Attaché, then U.S. Air's in-flight magazine, who asked if I would like to become that publication's monthly golf columnist. This seemed a marvelous moonlighting gig, and it so proved over the next decade. This regular assignment drew me into the world of golf, and once there, I found myself exploring different topics for other readerships, including that of my old alma mater, Sports Illustrated.

As to this piece, it seems, in placing it close by my preface to this book, to fit the phrase "by way of further introduction." It also is a picture of Tiger as a much younger man. Do you remember what he looked like and sounded like, when he looked and sounded like this—in August 1997?

I watched the beautiful Nike* youth come marching, marching, marching across my TV screen, bags in tow, and swinging, swinging, swinging—lovely, large, smooth swings—and declaiming, proclaiming, "I am Tiger Woods!" "I am Tiger Woods!!" and "I am *Tiger Woods!!!*" I thought upon *Tiger Woods* for a moment, upon his exotic heritage, his preternatural poise, his apparent intelligence, his unconscious concentration, his perfect swing, his impossible length, his bold putting, his Sunday charges, his minus-18 at Augusta—later those wide-margin U.S. and British Open wins—his seven-million-clams-plus years (not counting endorsements, just purses). I took a deep draught of beer, sighed, and said to myself, "Well, I'm not *Tiger Woods,* that's for sure."

Rather, I am the Walrus. *Tiger Woods,* in his very implausibility, shuts me out. The Walrus lets me in. He has long been my favorite professional player because as I watch him waddle up the fairway I can readily imagine, if only imagine, that there but for the grace of the golf gods go I.

The Walrus is, of course, Craig Stadler. His nickname derives, he readily admits, not from the fact that he sometimes blows and bellows like a walrus—though he does—but from the fact that, "like the walrus, I sport a heavy mustache with drooping ends, look lazy, and am characterized by a heavy layer of blubber."

The Walrus has a bad, 1970s haircut, an unkempt manner, and a passel of penchants. He has a penchant for grumbling, and for dropping, flipping, or even heaving the occasional club. In his 1995 autobiography, inevitably entitled *I Am the Walrus* (Delacorte Press), he gives lessons on what he calls The Fun Fling:

1. After flubbing your shot, maintain a narrow stance right where you played the shot from.

2. Hold the club almost as if in the address position, except that the clubhead is about one foot off the ground.

3. Use good etiquette. Check to make sure no one else in your foursome is within 20 feet of your target area.

4. Stand silently for a second, gaining explosive energy.

5. Keeping a perfectly still head and with no body movement, give the club a jerk upward, using a very wristy stroke and a full release . . .

I quote at such length only because I presume the Walrus book is out of print, having been pushed from the shelves by Mr. Penick's instructionals, a few Feinsteins and the four-score volumes that are about, "with," or by Tiger or members of Tiger's satellite community.

Which is not to imply that the Walrus himself has been nudged from golf. Not a bit of it. He's still out there, trolling for birdies. He's routinely Top 50 on the money list and top 20 in scoring, greens in regulation, birdies, and driving. He hasn't recently added to his career total of a dozen tour wins, but I've got a hunch that he will before he's through. He's only in his late forties, after all, and although Tiger makes that seem grandfatherly, the Walrus still can move the ball around.

We who admire the Walrus do so not for his evident success—Masters title, high seven figures in lifetime earnings—but for his essence. When I first noticed his standout presence on tour in the mid-1980s, I asked a friend who covered golf what she knew about Stadler. "Nicest guy out there," she said. "His wife, Sue, is a dream, and Craig is nice, mild, funny. Sweet, really."

I started following Stadler in the magazines, picking up a nugget here and another there. These only reinforced my appreciation of the man. He liked to ski. This is an odd pastime for a Professional Golfers' Association pro, but I like the cold slopes myself and so I was happy to hear it. He was a crusader for faster play. Who among us weekenders isn't? One year, his game was in the dumper and Sue suggested a radical remedy: fitness. The Walrus lost weight. He looked good—well, he looked better—but suddenly he couldn't sink a putt to save his life. He realized that, for the first time since high school, he had nothing to rest his elbows against as he maneuvered the flat stick. His arms were all aswim on the greens, flapping and flailing like, well, a walrus's flippers. So, happily, he started eating in Walrus quantities again, got his armrest back, got his touch back and, eventually, got his game back.

As I say, I found these things in the notes columns. That last one may well be apocryphal. The San Diego Open incident, however, is certifiable.

In the final round, 1987, the Walrus pushed his drive on the 14th well right, and the ball came to rest beneath the lowest branches of a small pine tree. Realizing he could play the shot from his knees rather than "wimping out" (as he termed taking a drop), the Walrus placed his golf towel on the ground and knelt. (It needs be noted how uncharacteristic this fatal decision was: The Walrus doomed himself by trying to *preserve the cleanliness of his pants*.) Anyway, a golf nut from Iowa, watching the tournament on TV, saw Stadler "building a stance," thereby committing a rules violation. The Iowa guy phoned tournament headquarters. The short of it is: By the time the Walrus found out that he was required to take a two-stroke penalty, he had already signed his scorecard. The only sentence available was disqualification. This cost the Walrus substantial second-place dough and, when the incident was re-reported and misrepresented in the press, an additional loss of dignity and reputation. Some folks thought he had "cheated." Did the Walrus rage and roar? He did not. He's a golfer, and knows you play by the rules. And when the pine tree became diseased years later and was slated for removal, he accepted the club's invitation, flew to San Diego, took up a chainsaw, and did the honors.

I was impressed not only by Stadler's sense of humor, but also by the fact that he could handle a chainsaw. Ah, but, then—this was no standard-issue golfer. This was the Walrus.

Now, as we plunge forth in the new millennia, we are led by Tiger. And such as Tiger—perfect, unapproachable, otherworldly— seeks to make the Walrus an endangered species in golf.

Or does he? I think that he does not. I've been watching Tiger pretty closely, as have we all, and I'm here to make an assertion that surprises even me. I am the Walrus, and so is Tiger Woods. Deep down beneath the swing and the torque and the physique is a genetic coding not unlike Stadler's. The old sea mammal and the sleek young cat are related.

Consider: Each looks odd in the whitebread world of pro golf, each comes from a middle-class Californian upbringing, each had a stick in hand at a young age, courtesy of Dad. Each thrived in college. Each has a green jacket. What Nike wants you not to know: Each is playful, each has a sense of humor, each is human.

A while ago—seems like ages ago, now—during the lead-up to Tiger's phenomenal here-I-am 18-under win at Augusta, a cover story appeared in *GQ* in which Tiger was overheard telling jokes of regrettable taste, some racial, some racy. Nike and IMG®, Mark McCormack's huge Cleveland-based management company that makes sure Tiger stays *Tiger* (and by doing so makes good on Nike's $100 million investment in Tiger), went ballistic, then went into a well-practiced damage-control mode.

Or tried to. For I noticed during the tournament's small moments that the kid's corporate handlers couldn't quite keep a leash on him. During early-round coverage on cable, Jim Nantz asked Tiger how he felt about his first nine as a pro at Augusta. "Pissed-off," Tiger said. Nantz was taken aback, and tried to temper the answer. Tiger just smiled. How he had felt was, clearly, pissed-off.

On Sunday, before the final 18, Nantz was narrator of the IMG-produced, Nike-sponsored paean to *Tiger* that ran from three to four P.M. "He accepts responsibility as a role model to minorities and to the men who came before him," Nantz intoned. Never mind that a child simply cannot be a role model to those who came before him, this show was an embarrassment. Nantz was describing Zeus, Hercules, Thor—some god. Nowhere was the kid who regularly gets pissed-off apparently, the fun-loving kid of the *GQ* piece, the one who chilled on the eve of his triumph by playing video games with his best buddy from Stanford.

Nike is marketing *Tiger* as black in America, as Thai in Asia. How inhuman—how inhumane—is that? He's *one* person, one 20-something person who sometimes misses four-footers. We've all seen that happen to him—live. And you know what? As Tiger stands and looks at the offending, non-dropping golf ball, his expression marks him as the lean, smooth-cheeked, black nephew of the Walrus. Tiger doesn't shrug at misfortune. He glowers at it. We'll see the Fun Fling from him before too long.

And when we do, someone at Nike will call someone at IMG and ask what the hell's going on out there. That's sad. It seeks to deny the kid his humanity, his essence.

Those of us who have long loved the Walrus have done so because he wears his feelings on his sleeve, he tells you how he feels.

I heard two great sound bites in the 19th-hole interviews during that first year of the *Tiger*. The first was the young lad's "pissed-off," and the other was the Walrus's response when he was asked what had happened on the back nine when he'd blown an early-season chance: "Well, not a heck of a lot, obviously."

I listened to that and I said, happily, "*Yes!* He is the Walrus. *I* am the Walrus." I looked at Tiger (not *Tiger*), the most human player to hit the tour since Stadler, and I said, "*You* are the Walrus."

I looked at Nike and IMG, those eggmen, viewing such pairings as a nightmare, and I said to them: "*Goo Goo Ga Joob!*"

Chapter II

Mikey MacMulligan's Plain Speaking

Eighteen Holes of Opinion and Criticism

The Backswing:
Every so often I would find myself wanting to get a few things off my chest concerning the state of affairs in our great game. Whenever this every-so-often arrived, I looked at myself in the mirror and saw there a cranky (but loveable?) old Scotsman. I gave that guy a name, split myself in two, and went out for a round of golf. Mikey MacMulligan made his first appearance, which follows right here, in October 1998.

It's always a happy occasion when I set out for a quick eighteen with my good friend Mikey MacMulligan, for Mikey is a man who talks sense. We trod along, thwacking away, jabbering between backswings about the issues of the day. Mikey and I teed it up just last week at the not-so-royal and not-very-ancient public course in Lower Crestfallen, and the afternoon proved to be rich in lively discourse, if not in birdies. For me, at least.

"Young Casey Martin!" Mikey exclaimed as I took my backswing on Number One. "Aye, God loves a snap-hooker, laddie, and ye've got a nasty one there to go try 'n' find. But as I was sayin', young Casey Martin! I think he should be allowed a ride."

"That so?" I said as I teed a provisional.

"I do," he said. "I do, I do. Me meself, I dunna like ta ride. I like the walkin', I like the exercise in me legs and the air in me lungs. But it's not as if our game is football out here, now, is it, laddie? Nae! An' there's nae use pretending it is! What's this nonsense about—'upsettin' the athletic balance'?! Have ye seen the pot on Young Johnny Daly, 'tween the hooch and the chocolate? Athlete, my ankle! Let the young'un Martin ride, till that hip o' his goes like Jack's, and he takes to the veranda."

"You do speak sense, Mikey."

"Aye, that is so."

So I'm finally free of the greenside bunker on Number Three, and after Mikey offers commentary on my shot—"Och, you're s'posed to take the sand *behind* the ball, me friend, an' not the ball itself, which, as ye see, goes flying younder o'er the green and into yon gorse"—after kindly pointing this out, Mikey attacked the issue of clubs: "Mine is the minority viewpoint here, laddie, but I'll give it to you square: I think the Tour should indeed get ridda the big-headed monsters. Ban 'em, says Mikey MacMulligan! Now, ye and me shall still be able to buy our Berthas and Boomers and all the other things that look like you're swingin' a turtle on a stick. But as for the laddies on the Tour, nae!"

"But the PGA's already backed down. And wouldn't that be a double standard?"

"T'wouldn't, and the PGA needs to get itself a spine in front of clan Calloway and the rest. What I'm doin' is protecting the courses. Young Tiger and such will eat them alive—if not this summer, soon, and for the rest of their lives—if somethin' is nae done. Your baseball players must use the wooden bats so that young McGwire and young Griffey don't make your parks and yards obsolete, while every wee Little Leaguer and big, fat softballer in the land uses alum'num. Is it not so, laddie? And so I don't see why young Freddie Couples canna be forced to use a regular-sized niblick even as you and I load the big lumber into the Sunday bag." And with that, he took his tight, compact swing at a ball in the hay and, without much effort but with a great assist from his new Heaven Wood, sent it zipping 150 yards toward the seventh green.

"Nice shot, Mikey."

"Aye, that is so."

"What," I asked later, meanly trying to place the interrogatory between his upswing and down on the 10th tee. "What do you think of Se Ri Pak?"

"She seems a fine lassie," Mikey offered, as he watched his pulled five-iron clip a branch and bound onto the green, nestling, finally, four feet from the pin on the tough Par Three. "Young Pak, is she nae but 20? Aye, 20. And she wins these major championships, and she has this nice swing that Mr. Leadbetter has helped her with, and she seems to like her mummie and she's bought herself a young beagle-dog puppy to keep her company and to try her English upon. It's a lovely story. Made in America! I like miss Se Ri Pak quite a little bit and, ahhhhh . . ." Mikey sank his putt. ". . . and she's got me watchin' the women again. I watched the Jamie Farr!"

"But on the men's side, it's the . . ." I lipped my four-footer.

"Ye'll not wanna be talkin' as ye putt, laddie!"

"Yes, Mikey."

"Ye were sayin'?"

"Well, I was saying—all the men champs are old. Mark O'Meara. Lee Janzen's not old, but he's not a pup. He's in his thirties. Tom Watson won again this year."

"Aye, I saw that. Forty-eight, and he takes Ben Hogan's tournament there, The . . ."

"Colonial," I said as I sent my drive on Number Eleven sailing o'er the pines on the right. "The Colonial. Mind if I hit another?"

"Ye go right ahead, laddie," said Mikey congenially. "Ye're hittin' three. And, yes, Old Tom wins at 48 and I have a theory about that. I think if ye split with the wife but give up the hooch in the same season, then it cures your yips."

"That's your theory, Mikey?" I said as watched my duck-hook plunge into the pines, left.

"Aye, it is," he said. "And ye're hittin' five now."

"I rely on you to keep track, Mikey," I said sarcastically as I waggled the driver.

"Ye can do that, laddie. I'll do whatever I can for ye."

"You talk about Watson," I said as we walked up the 15th fairway, following our perfect, perfectly equal drives. "Look what happened in late summer out on Long Island. Gary Player won on the Senior Tour, and he's 62!"

"Aye, so I saw," said Mikey. "Watching him and Lee Trevino walking together on Sunday really brou' me back. Made me feel a wee laddie again."

"Speaking of wee laddies, did you hear about that fellow in the Amateur Championship over in America?"

"I did, I did, I did!" said Mikey. "Eighteen years old, a wee bit over six stone. What was the laddie's name?"

"Erik Compton."

"Erik Compton it was! Six stone with a 10-stone heart. How does his story go again?"

I remembered, having been moved by it so: "He was 9 when the doctors found he had a bad ticker. When he was 12, he had a heart transplant, and about the same time his family's house gets blown away by one of those Florida hurricanes—the big one, Andrew, in '92. So the family relocates to an apartment at a country club, and to get stronger, Erik starts playing golf. At 15, he shoots a 65. And now he's winning the majors on the junior circuit. Amazing."

"'Tis what I love about this game of ours," Mikey said. "I love a story like that. Young Casey Martin gets his ride, and young Erik Compton gets a new heart." He was suddenly quiet, and the stillness was stunning. He looked at me, then at the ground. "Ye're away, lad," he said, and I saw that he was right. Not wanting to show him the way, I pushed my approach into the greenside trap, right.

"So what has made you saddest in golf this year?" I asked as Mikey prepared to tap out for a nifty, no-worries 76. "Aye, I missed young Jack at The Championship."

"Birkdale?"

"Aye, of course. The Championship. A good long run he had, young Jack. So many majors without a miss."

"Well, he'll be back to play all four in 2000," I said. "At 60 years old. He said he'll play all four at 60. We'll see him again."

"Aye, with his new young hip. Maybe young Martin and young Jack will be paired, each with a young new hip. "

"And what's made you happiest, Mikey? If Jack's made you sad, what's made you happy?"

"Aye, the smile of young Matt Kuchar."

"Well," I said, "we'll be seeing a lot more of that." I extended my hand.

Mikey hesitated.

"Laddie," he said, "Ye've a putt ye'll want to make first."

There are no gimmes with Mikey MacMulligan.

Chapter III

No Eden Without Eve

Boys Will Be Boys, Which Is Bad News for Women Golfers

The Backswing:

Well before there was a dustup at Augusta National, there was an issue about male-female inequities in golf. In fact, I remember learning as a fuzzy-cheeked youth that women couldn't play on Wednesday afternoons or weekend mornings at our club in Tyngsboro, Massachusetts, and thinking, "really?" That remained my attitude after I took up the game.

There have been some topics along the golfing way that I felt needed a bit more reasoned discourse than Mikey MacMulligan might offer, and this was one. The piece was published in May 1998.

Let me be plain: I am a believer in total, absolute, unequivocal equality for women as regards all aspects of, and all issues involving, golf. How strong a believer am I? When I'm playing for money with my sister Gail, the red tees are out of the question. How 'bout that for a liberated male? You can't ask for more than that.

And when I read about the rules still in place at some of our country's clubs even as the millennia change approaches—30 years after Gloria Steinem, 40 years after Simone de Beauvoir, 50 years after Kate Hepburn smacked it 200 yards down the middle to beat Babe Zaharias in the movie *Pat and Mike*, 432 years after Mary Queen of Scots was criticized for playing her beloved game of golf too soon after the death of her husband, Lord Darnley—well, I start glowering like Faldo. Men's-only tee times? Men's-only lounges? Men's-only locker rooms?! (That's okay, I guess. But the other stuff: T'ain't fair, I say, t'ain't fair.)

When I was a kid, growing up in the late 1950s and early 1960s, the world was a different place. Many clubs were strictly male: "Eveless Edens." Ancient, silly rules were indeed fading—"Women are allowed to use but one club, the putter"—but other prohibitions were proving more stubborn. Most of the women who frequented the club where my family played golf and tennis—a Massachusetts club very typical of its kind—did not work, and so they got in as much weekday golf as they could. Nary a peep was heard that all of the morning tee-times on Saturdays and Sundays belonged to the men, nor that the men's and women's grills were separate and hardly equal. The women seemed to accept that they were guests at their family's club, and would be treated as such.

Times have changed . . . outside the clubs. A woman's place in the work force has been secured, and various laws have been signed that seek to protect her equal rights there (even if her salary continues to unjustly lag). Women hold positions of power in business and on corporate boards. Moreover, societal stigmas attached to single or divorced women have eroded in most regions, and the single mom— or single dad, for that matter—is a phenomenon of modern society.

Many private clubs have turned a blind eye to these very obvious shifts in the lifestyles and status of American women. They've done so for the obvious reason: every right (or tee time) granted to a woman by the male-dominated club is a right (or tee time) ceded by a man. In a book published this month, *Breaking the Grass Ceiling: A Woman's Guide to Golf as a Business Tool* (Triumph Books, 1998), Cheryl A. Leonhardt, founder of the Business and Professional Women's Golf Association, writes, "Many country clubs are still culturally in the 1950s because when our high courts considered the value of equality, they also considered the rights of privacy and freedom of association and ruled that private clubs were exempt from the Civil Rights Act of 1964. So it is often the men who have the preferred weekend morning tee times; the ladies have their morning during the week, usually Tuesdays, and, of course, weekend afternoons. It is the men who hold office; it is the ladies who decorate the clubhouse for parties. It is the men who decide where the forward tees shall be placed; it is the ladies who must hit from them."

Clearly, this situation is not only Luddite, it's intolerable. Some states are saying so—a baker's dozen have enacted laws specifically governing discrimination in private golf and country clubs because the higher courts have had trouble applying the Civil Rights Act to these institutions. Some clear-thinking cities are saying so, too: A dozen major metropolitan areas have passed similar legislation. Moreover, activists in states without such club-specific laws have sued *private* clubs under other civil rights statutes that govern *public* accommodations at places in their districts, places such as restaurants and hotels. The argument is this: If a restaurant that hosts banquets, or that caters to a business crowd, cannot discriminate on the basis of race or gender, then how can a country club down the street, which rents its rooms for banquets, which daily encourages members and their guests to do business over lunch, continue to discriminate? The courts have, in the past decade, increasingly seen the wisdom in this argument. A landmark 1995 decision by the California Supreme Court accepted reasoning along these lines in asserting that the private clubs in that state are subject to California civil-rights law.

Legislation is well and good, but it hasn't always made things fine and pretty for women golfers in the trenches (and bunkers). There's a story, cited in Leonhardt's new book and detailed in Marcia Chambers' *The Unplayable Lie: The Untold Story of Women and Discrimination in American Golf* (Golf Digest Books, 1995), that seems so fantastic as to not be true—and yet it is. It's about a woman from Long Island who won her argument regarding weekend play, only to see the horror begin. In 1988 Lee Lowell, a former art teacher, petitioned her club, the Cedar Brook Golf and Tennis Club in Old Bronxville, New York, to change its rules regarding weekend tee times, rules that placed men first, men-with-guests second, *honeymooners* third and "Lady members with or without guests" fourth and last. Lowell pressed and pressed her suit—she clearly wasn't going to go away—and the club finally granted her permission to play. Her first early weekend tee time was in a shotgun, and she approached the 17th tee to find her playing partners. "The two gentlemen I was supposed to play with told me that they wouldn't play with me," Mrs. Lowell later recalled. She played the hole alone, then went to 18. In the middle of that fairway, she found a barricade fronted by the chairman of the men's golf committee. "They kept screaming that I could not play." Mrs. Lowell drove her cart toward the 16th tee, which was open. Chambers writes that the men "revved up their carts and went after her. They gunned their carts. That means that when they floored it, they were trotting along at a solid ten miles an hour. They cursed at Lowell from 150 yards away. Undaunted, she teed off." Her drive narrowly missed the men, and too bad that it did.

Now the men stole the ball! Lowell went to the second tee. Eight or ten men charged toward it, set up a new wall with their carts. One threw a golf ball at her. Another felt it was time to relieve himself in her presence. Lowell, finally terrified, fled in her cart. *The men gave chase.* They encircled her. "I was scared," Lowell told Chambers. "I felt like a child who was afraid of being maimed or hurt. I felt the rage in these men . . . And where was I? I was in a wealthy country on the fairways of a private country club."

The denouement was that Lowell made it to the women's locker room where she broke down and cried. She was suspended from the club, then shunned when she returned; both she and her husband received threatening phone calls: "You better not play or your life is at stake." Lowell carried her crusade forward. She pressed criminal charges against the leader of the Cedar Brook pack, but although a judge found that the man's actions in "bringing the enforcement of golf etiquette to the level of personal intimidation speak for themselves," he also found those actions did not constitute a crime. Of Cedar Brook, the judge bothered to add, "Perhaps it is best that a member with the integrity of Lee Lowell not be associated with such an organization." No problem there, writes Chambers: The club refused to renew the Lowells' membership. Lowell filed a complaint before the New York State Human Rights Commission and, in July of 1992, the commission found "overwhelming evidence" that the club had discriminated in its policies and in ousting the Lowells.

Reading the tea leaves at last, Cedar Brook changed its ways—it's got a mixed grill now, and mixed weekend tee times. The Lowells eventually moved to Florida and joined a club with no tee-time restrictions.

Up in Pennsylvania, Wynn Harris and her husband Bob know how the Lowells felt. Wynn already wasn't happy with the policies at the Meadowlands Country Club—weekend tee times, the usual—when she suffered a particular indignation by trying to do a nice thing on Father's Day. She invited Bob's dad to play as her guest, but because the grill rooms at Meadowlands were separate, her father-in-law had to eat breakfast alone in the men's grill, then sign *her* name to the check because he himself was a non-member. The Harrises complained, were shunned—in fact, they were booed after they won a tournament—quit the club in 1995, filed a complaint with the Pennsylvania Human Relations Commission, and eventually brought suit with the help of the Women's Law Project in Philadelphia. Meanwhile, the Women's Golf Association of that city was surveying the clubs thereabouts, and finding that Meadowlands was no exception in its policies. On the boards of the 43 clubs responding, there were 477 directors, only 34 of them women—seven percent. As Leonhardt writes in *Breaking the Grass Ceiling,* if the board is male-dominated, "be advised that this club is male-dominated and you have some decisions to make. You may look for another club to join, or join and then try to change it from within."

This latter course is the tougher one, but then it always has been for pioneers. I like pioneers. Though I hope, of course, that men everywhere stop behaving like cowardly, paranoid children, I hope as well that women persevere in their efforts to knock down ultimate barriers at America's courses and clubs.

I have a further hope, though this one seems more of a dream. I hope that every organization holding any sway in this great game of ours takes a stand on the issue, as they all did when Tom Watson made racial discrimination at America's clubs a hot topic several years ago. We know what the Women's Tour thinks. What about the PGA Tour? What about, for that matter, the PGA? The USGA? The Nike Tour? What about Nike? Nike makes a lot of money off the sweat of women's athletes. Let's hear from Nike on this? Let's hear from all of them.

And no more posses riding hell bent for leather o'er the far hill of the fairway, please. No more golf carts swarming in circles around the damsel in distress. No more war whoops. It's time to grow up, boys.

Chapter IV

Mulligans and Ms. Lewinsky

Why President Clinton's Golf Game Shouted: Beware!

The Backswing:

Believe it or not, the following words were deemed too hot for the airline magazine. Now, this couldn't have been because the Clintons flew U.S. Air—they had their own plane at the time, didn't they?—but anyway: This little sketch, killed by the in-flight mag, did develop a happy afterlife. It ran first in Sports Illustrated *in May 1998, then was anthologized in the* Signet Book of American Humor *(Regina Barreca, Econo-Clad Books, 1999). For my money, its appearance in those places was trumped by one other: A friend who's a member at the august Sleep Hollow club told me that a copy of the SI version got tacked to the men's locker-room bulletin board. I stand humbled.*

That there have been ethics . . . umm . . . let's call them *situations* with the gang in the White House, including the top hound dog, is not exactly breaking news. But what might be fun as we approach the three-quarter pole of the Clinton years is to assay and assess the various malfeasances and misdemeanors. Not-inhaling and draft-dodging seem like ancient history now; they should perhaps be wiped from the slate, having outrun the statute of limitations for public umbrage. (Of course, they *are* indicative . . .) Travelgate? That still ranks, and Web Hubbell rankles. I, more-often-than-not Democrat though I may be, would argue that Whitewater ain't done yet, not to mention Ms. Jones. She'll be heard from again before the closing gong.

And then there was the moment I first heard about Monica S. Lewinsky. I said to myself, well, sure, absolutely, no question about it. I can still, today, vividly recall an early discussion on this topic between my wife and myself. Luci was just finishing her take on the subject—" . . . and another thing, Buster, I don't care what the Bible says, that kind of behavior outside *this* household means *big* trouble"—when I followed with, "Of course, dear. Goes without saying, dear.

"And you know what, sweetie? Saying that this kind of thing doesn't *count* is precisely the type of wacky distinction our friend Clinton *would* make. It's just like with the mulligans."

My wife, not wanting an explanation, didn't ask for one. But I've thought about this further as time has gone by, and have become ever more firmly convinced: If the President's handlers—not to mention, We the People—had paid a little closer attention to their man's behavior on the golf course, they would've been more on their toes, and perhaps could've headed off not only probable impeachment but the Lewinsky mess entire. They could have spared the country a lot of pain back then. With a little watchfulness, we might avoid similar pain in the future.

You see, I had, before Ms. Lewinsky came onstage, been watching President Clinton's game—his golf game—for six full years, and although I'd seen his swing improve admirably—particularly the follow-through, which had become high and strong—I had noticed that the president had been unable to conquer his seemingly pathological mulliganitis. What did it say about a fellow that he just couldn't help but shave strokes, *even when the whole world was watching*? Did it, perhaps, say something *dangerous*?

Tim Russert, too, wondered about that even before the Lewinsky scandal. Russert chatted with the president on the 50th anniversary edition of *Meet the Press* earlier this year. On that show, the host first showed results of his program's exclusive poll of American attitudes toward Clinton—for instance, that many more of his countrymen pictured the president playing golf (40 percent) than saw him in jogging shorts or even eating at McDonald's; Clinton-as-golfer was second in image only to Clinton-as-saxophone-player (43 percent). I guess this wasn't all that surprising. The president is and always has been an enthusiastic, unapologetic golfer, nothing like the top-secret swinger that his idol, John F. Kennedy, once was. (JFK wanted to project a vigorous, energetic persona to the electorate to counter the country-club image of Eisenhower, Nixon, and the Republicans generally, so he kept his superb game—perhaps the best-ever of a U.S. president—largely in the closet.)

Anyway . . . On *Meet the Press,* host Russert steered the interview along the curvy roads of domestic policy and foreign affairs. And then, as time wound down, he started tossing softballs. He asked President Clinton questions about eating, about Martha's Vineyard, about daughter Chelsea and, finally, about golf.

"I've gotten better since being president," said Mr. Clinton unassumingly, wholly unaware that this was a pretty disquieting thought. *A president with enough spare time to improve his golf game?* Yikes. "It's mostly because I've gotten to play with better golfers." Oh, I see.

I was hoping Russert would follow-up with a question about the president's good friend Greg Norman—What *did* happen at the Shark's house when Clinton "slipped" on the stairs and broke his foot?—but Russert went on to handicaps instead. "Twelve, thirteen—something like that," said the president. *With any mulligans?* Russert pressed.

Mr. Clinton's eyes went steely, like they do. He took one of those pauses, as he does.

"One, now."

I believe that like I believe in July snow, in winged pigs, in my own ability to stay dry on the 16th at Augusta.

In trying to figure out the sitting presidential handicap for their 1996 book *Presidential Lies: The Illustrated History of White House Golf* (Macmillan), Shepherd Campbell and Peter Landau wrote, "The answer is clouded by the matter of mulligans, which he uses

23

freely . . . Clinton admits to one mulligan per round. But others put the number higher. It is said, for instance, that with friends in Little Rock the standard arrangement was for one extra tee shot and two extra fairway shots per nine holes."

Apparently, the loosey-goosey standards of the Rose Law Firm weren't the only values of some questionability that the Clinton gang packed along from Little Rock to Washington.

Do I think the president is still shaving six per 18? Frankly, I don't know what to think. I've tried for a while to follow the good reporting of CBS News' Mark Knoller, who is to Clinton's golf game what Boswell was to Johnson. Knoller says, for instance, that during Mr. Clinton's 17-day vacation in Jackson Hole, Wyoming, in 1995, the president spent 55 hours and 36 minutes playing 206 holes of golf, scoring an average of 85.1, whereas last summer on Martha's Vineyard he spent 48 hours, 31 minutes, playing 180 holes in an average of 82.73 strokes per round. By crunching Knoller's stats, we can learn some fairly certain things about the presidential game. To wit: that Mr. Clinton's foursome proceeds at a pace of five hours per round, a notion that would horrify the presidential predecessor, George Bush, who used to play a shoot-and-scoot game at Kennebunkport that the press termed "polo golf." (GHWB and three buddies once completed 18 holes in an hour, 42 minutes.)

But there are some things about Clinton's game that we simply cannot know—nor can Knoller. The first time the president reported breaking 80 was on a course in San Diego, Knoller told *Sports Illustrated,* "when no one was there to see it." The correspondent pointed out, "The press doesn't have access to most of the holes he plays, so a lot of times I have to take him at his word." Knoller's statistical model is, therefore—admittedly—flawed. Knoller said rather sadly that when Clinton claimed a Martha's Vineyard 79 last summer, "that was immediately cast into doubt because we saw him take three tee shots on the 1st hole."

Clearly, the man has not conquered his mulliganitis. Is this a big deal? Well, I guess . . . maybe not. According to *Presidential Lies,*

Lyndon Johnson, to take just one other example, had a golf game that was wholly constructed around the concept of the mulligan. If he didn't like a shot—any shot—LBJ just dropped and hit another shot. If he didn't like that one, he dropped again. Of course, Johnson didn't make public his goals. Bill Clinton's longing to break 80 was famous in his first term; it was considered an object of desire second only to health-care reform (and, apparently, one particular intern). Then too, if you asked LBJ how his game was, vis-à-vis mulligans, he would not have responded, "One, now, sonnyboy." He would have given a square answer: "Many as I want, I'm the goddam president!"

I was haunted by the image on my monitor: There sat President Clinton, all but wagging his finger at Tim Russert, all but saying, *"I have never, ever had as much as two gimme shots in one round of that game, that game of golf."*

I realized then with great clarity that there was, indeed, something—something critical, something *serious*—to be said about Mr. Clinton's mulliganitis. Something about duplicity, chronic self-delusion, a genetic incapacity for truth-telling. Also, as directly related to the Lewinsky situation: Something about calling a thing other than what it truly is, in fact calling it in a way that makes it vanish entirely, that makes it *not count*. Poof!—it was never there. Oral sex is not sex and so it goes away. It is erased. It is . . . a mulligan.

So, I'm thinking all this to myself, and I'm just about to delve further into a Limbaughian tirade of that nature, but then I think back to a Knoller observation, and I check myself.

"That was immediately cast into doubt because we saw him take three tee shots on the first hole."

Now, suddenly, oddly, I find myself drained of indignation and, instead, harboring tremendous sympathy for the First Golfer. You see, I can't stand to have my playing partners watch me in the first tee box, much less the foursome behind, the lunchers on the veranda or, God forfend, the vulturous presidential press corps. This bare concept—that the president of the United States, whoever he is, must play his golf in a fishbowl—forces me to ask myself a very pointed question: Would I, myself, suffer the hazards (the prying eyes, the slings and arrows of outrageous golf columnists) for the privileges (the instant tee times, the ever-wide-open fairways) that come with presidential golf?

And the answer is . . .

In a second. I'd take that trade in a heartbeat.

For I know just how good it can get, when you're a president who plays golf.

One night several years ago, I was ushered about on a private tour of the White House by a friend of mine who was in the military, and stationed for a while at 1600 Pennsylvania Avenue. We saw this room and that, walked hallways where Nixon talked to paintings and peeked under desks where John-John used to build forts, turning on lights as we went. And then we were in the Oval Office.

I can report that it is oval, smaller than you might think, beautifully appointed, Jeffersonian in feel, extraordinarily well-dusted: an altogether admirable room from which to orchestrate the world's well-being. I did the inevitable thing, of course—I strolled behind the great desk. And there, lo, I found a floor pock-marked by little holes.

"Ike's spikes," my friend explained, sort of.

"How's that?"

"Eisenhower's spike marks. He had a putting green in the Rose Garden. He'd putter around, then would come in through the French doors to sign a treaty, or to dash off a letter to Khrushchev."

Now, I don't know whether the floor's been mended, and, frankly, I don't know whether the tale is apocryphal to begin with. But it's a nice little story. And as I think about it now—a putting green in the back yard, and the absolute liberty to waggle the flat stick around for a bit and then come in to work without changing my shoes—I think to myself, wow, it must be cool indeed to be a golf-playing leader of the free world.

But where was I?

Sorry about that digression; we were talking about Bill Clinton, right? And I was going back-and-forth as to how I felt about all this, and had arrived at a point where I was worried there might be no moral to this story, and can a certain kind of sex be a mulligan, and what does it all mean? Let me try to tie this all together for us.

At the end of the long day, as you trudge to the 19th hole for requisite relief from the trials and travails of golf, there is reality to be confronted. And—sorry—that reality says a golf shot is not "a mulligan," it's a golf shot. Count it, count 'em all. Similarly, an act that might cause the spouse to shy some crockery at your head: count that, too.

That's the narrow moral, which is perhaps finally evident to Mr. Clinton. Perhaps not, too; I wouldn't bet either way, and it matters little, now, in any event.

As for a more general message that might be of some use to us as a society, as a Union, it is this: Let's pay attention. Bill Clinton's golf game fairly shouted for us to be *en garde,* yet we remained heedless. We were the antithesis of vigilant. It was our own fault, as much as his, what happened back then. It should never happen again.

Follow the golf.

Chapter V

Requiem for the Bag Toter

The Pipes Are Piping for the Late, Much-Lamented Looper

The Backswing:

I was never a caddy; my summer jobs were in tennis. But I did see them slouching over there by the shack, waiting for a bag, and theirs seemed a most amiable fraternity. In my adult travels, I've gotten to know eccentric, ancient caddies in Ireland, and smirking (this-guy's-awful), teenage caddies on Long Island—and at the end of the day, I still love the caddies. I love the whole idea of caddies. This essay first appeared in April 1998, and it has been with sadness that I've noticed a further decline in the caddy ranks since. It does seem the looper is the looming dodo of golf.

I predict that in the twenty-second century, there will still be caddy shacks on the grounds of St. A's, Augusta, The Country Club, Lahinch, Troon, Royal Melbourne—and just about nowhere else.

If I'm wrong, please do sue me.

Frankly, caddies are lucky to have limped into the new millennium. Bells began tolling for bag toters in the 1950s when the golf-cart infestation of America's greenswards took hold. Spreading like gypsy moths, the carts chomp-chomp-chomped fairway after fairway, leaving behind naught but the whitening bones of once-vital loopers. Let's say, for argument's sake, that there were a gazillion caddies employed in summertime America in 1955. Today there are maybe 20,000, according to the National Club Association, a trade group of 900 private clubs. There are something like 16,000 public and private U.S. courses today, and the betting of Bradley S. Klein, an editor at *Golfweek* and author of the book *Rough Meditations* (Gale Group, 1997), is that "only a few hundred private clubs and perhaps two dozen elite resorts [have] hung onto their caddies."

So, therefore, ergo, I maintain: Kaddies are kaputsky. But please don't think me harsh. This will essentially, eventually, inevitably be: A sentimental kolumn. I come not to bury caddies, but to praise them.

The caddies aren't going quietly into their good night. As recently as 1997, they fended off a grim-faced challenge from no less that the Internal Revenue Service. Yes, as if the IRS didn't have a big-enough lovability problem, it decided to go after lowly stick carriers, claiming they were "employees" of their clubs rather than "independent contractors." Never mind that caddies are paid by members—the golfers themselves—and not by course administrators. And never mind that a 1969 IRS administrative ruling had firmly placed caddies in the independent-contractor bag. Never mind all that, said a field auditor who was looking at the books of Westchester C.C. in New York. He issued a formal challenge that sought to require Westchester to start withholding taxes, and to pay tens of thousands of dollars in back taxes that hadn't been withheld. Rather than enter into such a bookkeeping morass, Westchester and most other clubs would probably have shuttered the caddy shacks. Fortunately, this was the quick realization of Representative Dan Burton, chairman of the House Government Reform and Oversight Committee and himself a former caddy. After he read tax attorney Michael C. Fondo's account of the IRS offensive in the *Wall Street Journal,* Burton acted as swiftly as Tiger's downswing and drafted the Caddie Relief Act of 1997. (By the way, it can be spelled either way.) This reemphasized that, in the eyes of the nation's lawmakers, bag toters were independent contractors. The IRS, putting a finger to the wind and reading which way it blew with rare perspicacity, quietly settled its differences with the WCC.

This was all good news, but make no mistake: It did not and does not represent the caddies' salvation. It represents a reprieve. As we know, golf is booming, and golfing fees are booming apace. The plain fact is, carts are cheap to maintain and are a great source of easy revenue for clubs. Carts are, I fear, the big wave of the present and the tsunami of the future.

This is a shame for myriad reasons. For one thing, carts are esthetically noisome, not to mention noisy. They look . . . well, they look just plain stupid, trundling down the paths toward the next tee box like a dodge-'em car escaped from the arcade. I like the fact that carts allow Casey Martin or an octogenarian on his third hip replacement to keep swinging, and I like nothing else about them.

Moreover, the institution of caddying is, on its face, an altogether good thing. To caddy is to be involved in a healthful, muscle-building enterprise, one that takes place entirely in the fresh air. Caddies often become good golfers (Ben Hogan), and sometimes become other types of talented and crafty players (Fidelity's Peter Lynch). Caddies are encouraged to go to college by such organizations as Massachusetts's Francis Ouimet Scholarship Fund and the Western Golf Association's Chick Evans Scholarship Program, which since 1930 has provided nearly 7,000 men and women with tuition and housing aid. Perhaps most significantly, the practice of bag-toting has, though the years, enriched mankind with a steady-flowing stream of fun and funny fellows. Harvey Penick worried in his first little book that, with the decline of caddies, golf would lose many of its most "colorful characters" who add "a lot to the spirit of the game" (*Harvey Penick's Little Red Book: Lessons and Teachings from a Lifetime in Golf,* Simon & Schuster, 1992).

As sweet old Mr. Penick implied, there is no need to be afraid of a caddy, though such fear is as common as the widespread terror of a veranda crowd near the first tee. My trust of—and, indeed, affection for—caddies came to me like an epiphany during what was surely one of the worst rounds of golf I ever played. I had been invited to The National to take part in a corporate round. I never play well in such circumstances, but this was The National, and so I boarded a train for eastern Long Island and, after enjoying the fabulous lobster lunch they serve there, I teed it up. I nearly broke a window on Number One, and by the third hole, my caddy was handing me long irons at each tee rather than the lumber. "Just until you find your rhythm," he said.

I figured he was humoring me, maybe even patronizing me. But as the day wore on and my game frayed further, I saw that he had genuine sympathy for his charge. He was taking this personally, and he grew activist. He picked up a three-footer for me, as if making it on that slick green would've been the easiest thing in the world. He gave me instruction on a bump-and-run—instruction that worked.

Somewhere on the back nine, I was facing an immense green and a 20-yard chip. "This side of the pin," said the caddy. "Don't go to the back of the green, and whatever you do, don't go *off* the back." Okay, fine. I chipped. The ball bounced and started to roll. It passed the stick about six inches left, and slowed gently. It trickled just off the putting surface, and I was thinking: Good A putt from the fringe, I might even get down in two.

Standing beside me, my caddy sagged. I had laid him low, and as we trudged forth, I found out why. The enormous thing started to come into view from its far lip; I heard the music from *2001: A Space Odyssey* in my head. Just beyond the green, nipped up right against the edge of it, lay the biggest, deepest bunker I'd ever had the honor to inhabit. I needed to climb down a ladder embedded in the front face of the trap to reach my ball. I opened the wedge flat-out, and felt fortunate to be released from jail after only two swipes. I think I took six or seven putts, I was so shaken. And what did my caddy say as we walked from the green? Not "Told you so" or "Should've kept it in front of the pin" but, rather, "That's a tough trap." He sounded as if he'd just played it himself.

Now, surely, not all caddies are such good fellows and true. A former boss of mine once had several dozen of us as guests at his club. Fishing, our foursome asked the caddy if he sometimes carried for the boss. "Sure," the kid said, then paused and smiled. "Not much of a tipper." He paused again, and added, "He kicks 'em out." As in, out of the woods. We were certainly pleased to be in possession of such useful information, but even so: I wouldn't want a caddy talking like that behind my back.

The boy from Ballybunion never would have. He was a soldier on the course, and a mate off of it. The rain that day in western Ireland was slanting in sideways, but my caddy and I fought stoically through the gale for four hours; I had come this far, I was *going* to play Ballybunion, hell or high water. I got both. But as we stripped out of our weather gear afterward, the caddy said obligingly, "A fair round, considering."

"Thanks."

"Fancy some snooker?"

I was surprised by the easy camaraderie. Back in the States, it would've seemed effrontery at the finer clubs. But I was taken in by the caddy's guilelessness, and I said, "Sure, as long as I can buy the Guinness."

"You're on."

I do shoot pool, but not snooker. It took me a while to get the hang of the big table, small balls, and new rules. During this while, my skinny young friend took three games and four pints off me. "Let's make it a World Series," I suggested.

"A wha?"

"Best of seven."

"Greeeeet," which meant great.

The fourth game was close, but I eked it out. The fifth was less close, the sixth was a cakewalk. I tried to call it a draw and leave it there. I think the lad thought I was trying to cheat him out of a stout—his eighth? his ninth?—and he would hear none of it. I beat him in seven, and he was entirely pleased by the turn of events. "You're a fine sportsman," he said. Actually, he said, "Yeeeer uh fiine sposhmun!" For my part, I remember that boy from Ballybunion as one of the finest golfing buddies I've ever had.

In the old book *Golf,* published in 1890 by his Grace the eighth Duke of Beaufort, it is written, "Wherever golf exists there must the caddie be found." No longer true. Less true each and every day. Already I hear the pipes a pipin' for the lonely looper. I raise a glass, and a silent toast to the bag toter.

Chapter VI

Nothing but Plums

In Praise of P. G. Wodehouse, Bard of All Bogey Men

The Backswing:

The riff on President Clinton, his golf game, and his intern was part of a hoary and hardly horrible journalistic tradition, wherein a submission that gets killed at one publication is subsequently placed at another. Everyone's happy. By contrast, this look at P. G. Wodehouse, one of a handful of writers who can make me laugh even while bowling me over (and Wodehouse would do something devilishly dazzling with that metaphor) with their manipulation of the language, is part of a second, far sleazier trick of the trade: double-dipping. I wrote about Plum's golf stories in Sports Illustrated *in October 1995, then again in* Attaché *two years later. Were these appreciations appreciably different? In revisiting them both for this volume, I found similarities and dissimilarities, and so decided to triple dip, and massage them into a single essay. What follows is the last word I'll ever offer on this subject. Probably. Well, possibly.*

I know the feeling, so do you.

And so did Plummie, who in 1926 captured it most felicitously: "It was a morning when all nature shouted 'Fore!' The breeze, as it blew gently up from the valley, seemed to bring a message of hope and cheer, whispering of chip shots holed and brassies landed squarely on the meat. The fairway, as yet unscarred by the irons of a hundred clubs, smiled greenly up at the azure sky; and the sun, peeping above the trees, looked like a giant golf-ball perfectly lofted by the mashies of some unseen god and about to drop dead by the pin of the eighteenth. It was the day of the opening of the course."

Nearly four score years later, and the feeling's the same on opening day. Seventy-one years later, and the prose hasn't been equaled, as regards putting quill to parchment with golf in mind. Herb Wind, Dan Jenkins, John Updike—fine writers all. But the bard of the links is and has been for quite some time, our Plummie.

The above longish quotation is from one of his early and best golf stories, "Heart of a Goof" (collected in a volume of the same name that'll fetch you a very pretty penny, if you can find an early edition). In re said quote (as Wodehouse's Bertie Wooster might've put it): It needs be noted that "a brassie" is—or, rather, *was*—a brass-bottomed two wood. "A mashie" was an approximate five iron. "A goof" was—and still is—"one of those unfortunate beings who have allowed this noblest of sports to get too great a grip upon them, who have permitted it to eat into their souls."

And, oh yes: "Plummie" is—or, again, sadly, was—Sir Pelham Grenville Wodehouse, P. G. Wodehouse by byline, Plummie or Plum to his wife and friends.

If Harvey Penick was golf's Socrates—the game's greatest teacher and philosopher—then Plum was golf's Shakespeare: its master comedian, romanticist and occasional tragedian. Wodehouse's world of golf was, usually, a sweet midsummer afternoon's dream, played out in an Arcadia where bliss is going 'round in one-over bogey, and where true love triumphs over a stiff wind.

Golf and love: Those are the two essential ingredients in the "golf stories" of P. G. Wodehouse. (His canon is so overlarge—94 novels in 94 years—that it is divided and subdivided. There are the dozen-odd Bertie-and-Jeeves novels, the dozen-odd Blandings novels, the very odd Psmith novels, the Jeeves stories, the Mulliner stories, the school stories, the golf stories. Then there's the miscellany.)

In the golf stories, we have golf and love, love and golf. To wit:

- "Reggie was a troubled spirit these days. He was in love, and he had developed a bad slice with his mid-iron. He was practically a soul in torment." (from "A Damsel in Distress," 1919)

- "You know how it is. If you have a broken heart, it's bound to give you a twinge now and then, and if this happens when you are starting your down swing you neglect to let the clubhead lead." (from "There's Always Golf," 1937)

- " 'You love her?'
'Madly.'
'And how do you think it affects your game?'
'I've started shanking a bit.'
The Oldest Member nodded. 'I'm sorry, but not surprised. Either that or missing short putts is what generally happens on these occasions. I doubt if golfers ought to fall in love. I have known it cost men ten shots in a medal round.'" (from "Scratch Man," 1959)

- "And so (said the Oldest Member) we come back to our original starting point—to wit, that, while there is nothing to be said definitely against love, your golfer should be extremely careful how he indulges in it. It may improve his game or it may not. But, if he finds that there is any danger that it may not—if the object of his affections is not the kind of girl who will listen to him with cheerful sympathy through the long evening, while he tells her, illustrating stance and grip and swing with the kitchen poker, each detail of the day's round—then, I say unhesitatingly, he had better leave it alone. Love has had a lot of press-agenting from the oldest times; but there are higher, nobler things than love. A woman is only a woman, but a hefty drive is a slosh." (from "A Woman Is Only a Woman," 1922)

The golf stories could just as well be called "the Oldest Member stories," as all but a couple of them are narrated by this veranda-sitting, tweed-suited gentleman who is possessed of "the eye of a man who, as the poet says, has seen Golf steadily and seen it whole." Routinely, in one of these stories, a young duffer will be climbing toward the clubhouse from the 18th green and the Oldest Member will diagnose in his demeanor something that is causing (1) trouble in love, (2) trouble in golf, or (3) trouble in both. By way of remedy, the Oldest Member will draw the youth aside and relate "from the innumerable memories that rush to my mind" a story, the moral of which sets things right. The stories are, if you like this sort of thing, hilarious. At the very least, the writing is always marvelous.

Or at least I thought so, two decades past, when I chanced upon a paperback of "Heart of a Goof" and thereby was ushered into the world of P. G. Wodehouse. I read each story twice that summer, howling as I went. Wodehouse was so funny, it made me wonder if he was any good. The prose certainly seemed fine and literate to my ear, but for anyone to be this entertaining, well . . .

One day I was reading serious stuff, a John Updike novel entitled *Of the Farm*. It's a good book; I recommend it. But anyway: I was reading it, and Updike's protagonist picks up a copy of something by Wodehouse. Finding this in Updike, I figured the author must be an admirer of Wodehouse, placing him in his book like that. I knew for a cert (as Bertie would say) that Updike not only loved golf, but was borderline obsessed by it. So I dropped Updike a line, asking if in fact this were so—that he thought Wodehouse a talented writer. And what, I added, did he think of the golf stories in particular?

Came the reply from Beverly Farms: "I read Wodehouse in my teens. He was a wonderful writer, and the golf stories seemed to me just as wonderful as the rest, and to this day they seem the best fiction ever done about the sport."

So there. Suddenly, I no longer had to consider Wodehouse just dessert, a bon-bon reward to be granted only after chewing through some gristly translation of one of those dour wunderkind from India. Wodehouse was a healthy meal himself—John Updike, no less, said so. If some critics might be right that certain of the golf plots were similar to Bertie-and-Jeeves plots, and that some of the golf gags were reminiscent of Blandings Castle gags, so what? Updike said Wodehouse nourishes.

What Updike did not explain to me, and an answer I would seek elsewhere, was, Why golf? What did golf mean to P. G. Wodehouse?

"Golf meant everything to him," said Peter Schwed, Wodehouse's friend and longtime editor, when I called upon him at his Manhattan apartment. "He was golf mad."

But not always. As a boy growing up in late-nineteenth-century England he was, I learned in yet another place, cricket mad and rugby mad. Frances Donaldson speculated in her Wodehouse biography that his background in sports served his writing: "It was important to Plum's later career that he was above average at games. In the school stories, both games and boxing are described with a practical knowledge, and an enthusiasm that only personal participation and enjoyment could give. And, although he took up golf too late in life to excel, his theoretical knowledge is immense." Wodehouse, for his part, implied with tongue in cheek that he wished he had spent more time playing, less working: "Whenever you see me with a furrowed brow you can be sure that what is on my mind is the thought that if only I had taken up golf earlier and devoted my whole time to it instead of fooling about writing stories and things, I might have got my handicap down to under eighteen."

But he did spend his time fooling about writing stories. And after the wheel-spinning, rejection-filled start that many writers encounter, he became one of the world's most famous, most prolific, and most highly paid humorists. His vision of crazy British clubs, antic country castles, and eternally sunny skies went down like sweet vermouth during the Roaring Twenties. At the time, he also contributed lyrics to many of the most successful Broadway musicals, including several with music by Jerome Kern. (Wodehouse words are still being sung nightly across the land: he wrote the lyric to the song "Bill" in *Show Boat*.) Not only was Wodehouse entertaining, but—as Updike said—he was good. In 1939, Belloc called him the greatest writer working in English; Evelyn Waugh referred to him always as "the Master." (If I'd read their bios at the outset, I wouldn't have had to importune Updike, and I wouldn't have felt any unease during those early years when I considered Wodehouse a guilty pleasure.)

The first golf story, "The Clicking of Cuthbert," appeared in 1916. By then, Wodehouse was playing the game himself, or at least playing at it. "He never made any presumptions of being anything but a duffer," Schwed told me. "He was a bum golfer." Wodehouse had at least one good day, and he wrote about it, years later, in the preface to *The Golf Omnibus* (Barrie & Jenkins, 1973): "I may have managed to get a few rays of sunshine into the stories which follow. If so, this is due to the fact that while I was writing them I won my first and only trophy, a striped umbrella in a hotel tournament in Aiken, South Carolina, where, hitting them squarely on the meat for once, I went through a field of some of the fattest retired businessmen in America like a devouring flame."

The Golf Omnibus, assembled in 1973, is the First Folio of Wodehouse on golf: It is what you need, and it is all you need. A collection of 31 stories, the omnibus includes several classics: "Goof," "Cuthbert," "Sundered Hearts," "Ordeal by Golf." In "The Coming of Gowf," Wodehouse explains how the game first arrived in the kingdom (the kingdom in question being Oom, where King Merolchazzar eventually declares golf the official religion). For all the silliness in the book, there is substance. "I think the golf stories are just about his best stuff," said Schwed. "Two things he was very shrewd about were golf and relationships. He was an acute observer of the species, and in the golf stories, the satire is right on the mark. Anyone who's ever golfed will have to laugh at the situations out on the course. This stuff really happens, as a golfer knows."

This seemed reminiscent of something else that Updike had told me, so I went back to those notes, and sure enough: "No two of the matches he describes are alike. I found them so delightful that when a few years later I had a chance to take up the game I jumped at it. Wodehouse was my first golfing experience." So, then: We have

Wodehouse to thank not only for his golf stories, but for John Updike's own fine and often funny collection *Golf Dreams* (Knopf, 1996). As Schwed and Updike implied, the golf stories of P. G. Wodehouse aren't just for Wodehouse fans, they're for golf fans—of which association Wodehouse was a dues-paying member. "How I loved the game," he once wrote. "I have sometimes wondered if we of the canaille don't get more pleasure out of it than the top-notchers. For an untouchable like myself two perfect drives in a round would wipe out all memory of sliced approach shots and foozled putts, whereas if Jack Nicklaus does a sixty-four he goes home and thinks morosely that if he had not just missed that eagle on the seventh, he would have had a sixty-three."

Wodehouse was 92 when he wrote that. He had long since given up the game; he rarely played after settling in Remsenburg, New York, a sleep-seeking village that lies a five iron from Shinnecock Hills and perhaps a full six from The National, on the belly of Long Island. It may seem surprising that the man who made Bertie Wooster's Drones Club world famous never pressed for membership at those hallowed courses, or at any of the other great links of eastern Long Island. But the fact is, Wodehouse harbored a lifelong loathing of clubs.

It was golf, the game, that he loved. He loved it sunny, he loved it pure, and he loved it flat-capped, argyled, and knickered. He loved it olden. And although the feeling of opening-day was unchanged over three-quarters of a century, other things about golf were evolving, and not all of this *progress* sat well with the great old writer. "Time like an ever-rolling stream bears its sons away, and with them have gone the names of most of the golf clubs so dear to me," he wrote months before his death. "I believe one still drives with a driver nowadays, though at any moment we may have to start calling it the Number One wood, but where is the mashie now, where the cleek, the spoon and the baffy?"

Wodehouse died in 1994. I think titanium did him in.

Chapter VII

The Return of Mikey MacMulligan

Eighteen More Holes of Opinion and Criticism

The Backswing:

A year and a half passed before I had enough peeves piled up to revisit the linksland of Lower Crestfallen with my buddy, Mikey. Maybe it was the bursting store of peeves, or maybe I just missed the old coot—your pick. This second go-round with the cantankerous Scot was first published in March 2000.

I can't line up a game in March unless it's with my good friend Mikey MacMulligan. The others in our little circle down at the not-so-royal and not-very-ancient public course in Lower Crestfallen shelve the clubs in October and won't buff their blades again until the birdies call in April. But Mikey, well, he's made of sterner stuff. He'll burrow after a ball in the leaf piles of November, and hack his way right through the holidays. "Nothin' like a bracin' nine on Christmas morn!," he has been known to exult. If there's any kind of thaw in January, Mikey will bundle up and bustle forth. "And February!" he says. "February—ye can tell ye'r gettin' more light! Ye can play till nigh on five o'clock!" So of course, in March, when I'm willing, Mikey is waiting. "It's high time ye returned to the wars!" he exclaimed as he saw me tying my shoes in the car park. "There was easy scorin' out here this winter, laddie, and it's truly sad how much ye've missed."

"Well, Mikey—the wife, the kids."

"Och!! Excuses!" He winked. Mikey's always had a soft spot for kids.

"So, then. The usual, Mikey? Fifty cents for the front side, double on the back, and lively discourse on the issues of the day?"

"I accept the arrangement, laddie!" Mikey said as we dragged our carts to the first tee. "I'll be pleased to take yer money! And such a sportsman as I, I yield to you the honors. Welcome back to the course!"

I teed the ball and limbered up as best I could in 30 seconds. There are no mulligans with Mikey MacMulligan, even on opening day in March, and there is no time "wasted" at the range. With my stick resting on my shoulders, wrists draped over each end, I performed a desultory stretch—left turn, right turn—then took my stance with an engulfing lack of confidence. "I'm sick of Silly Season!" Mikey exclaimed as I entered into my backswing. "Sick of it!

"Aye, God smiles upon a slice, laddie," he continued as he followed the dive-bombing path of my ball. "And ye've got a nasty slice there to go try 'n' find. But as I was sayin', Silly Season! It should be outlawed!"

"That so?" I said as I teed a provisional. "And just what is Silly Season, Mikey?"

"It's the season the laddies on Tour are finally done of," he said. "It's the season 'tween fall and New Year's when all of ye weak-kneed family types sit by the fire, while I'm out here workin' on me game."

We walked after our opening shots, I toward the fairway bunker, Mikey in the same general direction because his ball had carried the sand. "What's the problem with Silly Season, Mikey?" I asked.

"An embarrassment! An abomination! All these Skins games and Classics and tricked-up contests—I dunna mind that at all. Golf is a game, and games can be fun! It's the money, laddie! The money! Millions and millions and millions, and the players playin' half-baked but cashin' the checks regardless! Money for nuthin'! They should stay home on their duffs like ye do, if they're just in it for the money!"

He paused, red-faced, then added more measuredly, "At least young Freddie Couples gave a pot of his Skins loot to Payne Stewart's charity. A turrible sad thing, young Payne leavin' us so soon."

"It was indeed, Mikey," I said as I tapped in for a triple bogey (Mikey bothering to ask, "Seven, laddie, or did we build a March snowman?").

I was down two holes but finally free of the greenside bunker on Number Four. After Mikey offered helpful advice that he'd offered before—"Och, you're s'posed to take the sand *behind* the ball, me friend, an' not the ball itself, which, as ye see, goes flying yonder o'er the green and into yon gorse"—after helping in this way, Mikey returned to the issue of money. "Young Tiger made more than six million dollars last year, just by playin'! Goodness knows how much he made for sellin' his pretty mug! And they have golf sticks now filled with water . . ."

"LiquidMetal®, Mikey."

"Of water! And they cost hundreds if not thousands! Young Donald Trump is buildin' a course and it'll cost a half-million to get in! The greens fees at Lower Crestfallen are risen to seven-dollars-twenty-five in February!! Where's it going to end?!"

"What's your point, Mikey?"

"Me point is this, laddie: Our beloved game is settin' itself up for a fall! A fall, I tell ye! Do ye remember, laddie? When young Tiger appeared, it was goin' to become a great game of the masses. That has nae happened. The courses are more expensive, everything is more expensive. When the stock market crashes—and it will, laddie, it will—ye'll have all these links, and all these old niblicks made of water, and no one to afford them. The game will bust just as it boomed, says Mikey MacMulligan!" And with that he took a tight, compact swing with his seven iron—purchased second-hand about

15 years ago, I'd guess—and, without much effort, sent his nicked-up solid-core ball bumping and running toward the seventh green.

"Nice shot, Mikey."

"Aye, that is so."

"What," I asked later, placing my interrogatory between Mikey's upswing and down on the 10th tee. "What do you think of sore-legged Casey Martin making the tour, and being allowed to compete with a cart?"

"I wish him well!" Mikey said with a grunt, even as his clubhead struck squarely on the meat. "I said this before: hope he gets to ride each weekend, and I hope the tour does nae press this thing in court nae more!" His ball sailed straight down the middle of the fairway and looked like it might reach the water. As I was down four holes in the match, I found myself, gruesomely, heartened. But the stream was yet frozen, and Mikey's shot rolled across the ice and up to the lip of the green.

"Ah!" exclaimed Mikey. "Better to be lucky than good, laddie!"

"Yes, well," I said as I teed my ball. "What about that other court case—over in Massachusetts in the States? Did you read about that?"

"I did indeed, laddie!" Even as I proceeded to take my practice swing, take my real swing and take a clump of dirt from beneath the tee, Mikey proceeded to recapitulate the facts of the case, which were, in his rustic and highly emotional telling, unintelligible, but which were, briefly, these:

A jury in Boston unanimously decided that the Haverhill Golf and Country Club had systematically discriminated against female golfers and awarded $1.9 million in damages. In issuing its landmark award, the jury agreed with nine women, most of them spouses of club members, that prime tee times reserved for men and other inequities at the club were tantamount to discrimination under the law. Given the jury's decision, the Massachusetts attorney general's office asked a state judge to appoint a monitor to take over the club. While the club was retaliating for the decision by ex-ing one of the plaintiffs' husbands out of a fourball competition, Thomas E. Landry, executive director of the Massachusetts Golf Association, was taking a more level-headed view: "I think the impact is going to be felt not only by clubs in this state but also nationally. If clubs haven't been reviewing their bylaws and membership policies and privileges, the size of this award will certainly put them on notice." Indeed, in other, less dramatic court decisions across the country, club after club was being declared a "public accommodation" and therefore subject to various human rights and sex-discrimination laws. The Old Boys' Club bastion was under barrage.

"Och, and a good thing too!!!" Mikey summed up as he sank his putt on Number Thirteen, finishing a three-hole diatribe that, meantime, saw him go birdie-bogey-par (he plays wonderfully when he's angry). "It's time for this greeeet game of ours to be about sportsmanship and fair play in all ways, not just tee-to-green!"

"Well, the men are not going to go quietly . . ." I lipped my three-footer.

"Ye'll not wanna be talkin' as ye putt, laddie!" He had said this before; he would say it again.

"Yes, Mikey."

"Ye were sayin'?"

"Well, I was saying—the men will continue to fight. They like their Saturdays too well."

"Fie on 'em!" Mikey declaimed.

"You do have firm opinions, Mikey," I said as I sent my drive on Number Fourteen sailing o'er the yet-bare birches on the left side of the fairway. "Mind if I hit another?"

"Ye go right ahead, laddie," said Mikey congenially. "Ye're hittin' three."

"I know that, Mikey." I said as I watched my fade turn into a slice and plunge into the pines, right.

"I know ye do, laddie," Mikey said. "And ye're hittin' five now."

"I rely on you to keep track, Mikey," I said as I waggled the driver. I'm not good at sarcasm, but Mikey spurs it in me, each time out.

"Ye can do that, laddie." Said Mikey: "Ye keep track for me, I keep track for ye, and I'll do whatever else I can for ye."

Mikey had closed out the match on the 14th green, five-and-four, so we played the last holes for a quarter apiece. "It could net me another dollar!" Mikey had said. As we walked up the 18th fairway, he had earned himself 75 cents already, and was on the dance floor while I was in the bunker, each of us lying three.

"I love this game of ours," Mikey said as we strolled. "I love the game, yet sometimes I despair."

"You do, Mikey?"

"Ah, aye, I do. I dream of ours being the people's game, and I think it'll never happen. All the money, all the discrimination . . . all of the . . . Och, I do despair."

"What would make you happy, Mikey?" I asked as my sand save sailed the green and came to rest, unplayably, by a large oak.

"A day like it used to be in Scotland, back when Tom Morris was aboot, a day when the game belonged to the townsfolk. A day in spring with old men and dogs roamin' the course, and wee ones and ladies oot and aboot. The whole town oot for the golf. All comers!"

"Well," I said as I picked up my ball and dug in my pocket for two dollars fifty. "You can dream, Mikey. There's no club rule against dreaming." I extended my hand.

Mikey hesitated.

"Laddie," he said, "Ye've some puttin' to do before you're finished."

"You've won, Mikey. I yield. Surely you'll concede two strokes against the final score."

He said nothing, but waited while I took my drop and completed my round. In this new season, there are still no gimmes with Mikey MacMulligan.

Inside the Ropes

Chapter VIII

When the Whin's in Bloom

A Trip to St. Andrews, Birthplace— Perhaps—of the Game

The Backswing:

The word hallowed is an interesting word. A first definition in Webster's has it as "HOLY, CONSECRATED" and a second as "SACRED, REVERED"—which seems like hair-splitting to me, but then: that's what dictionaries are for, to split the hairs for us.

When those four all-caps words, five if we throw in HALLOWED itself, are applied to Gettysburg or the beaches of Normandy, the application seems apt. When they're applied to the pitcher's mound at Fenway Park or Centre Court at Wimbledon, I start to get uneasy. Perhaps no stomping ground in sports has more often been called hallowed than the Old Course at St. Andrews. Is it so? The answer is in the mind of the beholding golfer. This first ran in July 1998.

E ven as I was about to sit and write this account of my pilgrimage to St. Andrews, ostensible birthplace of golf, I was engulfed by a brief flurry of Andrewsiana. First, I was breezing through a golf-magazine story about properties that were on the market near great golf courses. There was a house for sale at St. Andrews. Its address was 7203 Ayrshire Lane, which surprised me since Ayrshire is on the western coast of Scotland but St. A's is on the eastern. Must be a long lane. "Seven-two-oh-three Ayrshire Lane is a recently completed twelve-thousand-foot residence with five bedrooms, eight-plus baths, Saturnia marble floors, coral walls and floor-to-ceiling windows that overlook one of the club's largest lakes and its East golf course." *East* course? Don't they mean Old Course?

"Also on the property's three-quarter-acre lot is a terraced swimming pool, rock garden and guest house. Property taxes are $19,000; homeowners fees are $885 per quarter."

Wow. I had met no one in Scotland who'd shell out that kind of dough.

"Gourmet markets and movie theaters are close by, as is famed eatery Maxaluna [Maxaluna ?!?], where dinner and drinks for four can run upwards of $200 [!?!?!]."

Okay, the punch line is this: "St. Andrews Country Club is a ten-year-old gated community of more than seven hundred single-family homes" in Boca Raton, Florida. Calling their McMansion community "St. Andrews" is what the Lexus set thinks of as a tribute, as an *homage.*

So, then, next: I'm in T.J. Maxx, rummaging like a Scotsman (or an *Attaché* columnist) through the clearance bin, which is where I get my golf socks. Up pops a green-and-white travel cup, one of those plastic hot/cold mugs. And on its mug is the crest of St. Andrews, *the* St. Andrews. Well, you never know what you're going to find at T.J.'s, but still . . .

It's marked down to a buck, so I toss it in the basket.

The point of all this is this: "St. Andrews" has clearly become something larger than itself. It's like "Ireland," our planet's great little exporter of humanity, which now exists largely beyond the borders of the Emerald Isle. There are perhaps 5 million Irish in Ireland today, but 44 million Americans have Irish blood, and the Diaspora has carried another 30 million Irish to ports-of-call elsewhere in the world. Ireland is everywhere. So, too, with St. A's. It exists in gated communities where palm trees sway, or on travel mugs, or on sweaters, or simply in the imagination, because the idea of "the birthplace of golf" is just too big to be contained by 18 modest, sometimes ungainly linksland holes on the windswept Fifian bulge of southeastern Scotland. More Americans "know" St. Andrews from having read *Golf in the Kingdom* (Michael Murphy, Viking, 1972) than from having been to the place, which is kind of like knowing baseball from having seen *Angels in the Outfield.* (Don't get me wrong, I liked *Golf in the Kingdom,* I'm just saying . . .)

All of this is perfectly okay, this transmutation of what St. A's means or stands for. Because, you see, St. Andrews itself—*the* St. Andrews, of the Royal and Ancient, of the Old Course, of Tom Morrises elder and younger—is something of a fraud. Birthplace of golf? Baloney. Golf was born in Rome, where Caesar's soldiers were whacking feather-filled balls around with wooden sticks; *Paganica,* it was called. Or, if you prefer, golf was born in Holland. Everybody knows that. According to auld Dutch literature, little Hanses and Franzes were "*spel mitten Colve*" (playing with club) or "*den bal mitta calven te slaen*" (hitting the ball with the club), and in more than 450 Dutch-master paintings, there are all these little villagers giving featheries a knock. The sport was called *Kolf,* and with North Sea trade flourishing in the Middle Ages, the game made its way across to Scotland. Right? Meantime, of course, the Belgians were playing a similar game called "chole"—*globulus ligneus qui clava propellitur* ("a wooden ball struck by a club"). And isn't the word "golf"—or, originally, "goff" and "gowf"—a Celtic form of "chole"? I think so. Don't you? Meantime, of course, the French were all agog over "jeu de mail," in which a player stroked a ball half-a-mile along a road toward a target, and also over "pall mall," which came from Italy, and of which Hieronymus Mercurialis wrote in *De Arte Gymnastica,* "*Hunc procul dubio inter exercitationes tardad atque remissas collocandum esse . . .*" (Apud Juntas, 1573). And on and on (you know how ol' Hieronymus could go on and on). Then there's a print dating to the Ming dynasty (1368 to 1644) showing Chinese ladies playing something that looks like golf. Looks like it to me, anyway.

Now as you might imagine, the Scots will hear none of this. Wrote Robert Browning in his *History of Golf* (Dent, 1955), which placed the Scottish "invention" of golf at or about 1100: "Scots devised [the game's] essential features . . . the combination of hitting for distance with the final nicety of approach to an exiguous mark, and the independent progress of each player with his own ball, free from interference by his adversaries." As to the most prominent of other claimants, Andrew Lang wrote about the Dutch back in 1880: "Clearly golf is no more kolf than cricket is poker." That attitude has maintained in the highlands and low for more than a century.

But I say: St. Andrews is the birthplace of golf like Cooperstown is the birthplace of baseball, and don't get me going on that one.

What St. Andrews *is* is the nursery of golf. It's where golf started to look like itself, learned to walk, began to realize its potential.

St. Andrews, by the way, wasn't even the first club in Scotland. Yes, the locals had been scything on the Old Course for generations in an informal manner—a parchment dated 1552 alludes to the "playing at goff" on "the common links . . . of our cittie, Sant Andros." But as far as formalizing goes, St. Andrews was beaten to the punch by the Gentlemen Golfers of Edinburgh (later the Honourable Company of Edinburgh Golfers) who founded their club and drew up the first set of rules for the game in 1744. (The Edinburgh Burgess Golfing Society claimed 1735, but that fraternity seemed to be more about rum-drinking than ball-sinking.) The Royal and Ancient was established as the Society of St. Andrews Golfers precisely a decade later than the GGE, in 1754. The St. Andrews gents loved to make rules, a trait they've retained for a quarter millennium, and Scottish golf evolved to something quite like what you and I play today, replete with tees (man-made, from wet sand), bunkers, greens, flags, stroke play (until 1759, all was match play) and mind-bending exasperation ("I cannae gowf in this haar!") When the St. Andrews course was changed from 22 holes to 18 in 1763, golf as we know it was ready for its close-up.

And if you go to St. Andrews today, that is the picture you see. That is what I saw: golf, pure, waiting for tomorrow. Golf that would become Shinnecock, Augusta, Pebble Beach, steel shafts, metal woods, long putters, IMG, Arnie's Army, Sharks and Tigers and Bears (oh my!), soft spikes, titanium, the Ryder Cup, the Dinah Shore, the Nike Tour, Casey Martin's lawsuit, gated communities, travel mugs—golf that would become all that is preserved in its original form in St. Andrews. The town and the R&A have done an absolutely magnificent job of protecting the essence of St. Andrews without turning the whole into a museum. St. Andrews is not a relic, it's a living thing. A beautiful old thing.

This is because St. Andrews is principally—surprise!—a university town. It is not a golf spa, it's an older Harvard across the pond. Wonderful grey-stone buildings loom above the narrow streets of town and, as you stroll these streets in late afternoon, you notice the lights are all on, the kids are at work. There's something about a college town: Its buildings can be old, intimidating Gothic constructs, but there's nothing musty or dead about the place. The students bring life to the scene. And another thing: The idea of a college town flies in the face of gated communities and the like. A college town feels smart and vital, not closed and self-consciously swank. It feels free and easy, not uptight. A college town can be as antiquated as St. Andrews and yet still smell of hope, of optimism, of promise, of youth, of tomorrow as much as yesteryear. A college town has blood flowing, not coagulating.

Better still, St. Andrews is a Scottish college town. This means that up the hill and overlooking the sea, you have your requisite castle ruin. Start there, would be my recommendation, then stroll down through the town. Suddenly—you'll be amazed how suddenly—you'll notice a building even bigger and more austere than most others you've passed, and you'll notice the land flattening toward the water. Then you'll notice that a golf green sits up near the building, and you'll go, "Oh!" For, yes, that's the Royal and Ancient Clubhouse, built in 1754, and the spot you're standing upon is in the lane where Allan Robertson and Old Tom Morris lived and fashioned golf clubs, when they weren't re-turfing and reconfiguring the course.

Old Tom Morris: He is the man. When the man had been a boy, this son of a St. Andrews weaver earned extra pence caddying the links. He was a terrific golfer and even more renowned clubmaker, and the Prestwick course over in Ayrshire snatched him away as its professional. Tom won the Championship Belt, precursor of the British Open, in 1861 and 1962, playing out of Prestwick. By then, St. Andrews's greenskeeper and pro, Robertson, had died, and the Old Course began efforts to lure Old Tom home. The lobbying was successful in 1864, and Morris set out his shingle in a former sweets shop near Rusacks Hotel. Then he moved down the road to a location opposite the 18th fairway, which is where you stand—where I stand—in the lane just before what is still called Old Tom Morris's, where you can still buy a club and many another doodad.

I'm looking across at the famous finishing hole, the way it crosses the burn and the bridge and the club's access road, then climbs to that majestic green fronting the majestic clubhouse. That hole was Tom's doing. The 18th used to finish down there, to the left, in the Valley of Sin. Tom filled in the valley to a considerable degree, and continued the hole's ascent out of sin toward redemption, toward the paradise of the verandah. I don't want to make too much out of that, but it's a nice thing Old Tom did with the 18th.

I'm thinking about all this as I cross the lane at dusk and walk onto the grounds. Impulsively, I turn left and head out over the links. I figure I'll stroll a whole, like the locals used to of a Saturday evening, because the course belonged to the town, to the townsfolk, to one and all.

Old Tom, who won the Belt twice more representing St. Andrews, was only called "Old Tom" after Young Tom came along. Y. T. was the Tiger of his day, a touched-by-God prodigy. He died young, thereby securing his legend. It was said he could bring forth "the music" that Old Tom so liked to hear from a supple, well-made shaft deftly used. Young Tom's younger brother, J. O. F. Morris, soldiered on after his sibling's death, and won his share of laurels at St. Andrews with his fine putting. But everyone agreed that he was no Young Tom. It was assumed there would never be another Young Tom, and perhaps there never has been.

The famous double greens are everywhere in evidence as I try to figure out whether the course is coming or going (the truest of true links courses—all of which are out-and-back—it is, of course, doing both). The seven double greens had already been built under the aegis of R&A Captain Hugh Lyon Playfair by the time Old Tom had come home from Prestwick, and Morris didn't touch them. He fiddled with the first and last holes, widened some fairways, but realized that the doubles allowed for play on either the original left-hand course or on the newer right-hand one, and that this had immediately become a popular thing. What's not widely realized: The first-ever Open took place on the right-hand layout. What we see as royal and ancient today was, in its own time, a nod to modernity.

As I walk past a sand-filled pot bunker and then a shallower, sandless one, I remember what I know about these traps: They were fashioned, first, not by Playfair or Morris, but by sheep seeking protection from the fierce north winds. Early golfers saw them as an accepted natural hazards, and later generations came to know their huge, beachlike, New World brethren as accepted unnatural hazards. How far we've come from the environmental science of the lambs! It's interesting that few traps in the United States, no matter how wide, are as penalizing as the deep pots or heavy-lipped bunkers of Scotland. Donald Ross and Robert Trent Jones had nothing on the devilish sheep of St. Andrews.

As I walk a hillside of gorse, I reminisce about past encounters with the stuff. Not here but on other courses in Scotland and Ireland I've been imprisoned by gorse just as securely as by any pot bunker. It's silly to use the term *rough* to describe the furze between Scottish fairways, gorse is way beyond rough. And it's awful without anyone trying to make it awful: No greenskeeper lets the gorse grow, and none try to shorten it. Gorse is simply inevitable; gorse and furze are as natural and immemorial a part of the landscape hereabouts as sheep's hollows. All of this leads to the conclusion that way before Caesar's men took up their *Paganica* clubs, the Deity had prefigured that golf would be a difficult, inscrutable game, a game to test humanity's mettle, courage, sense of honesty, relative goodness and badness. A metaphor for life.

There is compensation: The yellow and purple straw makes St. Andrews—and Troon and Prestwick and Portmarnock and Portrush, and so on—among the most beautiful places on earth to play golf. Today I'm not playing, and so I feel kindly toward the gorse. I bend, pick a golden flower from a patch of whin, attach it to my lapel. You can do this almost any time of the year. "When the whin's not in bloom," the saying goes, "love's out of season." Of course, you're not usually communing with poets when you're amidst the gorse, not unless your poet is Dante.

As I turn at the shore and head in, I find myself summoning not memories of Jack Nicklaus and Tom Watson—whatever I might have stored from the network rehash, whenever the Championship was last at St. Andrews—but, rather, I'm conjuring bits and pieces about local heroes who have trod this ground in eras gone by. I have, during this Scottish sojourn, read an odd, charming little book by the current R&A Caddie Manager Richard Mackenzie called *A Wee Nip at the 19th Hole* (Sleeping Bear Press, 1997), and so I'm filled with arcana. David "Auld Daw" Anderson, groundskeeper from 1840 to 1850, a fine golfer himself and father of two-time Open winner Jamie Anderson, used to have a ginger beer stand 'round here—out here by the turn—and he used to offer "a wee nip for the inner man" on days when ginger beer just wouldn't do. Willie "Trap Door" Johnson was another character who walked this way. He was a caddy who had a customized boot with a hollow sole that could hold a dozen golf balls. Working the gorse, he'd declare his client's ball "lost" even as it was sliding down his leg, through the trap door and into the boot. Stumpie Eye Archie Stump, half blind, nevertheless was a sought-after looper, and a more honest man than Trap Door. Archie advertised right up front, "I can carry clubs a' day sir, but ye'll hae tae watch the ball for yersel." In our time, Tip Anderson would have to be considered the preeminent caddy: 36 years on the job beginning in 1960, and he helped the Yank Tony Lema steal the 1964 Open. Poot Chisholm was a caddy, too: caddied for decades, and handed down sage advice for living to a ripe old age. He said on many an occasion, "Wi guid porritch and a wee nip, yer a' richt for life."

As I reach the burn and bridge again, I consider dropping in for a wee chat, perhaps a wee nip, with Rick Mackenzie. I'm sure he has other tales to tell about Poot, Tip, and Stumpie Eye.

Then I figure, nae.

For this was a roughhewn, private pilgrimage, not a formal one. It was spur-of-the-moment, and its purpose was simply to visit for an hour with some ghosts. You've no doubt asked: He didn't play? Why didn't he *play*? No time, this time. I'd been driving in Scotland, not really near St. Andrews, and something had beckoned. Trap Door and Auld Daw had whispered, perhaps. Suddenly I had said to myself, "You have to go there," and I had turned the hire car around.

Now, as I finish this, taking a last sip of coffee from my new plastic hot-cold mug, I emphasize: You, too, must go to St. Andrews, one fine day. The whin awaits.

Chapter IX

How to Watch Golf

Buy a Ticket; Go to the Course Early; Put on Sunscreen; Follow These Other Tips

The Backswing:

In writing on golf, I've been lucky enough to—or forced to—assay each of the classic forms of magazine journalism: the profile, the long-form report, the humorous take, the parody or satire, the editorial, the travelogue, even the service piece. Of these, "service" was the area in which I had the least prior experience. That is to say: none. But every now and again, on topics from dealing with the weather to bird-watching while you play, I gave it a shot. This particular advisory first appeared in February 2000. I will make no claims for its usefulness, but I remember being entertained while thinking it through.

We were deep within the maelstrom of Ryder Cup madness on that now famous September Sunday in 1999 in Brookline, Massachusetts.

Just to refresh your memory: The U.S. team had been woefully, hopelessly behind Europe when the first ball was struck on a bright, breezy Sunday, initiating the head-to-head singles competition. But very quickly, putt after putt began dropping for the Yanks, lofted wedge after lofted wedge settled hard by the pin, booming drive after booming red-white-and-blue drive found the lush, open-arms fairway as if pulled on a string. My sister and I were at the 14th green as Davis Love III closed out his match against the forlorn Frenchman Jean Van de Velde, the fellow who earlier in the summer had tossed away the British Open on the 72nd hole by going boink, boink, splash en route to a 7 when only a 6 was required. Davis lingered on the green, shaking Van de Velde's hand warmly, saying something earnest and encouraging—a bucko uppo, as Wodehouse would term it. This sportsmanlike moment remains keen in memory, particularly in light of what ensued later that day. It was the kind of moment a golf watcher savors because he was there: he saw it and interpreted its merit, rather than having it thrust upon him by a TV director, having its significance deconstructed for him by Johnny Miller or, goodness, Gary McCord. I do like TV golf, but I like live golf better.

In Brookline, things weren't bonkers yet, but they were en route to bonkers—you could smell it. Love's win brought the United States to 10–7 behind (Europe needed 14 points total to retain the cup it had won in 1997; the United States had to reach 14 1/2 to snatch the bowl away). But up ahead, three more Yanks were winning big, and just behind, Jerry Pate was beating Miguel Angel Jimenez. "This thing's going to be tied in 40 minutes," I said to my sister. "America's going to be ahead within an hour."

And so it would come to pass. All those big U.S. leads came home blazing, and of the matches that remained on course, Europe led only one comfortably: Spain's José Maria Olazábal was four up on Justin Leonard, and surely the reigning Masters champ was headed for victory.

We were deep within the maelstrom now. Cheer after thunderous cheer boomed from beyond the trees all around us— another great thing happening for the U-S of A. Mark O'Meara sinking one of his snaky putts perhaps, or Payne Stewart canning one of his uncanny chips. My sister and I, who hail proudly from the Boston area, got a little queasy about the jingoistic huzzahing: Our kinfolk certainly weren't being genial hosts. But there was nothing to be done. The United States was storming back, and Brookline was swept by the gale.

Where to go? I looked at the scoreboard and realized Stewart, in what would be the last truly great competition of his life, had pulled even with the blustery Scot Colin Montgomerie. "Monty's on 12," I said to my sister. "Let's make our way back there. He's always a good show when thing's get tight. Maybe he'll take someone's head off."

We were walking through the woods beside the 13th fairway toward the tee when, suddenly, we were stopped by a loud crack above our heads. We froze. Two seconds later, a golf ball fell through the branches of a tall fir and settled by our feet. "Don't move," I said to my sister. "Stay right here. Whatever this is, it's going to get interesting."

And that's how my sister and I were ringside for the pivotal moment of the great, storied Ryder Cup of 1999.

Serendipity has a lot . . .

No, serendipity has almost everything to do with pleasures gained in watching golf live. On television, thanks to the filter of a commentator's interpretation and the psychological hammer blows of taped replays shown a fifth and sixth time, it's the big moments that you remember: Jack Nicklaus's putt at Augusta, Larry Mize's chip in overtime, even Van de Velde's boink, then his splash. In person, it's the little things as well as the big, the surprises, the unguarded off-camera glances and grimaces that reveal the athlete compleat. These are what you file away, mentally, under Serendipity.

Having said that, I would caution: do not equate the notion of serendipity with happenstance or pure luck. You can do things on course to improve your chances of a serendipitous experience. And depending on the kind of golfing event you're attending, the things you do to better your odds vary. Here are a few tips.

How to Watch the West Oshkosh All Comers Classic

If you go to the course for a college match or city championship, pick a horse and ride it all the way. Most of these things are so scantly attended that you can stroll four lovely miles—a good walk unspoiled—while getting a caddy's eye view of the game. When I was an adolescent, tennis was my sport, but my friend Mark was good at golf. He would watch my matches at Shedd Park in Lowell during the city tennis tournament, and I would follow him during the city golf. One year, Mark had a good round at Mt. Pleasant and a better one at Nabnasset. He was only a couple strokes back entering the third and final 18 at Vesper. I walked the entire tournament with him and his brother, John, and I remember it as a drama building through scenes and acts. Mark progressed from being chatty and loose to being tight-lipped and resolute. His game changed: Sand shots became fraught, long putts became agonizing affairs. He finished tied for the title, so John and I walked with him—and, now, a hundred others—during an 18-hole playoff. Mark lost on the final hole; his opponent, a fellow named Joey, sank a long putt. I remember that City of Lowell championship, circa 1968, as one of my great sports-watching experiences.

How to Watch the Minor Leaguers

(These rules can often also apply to Thursdays and Fridays of Ladies Professional Golf Association (LPGA) and Senior Tour events, days when the crowds aren't too very large.) What we're talking about here is how to watch the erstwhile Nike Tour, rechristened for the millennium the Buy.com Tour (though not nearly as famous as such). Simply stated: Go nomad. You want to see a lot of players, you want to see some amazing stuff, and you don't care a fig about scores. So, wander. Get up close in the tee box on Number Three and listen to the stunning thwack these kids give the ball; follow the flight pattern as it shaves the bend of a dogleg. Watch 8 or 12 players pass through, then go to the landing area of another hole—any other hole, Number Six, Number Seven—and watch 8 or 12 approaches. Marvel at the height these lads get. Ask the club pro which green has the most treacherous undulations or, on a particular day, pin placement. Go there, and stay long enough so you figure out the breaks in the putts. Watch as players try to divine the knowledge you already possess.

How to Watch the Big Guns

Different rules for different days. Wednesday means practice rounds at PGA Tour events, and it's a great day to watch golf. My thinking is: On Wednesday, hitch your wagon to a star. Even if Tiger has a large crowd, it's nothing compared to what he'll have on Saturday if he's in the hunt. Take advantage, and get as intimate as possible. One year at the TPC tournament I followed Seve Ballesteros and Tom Kite during their Wednesday round because I wanted to see Seve's dashing, slashing style up close and personal. It was marvelous watching these two have fun on the course, though each was clearly trying to play well (and who knows how big the wager was?). They were gallant, giving each other putts; they were loose, laughing off bad shots, trying wacky ones. Once, late in the round, Kite's ball was shielded from the green by a tree, so Tom took a stance facing back toward the tee and banked a shot off a wide-trunked palm. On the carom, the ball settled six feet from the cup. Seve applauded the snooker shot wildly. Terrific stuff.

On Thursday, maybe you want to rest. Wear navy blue shorts to avoid grass stains. Settle for an hour by the green of a par three and watch the parade of pros come through. Settle in the bleachers on the home hole. Bring the binoculars.

On Friday make sure you visit the driving range. See how these guys work things out. Eavesdrop on Butch Harmon and David Leadbetter. See if you think these swing doctors are worthy of their reputations.

On Saturday, moving day, the competition heats up. Start thinking of this as a tournament, a contest. Keep an eye on the leader board and when you notice a golfer's score plunging toward red figures like the 10/18/87 Dow, go find that foursome. Witness what it's like when one of the best golfers in the world gets into the zone. Follow this guy to 18, then check the leader board again and seek out another hot golfer.

On Sunday, the game's afoot. I like to go out with the fourth pairing off the lead, then gradually drop back (or stay with a pairing, if one golfer makes a charge). I don't bring a folding chair because I like to travel light, but those umbrella-style seats look like a pretty nifty idea. I also don't use those cardboard periscope jobbers to peer over the tall fans. If I'm on site, I like to see the action with the naked eye or through binoculars. A new on-course aid that was in evidence at the Ryder Cup—new to me, at least—was a tiny radio with special frequency that gave constant updates from around the grounds. Ingenious, surely. But it seemed to me many of the fans were spending time concentrating on their earpieces rather than on what was ensuing in front of them.

By the time the cheer goes up somewhere else, buddy, you've missed it.

So, then: We have arrived back at the Ryder Cup.

The ball dropped out of the tree and my sister and I froze. Quite quickly, a crowd gathered, and officials started moving us back from the ball, clearing a prospective path to the fairway. Olazábal, very evidently concerned, strode to the ball and began surveying the situation. His pulled drive had come to rest fairly deep in the forest. He lay down on his belly, peering through the low branches to see if there was a way— any way—to advance the ball. It was high, immediate drama. Sadly, the fans who gathered were not nice—"I'd pick up!" laughed one twenty-something, while his beered-up buddies snickered. "Hopeless, José!" offered another. The incident became transformative in more ways than one: my sister and I decided, then and there, that we had to root for Europe. For José Maria's part, the dire straits forced him to concede that a punchout was his sole option. And thus he lost the hole and thus he began to unravel and thus Justin Leonard was even in the match by the time he sank a 45-foot putt on 17 to put unbearable pressure on the Spaniard and thus Leonard's unsportsmanlike teammates trampled Olazábal's line to the hole before he putted and thus did Olazábal miss the putt and thus did the U.S. of A. win the Cup and thus and thus and thus . . . and see you at the Belfry in England in 2001.

At which time the question will again become pertinent, a question that many golf fans insist has no satisfactory answer: *How Does One Watch the Ryder Cup?* How does one get anything at all out of an event that is happening everywhere at once, on a golf course that has allowed an impossible-to-manage 30,000 people to pass through its gates?

I would suggest there are two ways and two ways only. You stay home with the clicker. Or you go to the course and have a walkabout, like an Australian aborigine pursuing his mystical song line. You keep your eyes and ears open, and hope something good drops from the sky.

Chapter X

The Golfing Gourmet

In Cuisine or Facing the Green, the Red-Hot Emeril Lagasse Likes to Kick It Up a Notch

The Backswing:

The editor of Travel + Leisure Golf *called one day and asked if I could do a profile . . . on a chef. Well, sure, I said—it'll make my wife happy. I figured I'd get a round of golf and a good meal out of the assignment, but I was only half right. Emeril and I had a play date scheduled in Louisiana, but it fell through, and the deadline was looming, so finally the interview had to happen at a luxurious New York City hotel. This job's often tough. I will say: I did get to sample some Emeril cuisine in "researching" this piece, however, and it was splendid. This first appeared in* Travel + Leisure Golf *in November 1998.*

I first heard of Emeril when my wife Luci and I were in New Orleans and everyone told us we had to eat at Emeril's. Well, we couldn't. The place was booked solid. Tough beignets, baby. There's a lot of good eatin' in Nawlins, so we dined elsewhere and didn't think twice.

Until, that is, Emeril's sunny, smiley, broad and bushy-browed mug starts popping up all over Manhattan—on bus-stop posters, in the subway, in my dreams. Apparently Emeril has a show on the Food Network that's as hot as jambalaya, and a Friday morning gig on *Good Morning America* to boot. He's got about a kazillion cookbooks out and more on the way, plus new restaurants opening every week—one in Vegas, his third in New Orleans, another coming up in Orlando.

He's done Leno and Letterman. He's a cook, for crying out loud, and he's done Leno and Letterman.

By this point, I'm the only American yet to see him on TV, but I've developed a pretty firm impression of this guy Emeril Lagasse. I figure he's descended from four or five generations of bayou French, with Cajun blood coursing through his veins like Barry Sanders through Mike Ditka's New Orleans defense. I figure Emeril's a slimmer Paul Prudhomme, the famous Creole master who made Commander's Palace what it was before opening his own place across town (after all, Emeril followed Paul's footsteps precisely: eight years at the Palace, then he strikes out on his own with an eponymous restaurant). By now, I've got Emeril all figured out.

My wife and I have a cable package that democratically bestows upon our happy home two almost premium channels: The Food Network for her, the Golf Channel for me. One evening she wins the coin flip, so I am not watching a replay of the 1984 Greater Vancouver Invitational. Instead, she's watching *Emeril Live*. I'm practicing my putting on the rug, concentrating on a tricky 18-footer with a slight break at Caroline's Choo Choo, when all of a sudden a voice breaks my concentration. "Let's kick it up a notch!" the voice bellows. A crowd erupts, and everyone screams *"Bam!"* Caroline, having had the beejeezus scared out of her, starts to cry.

I've heard that voice—not Caroline's, the other one. "Wait a second," I say, as I glance at the tube in time to see Emeril throwing a fistful of something—pepper? parsley?—onto a plate of pork-something. "That guy's not Cajun!"

"He's from Massachusetts," says Luci absently. She adds, "Bam."

"He sure is," I say, for I am from there, as is Luci. "New Bedford, sounds like."

"Fall River," she says. "Lizzie Borden's town."

"No kidding?" I say as I try to calm Caroline.

"Yes," says Luci, able to talk for a moment as *Emeril Live* is in one of its post-*Bam* commercials. "He's 42, from Fall River. Father's

French, mother's Portuguese. Father worked in the mills for 35 years, mother was an awesome cook. Emeril always had his nose in the pot. Used to get in fights because he was always getting kidded about wanting to be a cook. A prodigy, though. He was fixing the family meals by the time he was in high school. Studied cuisine at Johnson and Wales down in Providence. Worked in Fall River, Boston, New York, Paris. Took over for Prudhomme at the Palace. Rest is history. Julia"—that's Julia Child—"thinks the world of him, so he must be the goods."

"You know a lot about this guy Emeril."

"Everyone does. He's huge. Two divorces—schoolteacher back home, then an actress/designer, normal pattern—two grown daughters with whom he's recently reconciled."

"What's he do in his spare time?"

"Nothing. Doesn't have any. Wellllll," she continues. "I guess he deep-sea fishes. And they say he likes to golf."

"Shhhh," she sums up. "He's back on."

From what I know of Fall River, Emeril is extraordinary. Portuguese/French kids from Fall River grow up to work in a factory, or make their way to New Bedford and become fishermen. "Breaking out" means they get into college, then find a job in Boston. Among the things they do not do is become world-famous critically acclaimed bone-fishing golf-playing chefs with ex-wives and reconciled children. Luci knows the resume complete, but I need to know more about Emeril.

So I call.

"Emeril's Home Base," is the way they answer the phone at the main office in New Orleans. Better than *Bam!*, I guess.

I talk with some exceedingly pleasant people and land an invitation to a taping of *Emeril Live* plus an opportunity to spend some time with the man himself. I tell the folks at Home Base that I want to talk about golf with Emeril, and they seem to think this novel approach will sit well with their already massively exposed boss.

Emeril is a phenomenon and so is *Emeril Live*. It's an hour-long party with a band, a wild-and-crazy host, a lot of good food, and nobody who doesn't really, really want to be here. One couple has flown in from Chicago for this New York taping, another from California. They get their money's worth. People dance during commercials; Emeril leads the clapping or sits in on bongos. Emeril's staffers, high-energy folks wearing *Bam!* T-shirts, scoot around with plates of food. Emeril has a heavy hand with Oreos and Snickers, targeting young kids in the audience, making them happy-happy (that's another Emeril catch phrase, along with *Bam! Kick it up a notch!* and *Pork fat rules!* Everyone knows these slogans and shouts them in unison, whenever encouraged). It all works magnificently. *Emeril Live* has supplanted the seemingly immovable *Two Fat Women* atop Food Network ratings in large part because the manner in which Emeril cooks—always throwing in more, always exuberant—is very obviously an honest expression of Emeril's soul. Essence and spice are part of who Emeril is in the same way that peonies and the Beatles-*Rubber-Soul*-period haircut constitute Martha Stewart: they're requisite, natural, defining, indicative. Emeril's a hot, kicked-up guy. Like parsley, he loves life. Like salt, he's driven. Like thyme, he's happy-happy. Like Tabasco, he shouts.

As now: "How 'bout them crabs?!" They're terrific: soft-shells perfectly fried, covered with a whispers-of-shrimp sauce ("Some people call this a *beurre blanc*," Emeril, man of the people, sneers. "It's a *butter sauce*."). The crabs are wonderful, illustrative that this showman is, first and foremost, one of the country's great chefs.

I leave *Emeril Live* wondering about this idea that personality expresses itself nakedly through art or other action: the idea that personality can't hide. This isn't news, of course. Picasso was a colorful guy, and Munch was a dark, tormented fellow. So of course, this would apply to cooking. Witness Julia and her big, rich, flavorful dishes. Wolfgang's pizzas are puckish, and Daniel Bouley's cuisine is simultaneously classical and modern—it's debonair, like Daniel.

And how about golf? Well, sure. Lee Trevino's ball—bumping, running, swerving, bouncing off trees—travels the course as Lee does. Jack Nicklaus's game is magisterial. Tiger's sky-high, toothy approaches soar and amaze, while David Duval's fly lower and quieter, behind dark glasses. Jim Furyk's got that sideways grin and putts cross-handed. Brad Faxon seems like a guy from New England who doesn't really belong at this level unless he sinks a tricky 56-footer, so he studies harder than the other guys and sinks it. Ray Floyd plays a burly, stabbing game from 60 yards and in. Fred Couples lumbers around half-lidded, bearishly, but when he rouses he does something scary—eagle tap-ins, holes-in-one.

I'm wondering about what kind of golfer Emeril is, and about the nexus of food and golf. I like both food and golf and, moreover, one reason I like golf so much is that you have time while playing to think about other things—like food, like what's for dinner—and also: Golf is the only sport that actually allows you to eat during the contest. I don't mean digest, I mean eat. Emeril must have some thoughts about food and golf.

He does. "Cooking and golf are nothing alike," he says. "Nothing." We are by now in the elegant dining room of the elegant Mark Hotel on Manhattan's elegant East Side, and Emeril is elegance personified: neat as a pin, a beautiful dark suit, a ten-pound Rolex, an attentive manner with his guest, a familiar but respectful manner with the servers, an unforced aplomb. He's not hyper as his TV persona might suggest, but is nevertheless enthusiastic. And he is, finally, from Fall River: The patois has not been overcome, and the cracked syntax of a kid from Massachusetts is, to another kid from Massachusetts, nothing but endearing.

"Well, I mean, they're something alike—they're both art, or whatever. Golf and cooking. But my observation is that, in this game, you're never in control. Maybe I'm not seeing something here. But, see, with cooking I know a carrot's gonna be a carrot, and I pretty much know what an onion's gonna do. With golf, I don't know where the boundaries are. In the kitchen, I feel in control. With this game, I'm wondering where the consistency factor is. Even with the better players, they have problems with this consistency factor. Different courses all the time, different conditions—feels totally different than the kitchen does. Golf's the one thing in my life I don't have by the throat. In the kitchen, if I say, 'Hey, let's kick this dish up a notch,' I know what'll happen. I go to the golf course, I have no idea where I'm gonna finish, how many balls I'm gonna lose. Some days you think, 'I feel good, had a nice wine last night, I'm gonna kick this course's ass.' All of a sudden, you don't."

Not kicking ass began for Emeril only about a year and a half ago, though he has the dedication of a lifetime player. "I've been able to travel the world, and for ten or twelve years I would go to places and see all these great courses, but I never played," he says. "Then, one time during our vacation from the restaurant, I was in Hawaii with all my chefs. We're at this amazing resort. One of the guys was a player, and one morning he says, 'Chef, we should play golf.' The other three of us didn't have a clue—we shot all kinds of balls and shot a hundred kazillion. But when I got back to the hotel I realized something had grabbed ahold of me, and ever since I've been going to a course or a driving range whenever I can, playing once or twice every week, reading all this stuff—where to play, how to play. My friends saw this and said, 'This is something Emeril's digging' and chipped in for a set of Callaways. Now, I feel, golf is the one thing I do that's really personal in my life."

From the get-go, even when shooting in the kazillions, Emeril with a club in his hand was quite like Emeril with a shaker. "Even in

Hawaii I could drive the piss out of the ball," he says. "I hit 250-plus out of the gate without blinking an eye. Before my drive went out of whack, I'd sometimes be within a hundred feet on a short par-four. I'm a long hitter, but very inconsistent. I'm aggressive. I don't lay up too often, I don't leave putts short." As mentioned, Emeril's drive has gone out of whack: "It's a mess, and I don't know what's happened. I go out there and slice all day and say, 'Jesus, what was I *doing* today.' Ten days ago at Timberlane, the club I go to across the river, I focused on the fact that the course is narrow and I shot an 89, which is very good for me. Next day, something goes hairwire [sic] with the drive again. It's a mind-boggling game. I'm just getting to the point where I'm playing for points, not just for distance—and that's a difficult phase. I went through the phase where you want to whack it further than anyone else in the first tee box. Now you don't have to be a smartass and hit it over a hundred-fifty foot tree where you don't have a chance, when you can punch a seven-iron to the fairway and save the hole. I'm just getting out of the nineties into the eighties, and I need help. I got this slice going that's . . . well, the game's just a mind- . . ." and here Emeril uses an inelegant adjectival phrase that his fans wouldn't like to see in print, and so they won't.

Golf has already been very, very good to Emeril. It has provided release for a man in desperate need of release. It has given a man who takes his pursuits seriously something that he can approach "with seriousness, but just for fun, too." It has even helped with the never-easy family life. His elder daughter, Jessica, has become a playing partner. "My daughters and I took a mini-vacation, and my new criteria for vacations is there has to be a golf course," says Emeril. "The younger one, Jillian, she could care [meaning, she could not care less], but Jessica has gotten into it—she took lessons at Cornell, where she's a sophomore. I'll tell you, it's very nice to go out as daughter and dad. There's a payback, though. I'm looking at her and she's very competitive like me, and I see her getting frustrated. When I play with her, it's like looking in a mirror. I'm getting paid back here in a three-dimensional phase."

This is not to imply that Emeril has a temper on the course. "I don't throw the bag in the water or anything. Really, I just love being out on a beautiful course. I can appreciate it just for that. I love everything about golf."

Almost. If there's one element of his new passion that Emeril would change, besides the presently hairwire driving, it is, yes, the food.

"It can be done better," he says diplomatically. "Basically the choice is chips, peanuts, hot dogs. They could really do a lot more with the 19th holes. Most of them have poor wine selections, and there's generally no offering of food—and that's a shame. They have, like, ambiance just built in: the most amazing views. But they invest in Trent Jones instead of a chef, and maybe that's right—it's about golf, after all. Want a restaurant, go to a restaurant.

"But you would think the membership of some of these clubs could afford a chef. It ain't like they don't have the cash." Emeril, as you might expect, has an Rx. "I've got this friend, Shep, who plays three or four times a week and is a serious foodie, too. I told him, if I hit the Powerball, I'd have a kitchen every four holes, like. A little shack, but with a real kitchen back there. You could do rasti. Griddled sandwiches. Soup is easy to do. It would be just awesome."

One thing Emeril does not have to do, of course, is hit the Powerball, so you may just see this gourmet greensward one day. The fellow from Fall River has already built things as improbable: an empire employing 650, churning out cookbooks, entertaining scores of millions of viewers, sending thousands of diners home happy every night, making dough of all sorts. "I'm not spread too thin," Emeril insists, answering a usual question. "I'm fortunate. I have great people, a great team to do all this. I have no regrets about how things are going." None at all? He stirs his cappuccino. "Well, I wish I could play more golf." He says it wistfully, in a whisper, not a bam.

Chapter XI

A Good Jog Spoiled

The Odd, Fleeting, Elusive Charms of Speed Golf

The Backswing:

This, too, appeared in Travel + Leisure Golf in the fall of 1998—in September, to be specific. What to say about it? Well, sometimes your ultimate take on a subject surprises you completely. I approached Speed Golf fully expecting to make fun of it, if not to ridicule it completely. It looked to me, from afar, hokey. Gimmicky. Silly. And then I witnessed it, and I was awed, nothing short of awed. I wondered if I might play better if I played that way: unthinking, always keeping the ball between myself and the pin, fast. I like to play fast anyway, but I mean: fast. This was hardly intended as a service piece, but you might hearken to the speed golfers. There could be some tips for your game here.

To some it might have seemed a good jog spoiled. To Jay Larson, it was the quintessential athletic experience. The best run he ever shot. The finest round he ever ran.

Whichever.

Both.

Larson had just posted an astonishing 111.55 at the Taylor Made Speed Golf Open, the crown jewel of the International Speed Golf Association (ISGA). This is not to say that the Open is the crown jewel of the ISGA *Tour,* because there is no tour—not yet. But there will be, if Jay Larson has anything to say about it. Ask him. "By next year, we'll have ten qualifiers leading up to the nationals. I'm going to Austria this summer to put on an exhibition, and we'll establish a European office there. We've got links to Japan, and they're going to be nuts about this. We're going to make Speed Golf an international thing."

So, you see, the International Speed Golf Association isn't really *international* yet. But it will be, if Jay Larson has anything to say about it.

Right now, it's pretty much a greater San Diego thing, which is where we are, at the lovely Rancho Bernardo Inn and Golf Course. We're on the veranda, and we're asking Jay Larson questions on the eve of his phenomenal run, on the eve of what will be the best round of Speed Golf ever posted in the history of the world—the whole, wide, international world.

A question: Jay, how do you feel?

"I feel good," he says. "A little tight in the shoulders. Could be nerves. But I'm running well. And my golf should be okay. I'm looking forward to tomorrow. Feeling good." Larson is looking good, that's for certain. He is in all probability the most fit 42-year-old scratch golfer on the planet, a former triathlete who still runs 40 miles a week at a six-minutes-per clip. He has those Southern California genes that decree a trim physique, a handsome smile, a flyaway sandy-haired haircut, and an ability to tan to a nice nut-brown turn. Not sepia, not mahogany—nut brown. As Larson talks and smiles his serene Southern California smile, he eats a training meal of chicken fettuccini. He drinks only water. "I'd love one of those beers, but not tonight," he says, yet dares to call himself a golfer.

Speed golfer, rather, and there's the rub. What Larson will do in the A.M.—in the early A.M., since speed golf is, for reasons we will learn, a crack-of-dawn enterprise—what Larson will do is rise, shine, tee it up on the first hole and finish 18 in less time than it takes Greg Norman to read the 12th green at Augusta. You can't do that after a sudsy night.

Jay, tell us about speed golf.

"Speed golf is regular golf done fast," he says. "It's a golf game, not a running game. The important thing is the golf—you have to be a good golfer. But it's a hybrid. You hit the ball, you run to it, you hit it. You sink your putt and run to the next hole. Simple as that."

It is and it isn't, considering that many golfers couldn't "run to the next hole" if their lives depended on it. Speed golf is inherently oxymoronic, the jumbo shrimp of sports. It is a slow game in a hurry, a calm game gone hyper.

And, in the modern age, it was a thing bound to happen. "It's certainly not for everyone," says Larson. "It's for those couple million out there who like to run, like to be fit, and like to golf."

The ideological founding father of speed golf—the Jefferson to Larson's Washington—is an exemplar of this kind of person, none other than the great miler Steve Scott. Curious about how fast he could finish a round and to what extent running would hurt his golf game, Scott added a clock to his scorekeeping in 1979 and ran 18 holes in 29.30, shooting 98. Larson read about Scott's fusion experiment in the paper and was intrigued. "I used to run against Steve in high school—I beat him sometimes in cross-country," he says. "I saw the score and said, I can top that." He had reason for his confidence. A superb athlete as a kid growing up in San Bernardino, Larson went to Loyola Marymount University on a baseball scholarship. An injury forced him from baseball, and he took up golf. He became good overnight, then very good. Then he got back into competitive running, and turned himself into a world-class triathlete. He was 11th overall (third fastest runner) at the 1986 Ironman Triathlon in Hawaii. He retired from that nutty sport in 1989, and drifted back into golf—he became a teaching pro—while maintaining his fitness. When Scott's flight of fancy proved beguiling to more than a few, no one was better primed for success at speed golf than Jay Larson.

"At first, we just did celebrity events and invitationals," says Larson. "Then we figured, 'Why don't we get more organized?'" The *we* was Larson and a business partner, Bob Babbitt, an X kind of guy who saw speed golf as an X kind of thing. But Larson intuited that running shorts and a dude 'tude weren't the way to go when courting country clubbers, and eventually he and Babbitt split, setting up independent web sites (what can you do, when you don't have a clubhouse?) and pursuing hypergolf in independent ways. Babbitt leaned toward the terms *extreme golf* or *Xtreme golf,* and Larson leaned away from them. Larson wooed and won buttoned-down corporate sponsors like Taylor Made, Titleist, and United Airlines, while hanging on to PowerBar*.

Both Babbitt and Larson have been very good at getting pub for their game; in fact, heretofore, speed golf has been more a media phenomenon than a real-world phenomenon. You may have read about speed golf in the *New York Times, Runner's World,* and *Golf Journal,* but have you ever really seen it? No, surely not. And why? Because it's against the law.

"Well, yes, sure, that's the problem," admits Larson, twirling a forkful of pasta. "The clubs don't want people running all over their course. You can't just play through everybody on every hole. So unless the club allows special early-morning tee times for speed golfers—the first slots on, say, every Thursday—then it's not going to really spread very fast. Right now, it's more of a tournament thing than a recreational thing."

That's only for right now, according to Larson. Tomorrow (meaning, within a year) he foresees a multi-round championship structure. The day after tomorrow, he foresees a seven-figure corporate sponsorship. The next day, he foresees a TPC-type club, with a speed golf house (fast food?) and a special speed golf course, foursome following foursome at four-minute intervals.

He has hitched his dream to a convenient horse, the nag named Slow Play. "This isn't just about playing a round in under 40 minutes, it's about getting all rounds to be under four hours," he says. "The worst thing about golf today is slow play. Everyone says so. The PGA says so. Well, we know how every round could be under four hours. I don't want to give you my formula, I'd hate anyone stealing my ideas. But what I envision is, we go from club to club, showing them how to speed up play. They would become ISGA clubs—we'd sanction them. I'm going to go to the PGA this year and try to get an endorsement. This will become a worldwide movement. You wait and see."

Larson is the Billy Graham of speed golf. He is also, as mentioned, the George Washington of speed golf. He's also the Mark McCormack of speed golf and, you might say, the Don King of speed golf. You wonder at times whether he's the P. T. Barnum or the Prof. Harold Hill of speed golf. But as you scan his last statement trying to separate what is clearly impossible from what is mere hyperbole, what is absolutely fantastic from what is merely fictional, a single phrase grabs you above all others, for you are a golfer and you know what is what: *playing a round in under forty minutes.* Yes, sports fans, no typos there: The big four-oh, the four-minute-mile of speed golf. That's the grail of the elite speed golfer. He quests after par, and he wants it achieved in less than 2 minutes, 12 seconds per hole.

Jay, how'd you sleep last night?

"Alright," he says. "Three hours."

He is at the club at 5:30 A.M. on the day of the Open to spend a couple of hours in his McCormack/King role before he tees off at 8:09 as the Tiger Woods/Michael Jordan/Mark McGuire of speed golf. Of course, Tiger/Michael/Mark could lose today. He lost last year's crown jewel event—it had some other name; this is a very young sport—when Dave Aznavorian, a former college golfer from Dartmouth, shot/ran an astonishing 112.11 at the Morgan Run Country Club, just north of here. Larson had a so-so day with a 115.39, but doesn't discredit Aznavorian's accomplishment: "His advantage is he's so quick on the trigger. I'm a faster runner, but he just gets there and hits it. If he's hitting the ball well on a given day, he's very tough."

Two words about the scoring: simplicity itself. You add the minutes it takes to complete your round to the total number of shots. Aznavorian shot a 74 in 38 minutes, 11 seconds while Larson carded a 76 in 39.39, hence 112.11 to 115.39. Got it? Look at it this way: One day, playing speed golf, Larson finished with a 75 in 39 minutes for a 114, while the day before, playing with friends, he came in at 76 in 4.5 hours, which would be scored in speed golf as a 346, which would be what speed golfers say it deserves. This is why golf aptitude outweighs foot speed in the sport: Every missed three-foot putt equals a full minute's running time, and a slice into the woods leaves the clock tick-tick ticking remorselessly as you hunt for the ball.

Of the 40 SG'ers in the field today, perhaps half a dozen are capable of breaking 120. These include a couple of amateur golfers who wish to retain their status for play in local United States Golf Association (USGA) tournaments, and a few pros who will compete for the grand prize of a grand (second place is worth $500 and third is $250). One person in the world makes a living at speed golf: Larson. Taylor Made is backing his evangelical mission, but even so, "I'm just squeaking by." Michael/Tiger/Mark will not be shy about cashing the check that Mark/Don hands over, should M/T/M prevail.

The amateurs go off first, at three-minute spreads, in seeded order (so that faster players aren't constantly running up the backs of slower ones). Rob Duncanson takes his mark. The timekeeper says "thirty seconds," and Duncanson bounces on his toes. She says "fifteen seconds," and he takes his last few practice swings of the morning. She says, "hit when ready" and Duncanson addresses his Titleist, however briefly—a curt "Hi Ball" to Art Carney's "Hellllooooooooo, Ball!"—then he gives it a whack. He schusses down the face of the tee box and runs into the deep hollow of the down-and-up par-four. The only way to express it is, "He's off!"—which is not a way you'd ordinarily describe a golfer following his drive on Number One.

Jon Levin will chase Duncanson. He takes a last chew of a PowerBar and grabs his driver. Levin, who finished ahead of Larson a year ago and just behind Aznavorian, wears a hybrid uniform for his hybrid sport: polo shirt, knee-length khakis, golf glove, double sweat bands, double pocket towels in his pockets, running shoes. *Thwack*, and there he goes. Carol Quimby's next. "Hit when ready." *Thwack*, and there she goes.

Leading each competitor is a caddy in a golf cart, driving ahead to the ball, executing deft, on-the-run handoffs, leaping out to rake traps while the boss jogs ahead to the green. Trailing each competitor is an official scorer in a golf cart because no golfer can worry about looking back and counting while proceeding to the next tee. Viewed from the veranda that overlooks much of this scenic, hilly (slope rating 122) 6,192-yard layout, there's a lot of buzzing going on out there, what with all the carts and golfers going as fast as they can. You think: There will be a terrible pile-up in speed golf, one day.

Perhaps as soon as today, for by the time she makes the turn, Quimby, in the midst of a fine round, has made up the stagger on poor Levin, who's flailing. Almost every shot, she's yelling "Fore!" and Jon veers right, then slants back to his ball, gives it another knock, gets out of her way again. Larson observes the action at the 10th: "Jon should have stopped there and let her pass. The passing rule is the most awkward one there is in speed golf." In fact, it's one of only two rules that differ in any way from real golf (what speed golfers call "regular" golf). The other customization is: Leave the flag in. This is not, as might be imagined, to save time, but to save the golf course, so that speed golfers aren't ripping pins out of cups and tearing the turf.

Levin and Quimby stay in lockstep through the entire back nine, and Quimby grows more and more frustrated. She catches a bunker at 16—"Shit!"—and another at 17—"Shit!!"—then finally passes Levin on the last hole, as his approach fades into the rough and he can't find the ball, jogging in place and peering desperately at the ground while Quimby putts out. There are a lot of undeleted expletives floating in the mist above the Bernardo course this morning, and Larson explains, "Speed golf is, in fact, more vocal than regular golf. You're talking all the time because you have to communicate with your caddy. And it's good to remind yourself that you're still breathing lightly enough to speak or swear, because if you're out of breath then you're going too fast. You'll never be able to get your heart rate down in time to putt."

"I don't cuss, but I'll talk to the ball all day long," says Duncanson, who talked to it this day for only 41 minutes, 46 seconds while carding a one-over 73—a superb 114.46 that iced the amateur title. Duncanson, another former triathlete, is a veteran at a nascent sport: He was playing speed golf before speed golf was born. "As a kid I'd go out at dusk on this nine-hole course in Pasadena and try to scoot around before the sprinklers came on. I guess that was good training for this." And now how does he practice the game? "You really can't. Sometimes I go out to a local park at 5:30 in the morning and hit a ball around the playing fields, running after it." A family man with a wife and two young daughters, Duncanson relishes the early-to-rise aspect of speed golf. "Take today, for instance," he says. "To break eighty and still be home for breakfast—hey, life is pretty good." Make a note, golf widows: Turn hubby toward speed golf, and strengthen the family unit.

The pro flight is set to go. "Hit when ready" says the starter, and Jay Larson does. As he runs—beautifully—toward his fade that has landed in the right rough, a dry-land armada of golf carts sail off after him. Press row in a speed golf tournament is a real hoot. The only way to stay with Larson is by cart, and so representatives of *World News Tonight,* a bunch of local papers, a couple of San Diego TV stations and, yes, your dogged reporter (driving prudently, staying to the right, using the proper hand signals) head off en masse. It looks like the most bizarre fox chase, with these squat, trundling golf carts representing horses and hounds, and the lithe guy up ahead with the stick in his hand—leaping over streams, bounding over bunkers—representing the quarry. Tally ho!

Larson's round turns out to be one for the books, so it's worth recording in detail. Here is how to shoot par in 39:55:

On the first, follow your errant drive with a mediocre approach, chip on and two putt ("Bogie out of the box," he mutters, stepping lively from the green. "No big deal."); hit an iron off the tee on the 167-yard 2nd into the greenside trap, right, sink a 10-footer to save par ("Here we go."); miss another fairway right on the 471-yard par-five 3rd, pitch into the trap ("Buried—goddam!"), eventually miss a short putt for your second bogey ("C'mon, this is a disaster!"); be short on the 178-yard par three ("Shit!"), chip 15 feet past ("Goddam!"), sink the putt; drive into the fairway bunker, right, on the 359-yard 5th, come out short of the green but nearly sink your chip, tap in; on the 356-yard 6th, snap-hook your drive ("God Almighty! This is awful!"), and then, back against a fence, punch a low bump-and-run between trees, chip on, sink another long putt for the save; drive into the right rough on the 412-yard 7th (skateboard kid by the side of the course noticing all the carts: "What's going on?" "A speed golf tournament." "*Dude!* Awesome!"), face a 20-footer to save par, sink it; find right rough again on 8, a par five, then whomp a 3-wood to the left rough, a chip, an approach, a tap; get it back to one-over at the turn by driving into the left rough on 9, chipping to the back fringe and sinking a 30-footer for bird.

(Old guy in a blue pastel sweater, standing on the patio by his course-side swimming pool: "There he goes, honey, look—God, he's gotta run up the hills, too!")

On the 387-yard 10th, drive into the right rough, for old time's sake, then stick your approach but miss the 10-footer; on the 145-yard par-three 11th, stick it again—15 feet from the pin—then take two putts, again; on the par-five 12th, find your first fairway of the day (please note: Larson is one-over at this point, could easily be one-under, and hasn't yet hit a fairway off the tee—till just now), hit your fairway wood to the front of the green, chip to four feet, lip the putt ("Doggone it!"); on 13 knock your approach to eight feet, sink it (give the crowd a Tiger piston-pump with your right arm); on the 421-yard par-four 14th, drive right perilously near the creek, take a long iron to just in front of the green, hit the pin with a 7-iron chip, tap in; on 15, drive into right rough (this is getting old), approach to fringe and take two putts; on 16, drive into right rough (real old), into a bad lie, then put your approach into the shallow greenside bunker, blast 20 feet past the pin, miss the saving putt ("Take bogie and get outta here!"); on the tricky, short, sand-laden, dogleg-left 17th, hit a 2-iron off the tee to the center of the fairway, nail your approach and take two putts; on the tough finishing par-five, drive into the fairway as if you're finally getting used to it, hit a five-iron to 60 yards, a nine-iron over water fronting the green, then dramatically sink the uphill 15-footer to return to par and stop the clock.

Simple. And you know what might be the craziest thing about the crazy sport of speed golf? Larson makes it *look* simple. Propelled by Reeboks° and calves of titanium, he goes his merry way, giving the ball spank after spank, hitting low shots that bump and run, never swinging more than three-quarters strength (the last thing you want in speed golf is a huge slice or fade that sends you running two fairways over), nipping after the ball again, knocking a three iron onto the green from 200 yards then zooming to his caddy's cart for an exchange (happiness is a long run with a putter in your hand), zipping o'er the hills like a sprite. "A fun round," he says when it's done. "A wild round. I was going too fast at first, with all the excitement. I did a terrible job with pace, and realized if I wanted to start doing better, I had to slow down."

He did, and thereby set a speed record. Very little in speed golf makes sense on paper.

Speed golf is a game of contradictory impulses, opposing forces. It's an athlete trying to take a nice, smooth, slow swing—and take it fast. It's a golfer putting, which requires stillness and calm, while his heart's racing and his breath is short. (In this, it resembles another weird sport, biathlon, wherein skiers try to settle themselves and, for goodness sake, shoot rifles.) Speed golf is a greensward full of lead-footed golf-cart drivers, which is no less absurd than, say, yield signs on the track at Indy. It's a big swinger swinging small, a natural sprinter pacing himself. It makes no sense on paper.

And yet . . . and yet.

It is a concocted game, yes, sure, admittedly. But cockamamie? Absolutely not. Speed golf has valuable lessons for all golfers. It, more than any other subspecies of the sport, proves the verities: If you want to score, trust your first instinct, temper your swing, don't muscle any shots, don't try to be too fine (speed golfers aim for the green, not the flag), keep the hole in front of you (speed golfers never fly the green), don't overthink your putts, don't agonize over your last, missed shot. Leave hazard and misfortune behind you. Onward—boldly, quickly *onward!*

And also: speed golf, as opposed to some golf, is about sport, as in athletics, as in jocks. There was a moment of some small pathos in the immediate aftermath of the Open at San Bernardo. Here, in this corner, were the SG competitors, still asweat, hydrating hungrily, lean, happy, great-looking, having burned some calories and built some muscle, ready to return to the respective bosoms of their respective families. There, in that corner (which was the first tee box), were four guys with four guts who constituted the first "regular golf" foursome of the morning, as the country club moved past this "speed golf" nonsense and reinvigorated its revenue stream. The boys limbered up in their lumbering way—club behind the neck and half a turn back and forth, a desultory practice swing—then launched their shots and drove off after them. Any other day, they might have looked okay. But after a morning spent spectating upon speed golf's elite, an observer found them a little . . . sad.

Would Jay Larson want to retire those guys? That's too harsh. Would he want to prod them with his pitching wedge, speed them up? Absolutely. And he thinks that you would, too. That's what he's betting on as he gallops into the future, taking the whip to Slow Play. A worldwide—an *international*—uprising against Slow Play will make speed golf a phenomenon like no one has seen since . . . what? . . . Foosball?

Well, no matter. Regardless of what happens with speed golf, we'll always have Larson's performance. Jay Larson has, on a misty morning in greater San Diego, turned in one of the more remarkable tournament golf rounds in memory. One-eleven-fifty-five on a hilly course: *What a score.* As Larson stared at the leader board, he had to have wondered, like Tiger after an 18-under Masters: Will I ever shoot another run like that? Or run another round?

Whichever.

Whatever.

Chapter XII

Laying Out the Layouts

The Heroic Notions Underlying Golf Course Architecture

The Backswing:

An aspect of golf I've become fascinated with since I began studying the game in something approaching seriousness is course architecture. I can now play—or stroll, or jog—18 holes and figure out many of the ideas that underlie this hole or that. And I now know what I like. I don't like highway golf. I don't like unfair tests, either of strength or mettle (operative word here: unfair). I like, almost as much as I appreciate a pristine fairway or a firm green, beauty—beauty born of contrast, of contour, even of conflict. I like a hole that spills forth from the tee box like a painting.

And, of course, I like a hole where I can make par. This ran in February 1999.

My friend Eric has gone nuts about the game, as have so many, and there's nothing surprising about that. He's been bagging work early, calling me about Thursday outings, heading for the driving range at exceedingly odd hours, chewing up his front lawn in Montclair with swipes at the Wiffle* ball. Again, as I say, nothing untoward, nothing worth worrying about. Lots of people are crazy about the game.

But we were lunching the other day and Eric told me he had been burning the midnight oil with a golf book. So what, you say. Well, the book was and is entitled *Golf Course Architecture: Design, Restoration and Construction* by Dr. Michael J. Hurdzan (Sleeping Bear Press, 1996). "I can't put it down," Eric said evenly. "I'm mesmerized by it."

It was a liquid lunch, so I figured: Maybe this isn't as bad as all that. Maybe it's the wine talking. But, no, it was Eric: "When I'm playing now, I'm on the tee and thinking, 'This is quite an heroic design.' Or, 'How am I ever going to survive a penal hole like this!' It's changed the way I think about the game. I appreciate genius out there, and I can see sloppiness too. Some courses make absolute sense to me now, and others seem purposelessly contrived. Hurdzan has opened my eyes."

Well, you'd have to meet Eric.

But his passion led me to ask the inevitable: Could I borrow the book? And so I did, and so I got hooked.

Like all else about golf in the boom-boom 1990s—as with all the booming business, the booming Berthas, the booming sounds from the thunderous hordes that trail after Tiger—there was a boom in golf-course architecture. Of course there was. In 1970, there were 10,188 facilities in the United States (4,248 daily fee, 1,321 municipal, and 4,619 private), and by century's end, there were at least half again as many. Someone built 'em, someone designed 'em. Recent years have proved to be good times for the Jones boys, Jack Nicklaus, Tom Fazio, and all the others.

But before we get to the modern day, let's deal with yesterday. What are the traditions of golf course architecture?

In the beginning, there was the land: the linksland, where they laid out the hallowed links of Scotland. Bunkers were natural sandy wastes by the seashore; a fairway was the gorsey hayfield you walked between tee and green. My copy of Horace G. Hutchinson's *Golf* (Longman's), published in 1890, has a nifty glossary that defines "Course" with economy: "That portion of the Links on which the game ought to be played, generally bounded on either side by rough ground or other hazard." I love that: *ought* to be played. You got that right, Horace.

Nothing essential has changed with the course since then, except that man has gotten involved—which, as we know, sometimes changes everything. Since before the births of Donald Ross and Robert Trent Jones—heck, ever since Old Tom Morris started reshaping the 18th at St. Andrews—debate has been ongoing about how much an architect should toy with the natural lay of the land. In a nutshell, that's what golf-course architecture has always been about. You've got a parcel, you're going to put 18 tee boxes and 18 pin placements on it. What do you do with the rest? Gussie it up, or leave it largely alone? As Hurdzan puts it, golf course design is the arrangement of starting and ending points, and if "in the process of arranging these points, the landscape is not modified or changed, then the golf course is merely 'laid out.' If the terrain is modified or changed, then the course is 'built.' If the building of a golf course follows a preconceived plan, then the course is 'designed.'" As is readily apprehensible, advances in technology, machinery and human ego have ensured that an ever-increasing percentage of all courses have been *built* and *designed* as the years have passed.

Greens came into being when it was decided to make hole-targets permanent, and a turf cover was built 'round them. The increasing popularity of golf led to the greens being trashed, which led to course maintenance men, which led to the need for architects, under Hurdzan's definition: "A golf course architect is one who has the technical planning processes to modify a site to maximize its golfing features, so that the completed site is fun and safe for the people who use it, and so that it accommodates reasonably priced, long-term maintenance of the finished golf course."

A word in passing: I'm relying on Hurdzan's book for much of this history and some of this lore. I do this not because it's the only source. The architecture boom has been accompanied by other terrific volumes. Just published is *Golf Course Design* by Robert Muir Graves and Geoffrey Cornish (Wiley, 1998) and recently republished is Donald Ross's wonderful memoir *Golf Has Never Failed Me* (1996). This was brought back into print by Sleeping Bear Press of Chelsea, Michigan, the firm that brought out Hurdzan's tome in 1996. But the short point to be made: I rely on Hurdzan because he was Eric's avenue to a fanaticism about course design (and hence to my somewhat tempered enthusiasm) and because other experts tell me that it is perfectly fine to rely on Hurdzan. In other words, he's authoritative.

The earliest architecture—the earliest large-scale foozling with the terrain—involved putting hazards where an improperly struck ball might land (hazard placement evolved apace with evolutions in the golf ball from the light-traveling, worm-burning featherie through the gutty to the wound and finally to our variously dimpled balatas and such). The creation of hazards (as opposed to the reliance upon natural hazards) led to the idea of penal design: manipulation of the greensward to reward the good and punish the wicked. The far extension of penal design, to give you easy reference, would be that green that looks like an oasis in the Sahara, where anything but a perfectly struck six-iron with just the right backspin buys you a piece of beach. The 15th at Cypress Point is quintessentially penal, what with trees left, ocean right, and sand all over. The knee-weakening 12th at Augusta is certainly penal, with water in front and trees in back of the green, but the aspect that famously makes the hole nasty—a green so firm and slanted that you can strike a pin-high tee shot and still go swimming—isn't really an aspect of penal design. The 12th's chief penalty derives from something other than a purposely placed hazard.

Early in the twentieth century, H. S. Colt started to move hazards back away from mid-fairway to catch the now-airborne drives and approaches, thus allowing the Saturday golfer a clear byway down the center. Colt's designs were popular, needless to say, and Colt was much imitated, as was the Old Course at St. Andrews, legendary birthplace of golf. It had long been a links famous for its bred-in-the-bones strategic design (meaning: there were various tactical ways to get from tee to green on each hole). "Strategic design in its best form rewards the good shot-maker without penalizing the less accomplished," writes Hurdzan, "and allows each to maximize the best parts of his game while minimizing the importance of his weaknesses. If a golfer does not drive the ball well, he may choose to play wide of hazards on his drive and rely on the sureness and strength of his iron play to make him competitive."

So with hazards being moved out to catch the modern golfer's dips and duffs, and architects on both sides of the pond trying to invent layouts that could be attacked by novices and pros in different ways, the seeds for the contemporary course were sewn. We are now early in the twentieth century.

A nice and undeniably dramatic tangent was that of "heroic design." "Its idea was to present a penal hazard but give each golfer a chance to carry as much of the hazard as he wanted to, as exemplified by the 18th hole at Pebble Beach," explains Hurdzan. "In good heroic design, the more that is risked the greater the reward." Picture yourself on the elevated tee of a dogleg-left par four. There's water left, tucked into the elbow of the dogleg. Up here on the tee, the breeze at your back, the whole world before and below you, you're certain that you can carry the water and leave yourself nothing more than a wedge. Or, of course, you can be a wimp and not a hero and play straight to the landing area. Were Clint Eastwood your playing partner, he would squint and ask, "Do you feel lucky, punk? Well, *do* you?" That's heroic golf.

America added "freeway golf" in the post-war years: long, rectangular fairways. Hurdzan thinks the courses are "lifeless," but they did and do allow course owners to keep a lot of traffic moving swiftly. And so they have proliferated.

But they have never been the stuff of the geniuses, the Colts and Alister MacKenzie's and A. W. Tillinghasts and Donald Rosses and, then, the Robert Trent Jones, Srs., and Dick Wilsons who showed great creativity and imagination—even wit—as they built America's mighty courses. From the vantage of the present, we can see that the visionaries have carried the day. Ross courses that have been tampered with are being restored to their original brilliance. (There's even a Ross Society, based in Connecticut, that dedicates itself to the perpetuation of the master's legacy and design philosophy.) MacKenzie and Tillinghast layouts are being preserved, or they're being studied by young'uns. The American Society of Golf Course Architects (ASGCA), co-founded by Ross, is a professional organization of affiliated designers, each of whom is tied to a greater or lesser degree to the ideas of the earlier experts. Cornish and Hurdzan are past presidents of the organization. Beyond these serious thinkers are other prolific designers—Jack Nicklaus, of course, and fellow still-playing pros like Ben Crenshaw, Ray Floyd and

Arnold Palmer, plus Tom Fazio, Pete Dye, Robert Trent Jones, Jr., and his brother Rees Jones—who are giving us great new courses each season.

"When I started in the 1960s, most golfers didn't know who Donald Ross was," says Fazio. "There was no widespread knowledge of architecture. I knew about it because my uncle had been one of the first good tournament players to cross over to designing, and I came up under him and learned a tremendous amount. But there was no general knowledge of Ross and Tillinghast and MacKenzie. Now, of course, it's heresy not to know about those guys and their ideas. Architects today are much more informed about the history of designing, and the golf courses are better for it."

Fazio, designer of some 175 layouts, is driving to the chewed-up site of his latest project in North Carolina as he discusses architecture yesterday and, particularly, today. "I've been in it now for four decades," he says, "and there are large differences in how things are done today and how they were done then. Not just the philosophy, but the method. Could you imagine doing your reporting stuff without word processors and computers? The same has happened in design. We use computer modeling now, and machinery has allowed us to create courses in amazing situations. In the 1960s, we would customize to the land. In the 1990s, we'll get land that isn't great for golf and we have to manufacture a natural setting. In 1988 in Las Vegas, we built Shadow Creek. There was no environment there at all. We had to build the environment."

John LaFoy of Greenville, South Carolina, who has been in the designing game for 30 years and has served as vice president of the ASGCA, built what *Golf Digest* called, in 1998, that year's best new affordable daily fee course. He carved it out of an old Nebraska rock quarry. "Quarry Oaks is an indicator," he says. "These days we're putting courses in what I might call environmentally challenged land—strip mines, quarries, like that. I think Nicklaus even did one in an abandoned copper mine out West. First, it's easier to get permission for such building because we're actually improving the land. You can get it cheaper. And a lot of the great old layouts were built on land that was clearly perfect for golf. One designer told me, 'If you want a nice, minimal golf course, show me a maximum piece of land.' That's about right. So a lot of that land is gone to golf already."

LaFoy is quick to add, "I don't think any industry has done a better job of being environmentally sensitive. We put native grasses in to give our courses a native look. Our use of pesticides is governed by sound principles. We've done an excellent job of going with the flow of what is right and proper, but also it's a product of not only the rules but who these guys are—the designers—and how they feel about these things." Hurdzan, who read Rachel Carson when he was studying turfgrass management at Ohio State University in 1961, is a champion of the trend toward enviro-sensitive golf. "Properly designed, built, and managed golf courses pose no threat to the environment," he writes. "In fact, they can enhance it." Modern designers try to accommodate or improve local standards of air quality, water runoff, or wildlife habitat. There have been problems with courses that don't do the right thing, certainly—particularly incidents of pesticide runoff into water supplies—but the ASGCA is foursquare and officially behind sound environmental building, and the United States Golf Association (USGA) and the Golf Course Superintendents Association of America have taken similar stands. All of this has raised standards nationwide.

The ASGCA has also formerly endorsed the move toward player-friendly play. This seems like a *duh* thing—well of course we want players to enjoy playing— but really it represents new thinking. In the 1970s and 1980s, some of the finest designers built gems that were all but impossible for a 15-handicapper to negotiate. With the golf boom, the ASGCA and others decided it might be nice to build some "friendlier" courses that would welcome the newcomers and encourage them to c'mon back for a second round. It's a return to the thinking of H. S. Colt, and it's popular once again. As LaFoy puts it, "No one ever complained to me about a course he had fun on and scored well on." What LaFoy and others do when they build a friendly course is put hazards out of the reach of higher-handicap players. They might, perhaps, eliminate tall grass that leads people to hunt for a ball for 15 minutes, slowing play for everybody (put a pond there instead; then the ball is well and truly gone). "Some designers, I hate to say it, design a course so it's got this dramatic look that will make the front cover of *Golf Digest*—they design it with that in mind," says LaFoy. "My attitude is to design the golf courses for the people who play 'em, not for the magazines. I'll tell you, I designed a little small-town club in Greenville, North Carolina, about eight years ago, and that course means as much to them in that town as Augusta means to its members. I take just as much pride and satisfaction out of that little town course as I do out of anything I've done, because the people enjoy it so."

LaFoy and Fazio both wonder whether all the new technologies and techniques add up to progress. LaFoy thinks Dye is one of the "true last innovators in course design," but says of stadium golf: "I don't really care much for the concept." He says further, "It's hard sometimes to distinguish creative from gimmicky. I realize that a lot of the more bizarre courses you see are the result of an owner wanting something unique, but sometimes it gets goofy. Every time I play a great old course by Tillinghast or Ross, I wonder what some of our modern architects are doing."

Says Fazio, "There's always a desire and a theory that you're getting back to the basics—that the past was better than what we're doing, and that it's good to keep a connection with the past. I agree with that. We're redoing Number Four at Pinehurst. I'll tell you, with the traditions of Donald Ross at Pinehurst, you can't do Pinehurst without thinking about Donald Ross."

Then, independently, Fazio and LaFoy offer a closing thought. "Personally," says Fazio, "I really don't think there *is* a bad golf course. How could it be bad if there's an open space to go out and walk and hit a golf ball?" Says LaFoy, "People take a ball and go out and play a golf course and have fun—that's a brilliant golf course to me. I don't see how you could ever call a golf course 'bad.'"

They are golf men. In the 19th hole in the sky, Donald Ross smiles.

Chapter XIII

The Week of Living Dangerously

All Aboard the Johnnie Walker Super Tour, the Silliest Event of Golf's Silly Season

The Backswing:

I am no Hunter Thompson (to which, from here in the hinterlands of Westchester County, I can hear the echoes: "He certainly is no Hunter Thompson!"). But I once found myself on assignment for Travel + Leisure Golf in the closest circumstance that our genteel game can offer to a Hunter Thompson Situation. Hunter would have supplied a higher degree of drug, certainly, and a far more grandiloquent proesy, but, well, anyway: Here this is, from November 1999.

Ladies and gentlemen, Captain turn on seat-belt sign for turbulence. Please to fasten seatbelts. Bumpy ahead."

You are, for no sensible reason, aboard the Johnnie Walker Super Tour, the weirdest, most wasteful, most wanton, most fun, most frenzied, stupidest, diciest, cleverest, craziest, nuttiest event in golf. As you click the seatbelt tongue into the buckle for the 5,781st time since Tuesday, you reflect upon a remarkable thing: That the Johnnie Walker Super Tour is in its third year is nothing short of amazing. *Amazing*. It can't be said that this is *incredible,* for you are undeniably here, and Ernie Els is undeniably over there, and Vijay Singh and Jesper Parnevik and the entourage and the flacks and everybody— you're all here, so it can't be unbelievable. It must be believed. But it *is* amazing. That the Johnnie Walker Super Tour has not yet crashed and burned—unfortunate phrase, that—is as miraculous as Mark O'Meara's putt at Augusta, as Brian Watts's sand save at Birkdale (oh, and there's Brian himself, sitting over there behind Ernie, buckling his seat belt. Good boy, Brian. Obey rules this week. Smart lad.).

What it is: The Johnnie Walker Super Tour is a four-round golfing contest involving nine players, lowest aggregate wins a hundred grand. Simple. Now you take this golfing contest and, for the edification of the fans out there, you spread it around. We'll play 18 here, 18 over there. Nice. Sort of like when the Crosby— with Spyglass, Cypress, and Pebble—involved a bit of commuting between courses. A different course each round. Nice idea. Like the old Crosby.

Like Bingle on steroids, more 'roids than Mark McGwire, Arnold Schwarzenegger, Hulk Hogan, the Dallas Cowboys offensive line, the Chinese women's swim team, the Bulgarian weightlifting team, and the governor of Minnesota have ingested in their cumulative lifetime. Tell us now: What'd the old Crosby tournament involve, a three-mile shuttle through a cypress grove? Sweet. The Johnnie Walker Super Tour bundles its troupe on and off airplanes something like 385 times from Monday to Sunday, earning everyone 5,562 frequent flyer kilometers on Air Niugini. What's that, about 4,000 miles? (And like you're going to fly Air Niugini again sometime soon!) This is not to mention the bus rides, which take up about a day and a-half. And all this is after you get to the starting line, for have we mentioned that the Johnnie Walker Super Tour takes place in Asia? Allow us to mention: It takes place in Asia, half a world away, and not just any Asia. It takes place in *Southeast* Asia (Niugini is how the airline whose charter you're on spells New Guinea, apparently). You fly first to Singapore, happy home of caning, and then you slip north to Johor Bahru, which is in Malaysia, sports fans, a place where at this moment the Army is dousing protesters because they don't like what's going on in the sex-scandal trial of some government leader (never happen back home, bucko), then you bop over to Bangkok—sure is good for your golf game, that place—then hop the four-hour charter to Taipei, then on to Hong Kong where you catch a bus for Shenzhen in the real China—one country, two systems, except when you're traveling and then it's two countries, six systems—then back out to Hong Kong and then . . . you head home. This itinerary doesn't look so bad, though, because CNN's telling you all week how rubber bullets are flying in Jakarta ("glad we're not in Jakarta this year; we were in Jakarta last year") and how the Philippines are about to explode over something or other ("our final round was supposed to be in the Philippines, but four weeks ago something . . . *happened*. Thank God for China"). So it involves all this travel, and it involves kings, other potentates, dragons, sponsors, agents, cell phones, bowling, and a lot—a lot—of whiskey. JW Black, some Gold, some 21, some Blue, not a drop of Red. The good stuff. The JW Super Tour is top-shelf, baby. Super Tour, super premium.

So that's what it is.

Why is it?

"Well, frankly, at the end of the day, it's all about selling whiskey, isn't it?" Whereas in America, a booze firm has to steer clear of sports sponsorships so as not to corrupt our impressionable youth—let 'em sniff glue, and we'll spend our dough on SI ads—in Asia, anything goes. United Distillers and Vintners—let's call it Johnnie Walker, let's give it a name we all understand—has a lot of clients in the area, about four trillion in Bangkok alone, as you might imagine, and JW wants to keep them brand-aware. Hence the Johnnie Walker Super Tour.

That's why it is.

How did it come to be?

"*Maaartin*, do you think you could get me a plane?" So asked Steven Foxcroft of his friend, Martin Hare, a few years ago as they sat sipping United Distillers and Vintners product on Martin's balcony overlooking Sydney harbor. "Certainly," said Martin. "Not a problem." Steven is the PR director for UD&V in Asia, and Martin, his friend, is the director of The Event Factory, a Sydney-based firm that makes things happen. So from the get-go, Steven's wacky idea had dangerous possibilities. Martin *could* get a plane, and did: a luxury jet that had once carried Michael Jackson on his Asian Tour and that had subsequently been cleaned. They were off, zooming about in what is called "true Johnnie Walker style."

"Which is a bit over the top," says Dave Cannon, a London-based photographer who is, right now, at this moment, traveling on his third JWST—and enjoying it immensely. "Johnnie Walker is into extravaganzas, mate." Cannon is standing poolside at the Palm Resort Golf and Country Club in Johor Bahru on the opening day of this year's Super Tour. Play is still underway, even though the nine competitors have finished their round. Parties count on the JWST; they count just as surely as chips and putts, and have an equal impact on scoring. There's a party going on right now—an extravaganza—here by the pool. "Extravagaaaanzas," Cannon repeats as he puts the lens to his eye and snaps a few shots of Toddy—Gary Todd, Ernie's best friend and his caddy this week. Toddy has a hostess perched on either knee. Ernie surveys the scene and smells trouble brewin'. "Toddy," he says, "come have a beer." Toddy has a beer already and doesn't budge.

Suddenly the lights go off around the pool and drums start beating. A giant, multicolored dragon rises above the heads of the partygoers at the far end, and the music becomes frenzied. The dragon—one of those paper deals, on sticks—is chasing a ball, trying to eat it. Finally he does, and the lights go back on.

"As foreigner, did you like?" a gentleman asks.

Sure. Good dragon. Did you like it?

"Oh yes. He's the best." In Johor Bahru, there are dragons, and there are dragons. "I hope the kings liked."

There are kings here?

"Two. Two kings."

On to Bangkok, international capital of fear and loathing. All players and personnel are still accounted for—checked, checked, and double-checked at the airport. Steven and Martin, lords of this dance (or as Martin puts it, "in charge of the nightmare"), do not take their checklist lightly. "A journo went missing in Bangkok—or was it Manila?—last year and that's something we'd like not to repeat." It seems that, circa five on a bright and shiny Bangkok (or Manila) morning, last season's JWST traveling squad departed a bar *sans* one reporter who, between four and five, had fallen in love—apparently with "a boy," though accounts differ. Some aren't sure who the object of affection was, and some who think they're sure aren't at all sure it was "a boy." Later in the A.M., the plane had to leave, lest the Tour come unhinged. The intrepid journalist chased up the Tour three days later, having done a nifty bit of island hopping and goodness knows what else.

"Oh!" says Steven. "Don't put that story in your article!" But he is far too late, since everyone who has been *en tour* before is all too happy to relate "The Tale of the Journo Who Went Missing."

Or to recite the heroic ballad, "Legend of Woosie." Ian Woosnam is not here this year, and most everyone—*most* everyone—thinks that's too bad. Woosie was aboard Super Tours I and II, and most everyone agrees he was the star, though he never won the golf tournament (have we mentioned that this is about a golf tournament?). The little Welshman with the world's most suitable nickname erected his JWST reputation slowly, as he elegantly built toward the Borocay Crescendo. The first year he behaved well enough, in fact, to force a playoff with Ernie—a playoff at the golf. He lost, but had helped get the Tour off to a terrific start: Its two most engaging, fun-loving competitors had gone all the way and then some. Ernie and Woosie were back for JWST II, a more potent cocktail. "A wild year, last year was," remembers Dave Cannon. "We started in Jakarta on a day the country crumbled. I changed fifty pounds in the morning, and it was worth thirty in the evening. I've still got some of it in my wallet and it's probably worth a bloody cent." Some Jakartans, seeing this circus with its gay and high-spending ways pulling up stakes even as banks were going bust, grew sad. They implored their friends to stay. "Yes, that was quite something," says Martin. "The plane's on the runway, and these fellows are demanding we pay extra per head." Liezyl Wehmeyer, Ernie's fiancée, was there then, and is here now. She recalls pleasantly, "We were all being held in the bar"—not a bad or uncommon thing on the Tour, but for the fact that those doing the holding were in this instance also holding "these mighty guns, these AK-47s." It is testament to the diplomatic *savoir faire* of Steven and Martin that last year's Tour made it from Jakarta to Bangkok, and that Ernie, Liezyl, and Toddy, as well as Jesper, last year's winner at the golf, are back this year.

But this was a story about Woosie, who, as we say, is *not* back this year. "Borocay was his Waterloo," says Dave. "Lovely, lovely Borocay."

It is an island, a small, tropical, beautiful island belonging to the Philippines. Think Bali Hai. It had never welcomed an international flight to its shores, but Steven and Martin, highly imaginative impresarios, imported some customs agents and turned Borocay's little airfield into Borocay International. The Tour's arrival on the island was preceded by a long, perhaps too long flight from Bangkok, a flight memorable for the putting contest and for Ernie and Woosie's frenzied *pas de deux* on a tabletop (last year's jet was a customized jobber owned by some sultan; this year's Niugini edition has real seats, alas). The gang waltzed through customs in Borocay—and why not, because customs was in the gang's employ?—and immediately fell in love. "A lot of falling in love that night," remembers one who was there, wistfully. A lot of falling in love, a lot of singing, a lot of midnight swimming, a lot of very nice whiskey.

And in the morning, the sun rose, as it will do above Borocay. The day waxed hot, then hotter. Poor Woosie, as prodigious a quaffer as Ernie or Toddy, but half their size, wilted in the sun, and could not, simply could not, finish his round. He was out of the tournament and off the Tour for good, because even Johnnie Walker must preserve the pretense that this is about playing the golf.

Speaking of which: On this year's Super Tour, the golf is scheduled for Tuesday, Thursday, Saturday and Sunday, and today is Wednesday so there is no golf.

Well, that's not quite right. At 4:30, down by the pool at the Shangri La, they will stage the Super Tour Shootout. The players and three Bangkok celebrities will gather poolside and try to knock a ball onto a smallish green that is afloat in the middle of the Chao Phraya River.

The shot is not an easy one: 125 meters with a strong upriver breeze and a difficult atmosphere in which to concentrate, what with barges and tourist boats bobbing about, and the ice of a thousand cocktails providing background music in the tee box. Vijay is long of the green, long again, then short with his three chances. One of the local personalities sticks it two meters from the pin, proving it can be done. Ernie is long, long, and longer. Jesper misses three times. The Asian pros miss too.

The proceeds, should a golfer score a hole-in-one, will go to charity, but still there's something . . . what? not quite unsavory, not quite unseemly, but let's say *colonial* about all this. One kilometer from here, in the arterial canals of this mighty river, Bangkok's teeming citizenry is spending the hot afternoon washing clothes in the muddy water, sweeping out tin-roofed shacks and meager, ramshackle houseboats that are moored one after another in a stream of poverty. Here, the city's moneyed class, much of it with blood from what once was the Empire flowing in its veins, has been invited to a party with world-famous athletes. They eat fancy hors-d'oeuvres—little quiches alongside little egg rolls—and imbibe an endless supply of scotch and soda. The British brought golf to Asia long, long ago—some of the clubs hereabouts are nearly as old as St. Andrews—and in the recent golf boom, new courses have burst from the Asian landscape. Ah, but you sense there's trouble afoot. The economies over here have famously gone bust, and as you watch famous golfers plunking ball after ball into the river while the smart set applauds and laughs, you start to wonder how much Johnnie Walker has spent on all this—not the balls, but the whole bash, the booze, the quiche, the hotel rooms, the buses, the airplanes. You wonder whether it can possibly continue. Isn't there some whistling past the graveyard here? You wonder these things aloud. Steven Foxcroft politely demurs regarding the cost, and as to the future of his tour he offers: "Good question."

Brian Watts saves the day. The Oklahoman who is having "an absolute ball" on his first Super Tour, is right of the green with his first attempt, wet left with his second, but—with the pros' very last chance to top the celebrity, whoever he is (and none of the westerners know)—Brian nearly holes it. Sixteen centimeters is the judge's report. Brian grins widely, the crowd cheers wildly. The shot will be shown over and over tonight as CNN's "Play of the Day," making Johnnie Walker very happy. Brian is clearly very happy. He announces that he will donate his prize, a three-gallon bottle of Johnnie Walker, to a worthy cause, which will make some needy Thais very happy (or very drunk).

The next day, everyone plays a round of golf—we'll report on the golf, promise—and then repairs to the hotel for a second night in Bangkok.

Now, there have been clear warnings that this is Bangkok. One who is staying here needed a massage, nothing more, but was hard pressed to stop the young masseuse from pressing further. But some of the gang, heedless, venture out. Woosie is back in Wales, so Ernie is on his own as ringleader. He, Liezyl, Brian, and a few others dive into "World Famous Pat Pong Road," as the green neon sign boasts. Everyone knows what it's famous for, and it's not karaoke. Still, as all the beer and whiskey goes down and the night winds on, it becomes clear that, for these bulletproof folks, karaoke is and will be the extent of the entertainment. Dave Cannon and Ernie do a particularly nice job with "Hey Jude," and not too long thereafter—sometime after three, but before five—the gang calls it quits. There is another song claiming that one night in Bangkok humbles a man, but the Johnnie Walker Super Tour 1998 edition has taken on the town and survived.

If barely. Andy Fuller, Brian's caddy, was not, unfortunately, keeping score of his drinks, and now it is 8:15 A.M. and Andy is aimlessly wandering the lobby in his hotel slippers, having slept through two alarms, hoping against hope that the eight o'clock bus has not left for the airport. He has heard "The Tale of the Journo Who Went Missing" and is in despair. He is also in luck. Martin is doing a bit of mopping up, and now he mops up Andy, caddies him to the waiting bus. Martin suggests gently, "Shoes?"

On to Taipei!

This is a near-four-hour flight, and affords a moment for a roster check. There are, as mentioned, 9 golfers among the 40 or so Johnnie Walker Super Tourists. Four of them are stars of the Asian tour, one each from Malaysia, Thailand, China and the Philippines, and they are uniformly pleasant, polite, and pleased to be aboard. Although some are good with the English tongue, they largely stick to themselves when not on the golf course. At the breakfast buffets, the "international stars" eat their cereal and eggs at one table, while the Asians eat their congee and rice at another.

That certainly has nothing to do with any standoffishness on the part of the tour's marquee attraction, Ernie Els, who is as friendly as he is charismatic. Proper billing would make this "Ernie Els' Super Tour, brought to you by Johnnie Walker." The dates of the tour have twice been changed this year so that Ernie could participate. Ernie draws the biggest applause at every stop, the most oohs and aahs with his mammoth drives. As he did last year, having figured out what the JWST was about, Ernie has brought along not only Liezyl but his best mate Toddy, who is carrying his bag this week and will lug the ring for him and Liezyl on the big night. During flights, Ernie is constantly shuttling back and forth between first class, where he and

Liezyl have seats, and coach, where Toddy holds down the bar. It's 10:45 on the morning after Bangkok, and Ernie, Heineken in hand, is on his way down the aisle right now. "Toddy!" he says, smiling. "Hawya feelin'?"

Brian Watts has been bonding with Ernie. He enjoyed their round together in Bangkok, he's been schmoozing with him on the putting greens, he's been taking meals with the South African contingent. This tour is so international, Watts is its idea of an American: a 32-year-old from Oklahoma who's been playing the Asian and Japanese circuits for nearly a decade and is known by the folks back home only through Scotland—through his exploits in the summer of 1998 at Royal Birkdale, where his thrilling up-and-down from the sand forced a playoff with Mark O'Meara. O'Meara won that British Open, of course, but Watts' second-place paycheck was enough to place him top-125 among PGA players and earn him a year's exemption on the American tour. "I'm psyched about coming home," says Brian, who will bring Andy, a former National Association of Intercollegiate Athletes (NAIA) national champion from Texas Wesleyan, with him. The golf boom and its bigger purses worldwide has created a vagabond class of pros and caddies—golf tinkers—whose while it is worth to spend a few years overseas playing and dreaming. Brian, with Andy by his side, held up under four days of intense pressure in July, and now the dream is real. "I've got a 15-month old boy, and he and my wife never did settle in Japan with me," says Brian. "So you can imagine how good this is to be able to come back." You hope he does well enough in the '99 season to keep that Tour card. If not, he'll face the unpleasant option of re-expatriation.

For two years, the JWST was a boy's club. This year, Laura Davies is along. She's finally starting to enjoy herself. She arrived in Malaysia at four A.M. on Day One of the Tour and had to tee it up at 10; she had a rough time on the course, and her woes continued in Bangkok. She's hitting from the back tees, which is making the courses 700 to a thousand yards longer than the ones she plays on the LPGA Tour, but that's not the problem. Laura is long enough, always has been, and her irons are as accurate as anyone's out here. But her putting, all yips and dips and yanks, would make Tom Watson look like Ben Crenshaw. She admits she's feeling the heat. "For the lads, this is fun time. But because I come in here as a woman I'd like to make a good showing, and it's been a lot of pressure." Now, after a few days on the team, she's settling in. She's realizing that Ernie is as matey as any of the guys back in England—Laura was along for Ernie's crawl in Bangkok last night—and Vijay's been helpful on the practice green, trying to teach her the cross-handed style that turned his putting around last spring. The crowds love her above all others, except maybe Ernie, and the gasps at her tee shots bring a wan smile to her lips. "Everyone's been great," she says wistfully, "I'd just like to show better." Maybe tonight. At the Ta Shee Resort in Taiwan there are, it seems, a couple of bowling lanes, and competition is being arranged. "Wait'll you see," says Terry Mundy, Laura's caddy and fellow Brit. "She'll be useful, she will."

Laura is chatting with Jesper Parnevik as the plane zooms eastward. She's probably doing most of the talking. Parnevik is very Swedish in the way of being Swiss with more quirks. He's not dour like a Norwegian nor reticent like a Scot nor elfin like an Irishman. He's Swedish: polite, smiling, a little odd. He's there and not there, almost invisible. Jesper's dad was a Swedish comedian, which probably means he was pretty funny—not really funny, but funny enough—and Jesper is his father's son, a jester off the old block. The retro pants make him appear either cool or dorky, take your pick, and the same goes for the cap with the upturned lid. Jesper knows this. Watching him, you have no question but that he's fully aware of the image he casts. When he says his special diet consists of volcanic ash, he knows how this goes down with the press, and knows that it will get printed. He needles the others, particularly Vijay, during post-round press conferences: "He's two up with two to play, which is nothing. We will catch him, sure." He's puckish without really seeming fun-loving, but it appears he's having a good time. He very much enjoyed the Tour last year, when he won it, and had planned to bring his wife along this year. But she's four months pregnant and so is back in the gated community in Florida (the JWST is no place for a woman in a sensitive condition). Seeking alternative companionship, Jesper phoned his friend Mike Chadwick, a computer software salesman who lives in Orlando and used to compete against Jesper when both were in Florida junior colleges. Would Mike like to come along, caddy, pal around? "I hadn't carried someone's bag in two decades, but how could you refuse something like this," says Mike, who has been wide-eyed like a little kid since touching down in Singapore. Jesper has been exceptional at keeping Mike involved. It was sweet watching the two of them, alone, in the Olympic-sized pool at the resort in Johor Bahru, seeing who could hold his breath and swim furthest under water. They had great fun that day: Earlier, they had won a practice match over Vijay and Clark Jones. Clark is, essentially, Jerry McGuire. He's a young American with a cell phone, a walkie-talkie, and a task: to keep IMG's two big clients on the tour, Vijay and Jesper, happy. Here's a snapshot of sports in the 1990s: At opening ceremonies staged along the way, the lineup standing at the first tee box includes nine golfers, Steven Foxcroft, sometimes Martin Hare and almost always, Zelig-like, Clark Jones. You just know Asia's golf fans are going "Who's he?" If you explained, "agent from famous American sports-management firm," they'd probably ask for his autograph.

Vijay has just told a journo to talk to Clark. The journo, who is covering the tour for an Asian magazine, has asked Vijay for a sit-down about the new course Vijay is designing in his native Fiji Islands. "Sounds good," Vijay says of the subject matter. "Talk to Clark. See what he thinks."

As you watch Vijay return to his seat, you can't decide if he's having fun. He probably is, in his fashion. You bumped into his wife, Ardena, in the health club, and she assured you that they're loving the tour. She must be, she's Malaysian—she's getting to visit family. And Vijay used to compete in these countries, and acknowledges that he's seeing a lot of old friends.

That's the good part, and perhaps the bad: Vijay used to play in these countries. "You'd expect that he'd be popular over here, but you'll notice he's not," says a journalist based in Asia. "They love Laura, love Ernie. But Vijay—to them, he's still a cheater." It will raise its ugly head as long as Vijay sets club to ball, the 1985 incident at the Indonesian Open in Jakarta that got him suspended indefinitely from the Asian circuit. Vijay has always denied he cheated—it was ruled that he had improved his score by one stroke before signing his card—but over here everyone is sure that he did. He says he will discuss it no more; he reiterated that after his win at the PGA last August. But as more famous men than him have learned, denying a thing or not talking about it does not make the thing go away.

As you watch Vijay pass beyond the curtain, you wonder whether he's having any fun—and why he agrees to come back and play this crazy tour.

Taiwan—and the itinerary picks up steam. It is 7 o'clock at the Ta Shee Resort, and the next 48 hours will involve dinner, bowling, sleep, golf, a dash to the airport, a flight to Hong Kong, a shuttle to Shenzhen (hoping to get across the border by 10 P.M., when mainland China closes for the night), sleep, golf, a final press conference, a dash back to Hong Kong and then . . . home, wherever home is. This is the Johnnie Walker Super Tour's sprint to the finish.

Perhaps because of the accelerated schedule, there is tension in the air. Vijay sits at table downstairs in the Starz restaurant and proclaims the menu that has been specially selected for the Johnnie Walker folks unacceptable. There are two choices of entree, and Vijay wants "choice." Ultimately, he and Ardena, Jesper and Mike and a few others dine upstairs, where the nightly menu offers choice. Downstairs, the Ta Shee chef chooses to murder Vijay, but Steven

Foxcroft convinces him that live-and-let-live is a wiser choice. And meanwhile, in Starz, Ernie and company chow down with the journos and don't think twice about it. It's not at all clear they even know which choice they've chosen.

Going to bowl tonight, Ernie?

"Yeah, sure, 'course."

Dinner finished, the athletes and others head for the lanes that are buried in the health club. Here, there is no bar. Martin Hare seizes upon this disturbing fact, and tells the befuddled bowling attendant, whose job it is to rent shoes, "I would like 24 beers." Martin has done some math: Twelve times two. But now he says to himself "What am I thinking?!" and to the attendant, "Make that . . . 50 beers!"

Even before the beers arrive, Laura Davies proves that, at the lanes, she is very, very useful. She has a confident approach and professional spin on her ball. She rolls 184 out of the box, and the boys are agog, laughing at and reveling in her success. "Back in England, me mum and stepdad and me played in a Sunday league," the big woman explains unassumingly. After a week of 300-yard drives from nearly everyone in the room, approaches stuck to the pin and holed 50-foot putts, someone marvels, "*That* was the most magnificent athletic performance I've seen on this tour." Everyone laughs, and Davies is obviously cheered by the good fellowship. It's nice to see.

What's also nice to see: This is not just photo-op bowling. The beers arrive, and Jesper, Vijay, Ernie, Laura, and assorted others stay for three and four strings. They are kids at the lanes on a Saturday morning, at play. Another point to be made: They are jocks. Even those who roll the ball flat—Ernie, Jesper—are scoring above 150 by the third string.

The merry partiers leave the lanes crew with a lot of empties and a sense of wonder: "Who were those guys?"

In the morning, at breakfast, all the talk is about Laura's bowling. That a world-class golfer might be buoyed on the course by her performance in a silly thing like intramural bowling seems absurd, but that's what happens as Laura cards a one-over 73, her best round of the Tour. "Started to get me confidence back with the first string," she says. Sports can be strange.

It's becoming evident that Laura—like Ernie and Brian, as other examples—is right for the Johnnie Walker Super Tour. She has a sense of adventure, a sense of humor, a sense of tolerance. She's a bloke, a mate, a good 'un. It makes you wonder: Has anyone been caught on this thing who clearly was in the wrong place at the wrong time? "Colin," Martin Hare acknowledges during the flight from Taipei to Hong Kong. "Colin Montgomerie was along the first year, and poor Colin—that was a mistake. You might be surprised to learn, he wasn't really into the partying. And it turns out he hates to fly."

When was it evident there was a problem?

"About 55 minutes in, as I remember."

But he stuck it out?

"Wellllll, yessssss." Martin pauses. "It wasn't all smooth. Things seemed to go from bad to worse for poor Colin. Whenever the plane hit turbulence, everyone would yell out 'Colin!' That wasn't very nice. He was already pretty upset when a bus was late at one point—in Bangkok, maybe, or Taipei. Somewhere. So Colin was upset, and we scrambled and arranged a car for him and he took off to get back to the hotel. The car, sadly, went left, and we watched it drive off in the wrong direction. It took Colin 4 hours to get back, not 40 minutes, and of course, we were well along with our party by then. Colin comes walking in pretty fumed up. I think we knew at that point that poor Colin wouldn't be returning to the Tour in the second year."

JWST III barrels through Hong Kong's beautiful new airport, is herded onto buses, and follows a police escort to the mainland border. There, a second round of Chinese Customs must be passed, and this before 10 P.M., when this sleeping giant of a country beds down. All hands are cleared by 9:37—23 minutes to spare. "That went nicely," says Steven, as he buys a dozen Carlsbergs at a little stand in the Customs depot that is marked "Deli." Welcome to the new China: Delis and Carlsbergs.

Everyone's tired by the time the Tour reaches the Mission Hills Resort, a massive spread of hotel rooms, an adjacent little Levittown of golf-resort houses—"Hillsborough"—that might have been transplanted from Myrtle Beach, 50 tennis courts, a bunch of swimming pools and 72 holes of golf, many of them lit at night, designed by folks named Faldo and Ozaki and Nicklaus. A million Chinese live within an hour of the resort, and an ever-increasing number of them have real money. Some are out playing golf right now. But except for a few stragglers at, yes, the bar, the Johnnie Walker Super Tourists head for bed.

Next morning, Jesper asks Vijay when tee-off time is. "Yours is noon, I think," Vijay says. It's a joke, and there is general, mild laughter. Jesper's appointed time is, in fact, 10:45, as is Vijay's. But Vijay wouldn't mind seeing Jesper show up late, for then Vijay would move back into first place in the tournament.

Ah, yes, the tournament. The golf tournament. What's been happening with the golf tournament?

On Day One, the hotshots were all a little 'lagged, and their games were lacking. A Chinese pro named Michael Chang led the tournament. None of the Asian press seemed taken with the fact that an athlete named Michael Chang was leading a golfing contest, not a tennis one. There is precious little irony afoot at the post-play press conferences on the JWST, where most of the questions seem geared toward next-day headlines that shout THEY APPROVE OF US! ("How you like our course?" "How you like our swimming pool?" "How you like our greens?"). Vijay liked the greens fine at the Thailand Country Club, where he scorched the course on a hot day, shooting a six-under 66 and restoring order atop the leader board. No one liked the greens at Ta Shee, though they were polite during the press conference—Vijay smiling for many seconds before finding something he could laud about the course, this being its beautiful setting in the mountains. Jesper was close enough with his irons to sink several short, bumpy putts at Ta Shee; he shot 65 and led by two.

Suddenly, the JWST was starting to look like an athletic competition. Vijay acknowledges as much at breakfast on this, the final day. "It's a crazy thing, this tour, and it doesn't really feel like a tournament day to day," he says. "Then we get out on the course and it becomes golf and it gets really serious."

How could it not, when your final three-ball involves Jesper Parnevik, Ernie Els, and Vijay Singh, hitting in that order? After a disappointing opening ceremony at Mission Hills—the first one of the week not to involve a little-kid dance troupe in native dress and a lot of throbbing drums—the three drive long, approach accurately, and face birdie putts. Vijay and Jesper make, Ernie misses. The battle is joined.

And it's quite a battle. The last thing you would dare ask of the Johnnie Walker Super Tour, a tour that offers you so very much, is super golf, but that is what you get on this final day. Vijay is scintillating on the front nine. He goes birdie, birdie, birdie, eagle, birdie as an opening salvo; there are murmurs in the crowd that he could be headed toward a 59. Jesper tries to hang in. He's still accurate with those irons, still sinking the occasional 30 footer. Ernie sits back and marvels; he'll finish third, and he knows it.

Jesper is one down at the long par-four 16th when Vijay drives into a fairway bunker left, clears the water to another bunker, comes out to the fringe. There seems hope, but Vijay, who has been the hottest player on the planet since the PGA, calmly chips in. Jesper will shoot 66 and lose by two, because Vijay finishes with a 62. Thrilling stuff.

There are not usually two-handed handshakes, hugs and kisses at the end of a golf tournament, but there are at the end of the Johnnie Walker Super Tour as everyone disperses—Vijay to the match-play playoff in Hawaii where he will lose in the final to Tiger Woods; Ernie and Brian, who finished fourth, to events in Japan, where Brian will win the Sony World Open; Jesper to his pregnant wife's side in Orlando; Laura to Florida, too, where her putter will remain balky but her long game, fortified by competition with the boys, will be enough to thrash the girls in the LPGA Tournament Championship, Laura's first win in a long while. A nice afterglow to her first Johnnie Walker Super Tour.

As for you, you just head home. You've got time on the long flight for some remembering, some way-belated postcard writing, some figuring. Playing with the statistics, you realize that the Johnnie Walker Super Tour can, in fact, exist in nature, for $T\text{-}G/T\text{-}S = TT/T\text{-}D^2$ (which is to say, the ratio of time golfing divided by time sleeping is precisely equivalent to travel time over time spent drinking, squared). Happy with that knowledge, you turn to reminiscence. First, of the golf: Laura in a grass bunker on Day One, downhill lie, booming a seven iron on a line, over water, finding the green—as fine and forceful an approach as you've ever seen by a golfer. Same day, dogleg four over water, Jesper, Vijay and Ernie not thinking twice and driving the green, while the Asians in their company take the long way 'round, the crowd giggling and whispering "cheeken," the action saying all that you have to know about the difference between the Asian Tour and the PGA. The serene 15th green at Ta Shee, set in a grove, Jesper dropping a long putt as chanting wafts down from a monastery on the hillside, feng shui golf. Ernie, Vijay, and Jesper sitting on the fairway on the last day, waiting for the green at 15 to clear, joking with one another, having fun.

Fun. You try to seize upon the one image that says it all about the Johnnie Walker Super Tour. You try this one: Malaysia, you go jogging from the hotel, hang a right at the entrance to the extravagant club, run past little kids shouting "hello" in English, find yourself amidst shacks and shanties, clotheslines, grandma swinging on a rickety swing, cats and dogs and kids everywhere.

That's not it. Too political.

You try this one: Raining out on the course, and a nice fellow, obviously local, shares your space beneath a tree. "La Nina," he explains. Ah. He's exceedingly friendly. By the time the storms clears, maybe 10 minutes, you have learned that he does not golf, has three girls aged eight, six and "maybe two, maybe three" and wants one more child as long as it's a boy. He agrees that girls are good, but they fight all the time and he wants a boy. You also learn that what you're reading about the sex scandal is already filtered. "In America you're free to write. Here not free."

Too political. Think about *fun*.

You recall this: The Air Niugini charter is taxiing to the gate—somewhere, in some country—as Ernie's friend Toddy—sweet, buzz cut, immense Toddy—appears from the forward cabin with a Heineken in his hand. He's heading to his seat with a big smile on his face.

Where ya been?

"I landed the plane, mate. Just took the controls there at the end. Fun."

Great fun.

Chapter XIV

"Then There's a Blind Approach to the Green..."

Seeing Is Believing, as We Travel 18 with the Masters of Sightless Golf

The Backswing:

I first wrote about blind golfers in the late 1990s and then was pleased to have the organizers of the Ken Venturi event ask me to redo the piece for their 2000 program. As a bonus, I got to play in a second Monday round with the blind golfers. I stunk as usual, but bizarrely and rather unbelievably saved my one good shot for the moment juste. I was faced with a 40-foot downhill left-to-right-breaking chip, and as I popped it, Venturi himself, hopping hole to hole in a golf cart, came over the ridge. He started to call the shot in his CBS voice: "... and it slows and leans towards the cup and it ... drops!" I was thrilled, of course. I only wish I had the moment on tape!

The replay was shown over and over again on nightly newscasts nationwide. A golfer named Worth Dalton drew his iron back and proceeded to strike the ball well and true. It landed in the center of the green on the par-three hole, and backed up neatly into the cup. Worth Dalton had his ace.

But why all the hubbub, why all the stuff and bother over Worth Dalton's hole-in-one? Well, what commentators from Maine to California, Minneapolis to Miami could not get over was: Worth Dalton is blind.

Get over it. Believe it. Worth Dalton is not only for real, he's not alone. At millennium's end, variously disabled Americans will be denied no opportunity, and blind golfers will not be denied their tee times!

It's not an oxymoron, blind golf, and it's not really a new thing, either. Much as competitive disabled skiing, which would eventually grow to be included as a demonstration event in the Winter Olympics, sprouted in the aftermath of the Vietnam War, as returning veterans strove to continue in a sport they had loved before being wounded in action, so too, earlier, did blind golf emerge in the years after World War II. If Alexander Cartwright and Henry Chadwick can each be called the Father of Baseball, then so too can Joe Lazaro and Charley Boswell share the title Patriarch of Blind Golf. Both men lost their eyesight during the war, then were discharged and returned home—Lazaro to Massachusetts, Boswell, an Alabaman, to new, temporary digs at the Valley Forge (Pennsylvania) Medical Center, where he recuperated and was trained along with other blind soldiers. Lazaro had played some golf before the war, Boswell had not. One day Lazaro was over at the Wayland Country Club where he had caddied as a boy, and the pro, Phil Farina, saw him fooling around with a club. "You swing well enough to break a hundred," Farina said.

If Lazaro and Boswell are the Cartwright and Chadwick of blind golf, then Farina is the Annie Sullivan (which I guess makes Lazaro also the Helen Keller; this is all getting very confusing). He's the miracle worker. He told Lazaro that he could help him re-learn the game, but not until he himself devised a proper way to coach a blind golfer. Diligently, Farina worked at perfecting a blindfolded swing, then figured out how to set up a player, get the stance right, place the club head behind the ball, estimate distance and direction without getting the client all bothered about bunkers or ponds. Farina became an accomplished pseudo-blind golfer, then passed on his learning to Lazaro.

Charley Boswell, meanwhile, was rehabbing in Pennsylvania. "They had some of us hit golf balls as part of their recreation program," Boswell, who died a couple of years ago, once recalled. "They got me square over the ball, and I hit it squarely on the first time. We hit balls for more than an hour. Forget it, I was hooked. I never took another Braille course or another typing course at Valley Forge."

It's too much to say that the United States Blind Golfers Association (USBGA), founded in 1949, was, in its earliest years, much of an association: It was Lazaro, Boswell, a few others, a passion for the game and a couple of organized events per year. From 1949 to 1974, only three USBGA national championships were not won by either Lazaro or Boswell; they were the Ben Hogan and Arnold Palmer of blind golf during that era. They could shoot in the 80s—Lazaro once carded a 77—and others, while game, had trouble breaking a century. So Lazaro and Boswell dominated the competitions. But even if the tournaments had slight fields and routine outcomes, the sport did gain some note, not least because it seemed like such a remarkable thing.

Think about it again, for just a second. Blind golf. Remarkable, simply remarkable.

I know for a certainty precisely when I first heard about blind golf—it was the first time I heard that joke. I was a kid, it was in the 1960s, and Bob Hope was telling it. He was on TV and either Lazaro and Boswell were alongside. Hope told the audience what these men were about, blind golfing, and then they put on a little demonstration. Then Hope told about how they had challenged him to a match. He didn't want to pick their pockets, but had finally agreed. "Okay," Hope said that they had said. "Meet me at the first tee—at midnight."

Ra-to-boom.

Hope did that patented deadpan thing where he sort of rocks on his heels, and the audience howled. I've heard the joke a dozen times since, but never told as well as Hope told it.

I heard it, most recently, in Westchester County, New York, when the 15 best blind golfers from throughout the country, plus the best blind player from Britain, convened for a two-day event, the Ken Venturi Guiding Eyes Classic. On Sunday, the golfers were to compete at the lush Mount Kisco Country Club in the Corcoran Cup, an invitational that is known as "the Masters of blind golf." (There are now blind golf tournaments played annually in Canada, Europe, Australia and Japan, plus four "majors" in the United States; because the Corcoran Cup limits its field to 16, it stands in as the highly selective Masters.) On Monday, the equally beautiful and even more hilly Donald Ross/Charles Banks course at the Whippoorwill Club, just down the street, would get into the act as part of a charity shotgun event to raise money for Guiding Eyes, an organization that trains guide dogs for the blind. The athletes are playing for their people: All blind golf tournaments benefit one cause or another having to do with the blind or disabled.

I and a whole lot of other sighted folks took part in the Monday shotgun, which was wonderful fun, but I want to tell you about the tournament itself. That was the special event.

We are at the Kisco course, then, on a warm and sunny Sunday.

I follow, first, the twosome that includes Walter Dietz and his brother Ed, and the Brit, Ron Tomlinson, and his wife Stephanie. That sounds like a foursome rather than a twosome, you might say. Well, it is and it isn't. Walter and Ron are the blind golfers, Ed and Stephanie are the "coaches." Don't call them caddies. They drive the cart, lead the player to the ball, set the alignment, calculate the distance, assess the practice swing ("a little more backswing . . . once more . . . *that's* it!"), place the club face immediately behind the ball, line up the putts, lead the cheering ("Here we go—right in the bunker!—no problem . . . Sun's out, breeze is blowing, time for a birdie!"). Every blind golfer will tell you that the coach is the most important part of his or her game. (This year, for the first time ever, a woman is competing in the Corcoran Cup: Sheila Drummond of Lehighton, Pennsylvania.)

On the first tee, Walter Dietz holds the club horizontal at the belt and his brother sights down the shaft and helps Walter align. Walter takes a large swing—he's one of the biggest hitters in the game—but hooks the ball. Tomlinson, with his turn, skulls one. Both men will improve; they're just off to rocky starts. Tomlinson winds up in a trap on Number One, which is not a place any golfer, sighted or not, wants to be if he's not yet loose. The only rule that is different in blind golf is that the player can ground his club in the sand, for obvious reasons. Tomlinson is out of the bunker with a single swing; I, for one, would not have been. Dietz proceeds to pace off his chip shot, holding his brother's arm. He gets up and down. Tomlinson struggles with his putting. It's hard to watch a blind golfer three-putt from four feet, something that happens more than a few times today, but eventually the cringe factor wears off, and the spectator simply celebrates the will, effort, and ultimately, the accomplishment of these athletes.

I walk ahead on the course and catch up to the twosome that includes Pat Browne, Jr. If Lazaro and Boswell were the Hogan and Palmer of blind golf, then Browne has been the Jack Nicklaus: He took over from them and became the greatest the sport had ever seen. The long (6'4"), lean fellow from New Orleans was a one-handicapper when he played at Tulane, before losing his sight in 1966. Sightless, he once shot a 74 at the Mission Hills Country Club in Rancho Mirage, California; he has won an astonishing 21 USBGA national championships; he has won the Corcoran Cup 17 times in 18 tries. He was coached for years by Gerry Barousse, a former All America golfer at Washington and Lee University, and they were an indomitable team. Browne, now 66, is coached this year by his boy, Pat Browne III, and it is undeniably touching to watch the child as father to the man: giving him the distance on a par three, lining him up, bending to watch the flight of the ball, exulting as it finds the green and rolls to a stop 20 feet downslope of the pin. "Great shot, Dad."

The golfers out here are full of jokes. "I've never seen a trap!" "Wow, look where that went! Well, it's lucky you can't."

"Never have to worry about water." Browne says, as he has said a thousand times, "I've never faced anything but a straight putt." It's the truth. A player will, usually, pace off a putt with his coach. But when these coaches see a 40-foot, downhill, double-breaker, they will determine that the thing to do is hit it to this spot, here, with enough pace to carry it six feet—then let the green do the rest. They'll line the player up, and ask for a six-footer. The player does as told, and it's astonishing how many of the long putts are close. I watch, and determine to putt with my eyes closed next Saturday.

I skip ahead to the twosome including James Baker of Nashville and last year's Corcoran champ, Keith Melick of Longwood, Florida. Baker comments on the 17th tee that he's "playing like a dog," then creams a 260-yard drive to the center of the fairway. Melick made the turn in 44 but is struggling on the home holes. "After that bad shot on 10, I haven't been able to get started again—it just took the wind out of my sails." We all know that feeling. But he hits tremendous fairway woods on both 17 and 18, gets up and down from creek side on the final hole, and finishes with a very respectable 104.

Melick pulled a Bobby Jones last year—he won all of the major tournaments. I ask him what he feels is the hardest shot for a blind golfer. "Pitching over something. Lobbing the ball is very tough."

"But," his wife and coach, Jean, interrupts, "Keith's very, very good from 150 yards and in. His short game and his putting are his strengths." Melick won the national championship in a playoff last year, becoming, at 68, the oldest player to claim the title. He's playing better than ever, and gives the credit to "the Scottish lass. Without Jean, I am nothing but another blind man. With her help . . ." He leaves the sentiment unsaid.

I ask the great Ken Venturi how he got involved with this gang. "I was friends with Charley Boswell, whom everybody loved," he says. "Twenty-three years ago, he asked if I'd come up here for this event and I said, 'For you, Charley, anything.' That was 23 years ago and the only year I missed was last year when my wife, Beau, died. We've put 350 dogs in the hands of the blind with this event.

"You know," he continues, "I'm always thinking about the guys who are here today. If you listen to my commentary on TV, I tend to over-explain some things. The reason is, I'm explaining the action for my blind golfers."

I determine to listen more closely, next time Ken is commentating.

The word comes in that David Meador of Nashville has finished at 104; a playoff is ordered. As dusk begins to settle in Mount Kisco, Meador and Melick return to the first tee. Most all of the blind golfers return in their carts with their coaches to watch, as they can, the action. After tee shots and approaches, Melick is in the trap, right, while Meador is in a bush, left. It seems the sentiment is with him: He won the national championship at Firestone in 1977, but has been second in the Corcoran Cup no fewer than 20 times. That's hard cheese.

Melick blasts to 18 feet. Meador goes over the green, then chips back to 6 feet, but he's hitting six. In between shots and putts, there's constant whispering as the various coaches tell their players precisely what's going on with the match.

Melick gets down in two, and he has defended his title. Handshakes and hugs are general, as is commiseration for David Meador. But not from his coach, Everett Davis, who remains resolutely positive. "A good day, David," he says. "Long day. Now we can put those clubs in the trunk."

"That's right," says Meador. "It's been a good day."

Chapter XV

Clint Eastwood's New Courses

Almost 70, the Actor Concentrates on His Home Holes

The Backswing:

I remember dashing for the airport after a day at the office and being so late for my plane I was told, "You can make your flight at the gate, but your clubs might not be on the plane!" They were disappearing even then into a hole that would lead to a tunnel that would take them to a transport that would deliver them to the jet's cargo bay. "But," I said. "But . . . They have to get there. I'm playing tomorrow with Clint Eastwood!!" When I arrived in San Francisco, the clubs were there, too. Clint makes things happen even when he doesn't know it. This was published in Travel + Leisure Golf *in January 1999, which explains why you'll not be reading about the most recent masterworks—*Mystic River, Million Dollar Baby, Letters from Iwo Jima—*in Clint's continuing string of* extraordinary *filmic successes.*

The big man comes riding over the hill, squinting in the bright western sun. He pulls up suddenly and dust flies into the air, blowing onto three grizzled hombres nearby. Clint Eastwood looks at the men with that gaze of his and he says . . .

"Sorry."

There are several things wrong with this picture. Eastwood's riding not a big stallion but a golf cart called E-Z-Go. He's wearing not a sombrero and bloodstained oilcloth coat but neat slacks and a corduroy-cotton golf shirt. He is shod not by Justin but by Footjoy. The weapons he's packing are not a Remington rifle and a Colt six, but a bubble-headed driver and an assortment of oversized irons; they're used for shooting Hogans, not desperados. Most disorienting, on his face there's no sign of the hallmark snarl, but instead a sheepish, little-boy's smile. And finally, being Clint Eastwood means, if it means nothing else, never having to say you're sorry.

Yet Clint the man—as opposed to Clint the cowboy or Clint the cop or even Clint Eastwood the icon—apologizes all day, every day. "Sorry I'm late." "Sorry, I've got to go." "Sorry, I can't remember." "Uhhh, sorry, I think I stepped in your line." He is an unfailingly polite, gracious, charming man. A gentleman. Having agreed to a 20-minute photo shoot—actually his people handle agreements, subject to Eastwood's approval—he gives the photographer two hours and is willing to give more. He tells the shooter, "Whatever you want, my dove." (To reiterate: Dirty Harry tells a shooter, "Whatever you want, my dove.") When people who have spent a day with Eastwood compare notes over nightcaps, their critiques include "a real sweetie" and "what a doll," and "he's so *nice*." These are comments from paid assassins (well, magazine journalists) instinctively quick on the trigger with "typical Hollywood asshole."

"Uhhhh, sorry guys," Eastwood repeats as *tres hombres* brush grit from their clothes.

"It's okay, Mr. Eastwood," says one.

"Hey Mr. Eastwood," says another, "Congratulations on the hole-in-one."

"Thanks," Eastwood says as he dismounts E-Z-Go. "That was a real one. I had one before on a short course, but that was the first real one of my life. It was over at Carmel Valley Ranch."

"Seventh hole?"

"Yeah."

"I'll set the pins, next time."

Everyone laughs. The boys are clearly respectful of Eastwood but know they can kid him, even though he's their boss. They're part of a construction crew that's been working for him up here, high in the beautiful Carmel Valley. They are molding a lovely thousand-acre meadow into a spectacular golf course, with equestrian center, clubhouse, and three-dozen luxury homes attendant. The course will be called Tehama but that's a technicality. Already, even though only 14 holes are finished, it's known as "Clint's course." A more accurate phrase would be Clint's Club, for membership will be restricted to 300, each of them having received a personal invitation from Mr. Eastwood. There will be no tee times at Clint's Club. If you're in, you're in like Flynn: You show up, and you'll be served. "It'll be a nice place," says Eastwood. "We'll have some fun up here."

Fun. Think about fun for a moment. When you were a little kid, you played in the backyard, yes? One day it was cowboys and Indians, next day you built a clubhouse, next day you laid out a raggedy golf course. It was fun. This is Clint Eastwood's backyard—he has owned most of this meadow for years—and, at 68, with a lifetime of cowboy and Indians behind him, he is still the biggest little kid in the world. "He's having fun with this," says Bob Hickman, who will be the pro at Tehama, having been lured from an assistant's post at Pebble. "Mr. Eastwood just goes whistlin' through life."

His tune has never been sweeter. There are only a few things that matter greatly to him, Eastwood says: family and career, then somewhat lesser passions like music and golf. Never previously have the stars in all galaxies been so favorably aligned. Married for two years now to Dina Ruiz, a Salinas newscaster, Eastwood became, last year, a father for the seventh time. He says he has "never enjoyed doing the father thing more." He participates in "cleaning up the goop" and is absolutely smitten with his wife, who is openly 36 years his junior. "She's a great girl," says Eastwood. "She's off taking a lesson today. She swings the club almost every day now. She's a good athlete and is going to be good at golf." He says he can't wait for that, because then they can play together all the time, out here in the backyard.

In the wide world of golf, there exist men—you know who you are—who use the game as a means of getting away from the wife and kids. Eastwood, the last real man (no apologies to James Garner), sees the sport as a family affair. "My other kids don't play, but the younger ones love to drive the carts," he says. "They'll love this course, with all these hills."

Eastwood steps into the first tee box on this course, ready to play a few casual holes—the ones that are finished—and talk about the abundance of good fortune that besets him right now. It is immediately evident that he's a man who is past giving a damn, and will talk freely. Interviewers have, during more turbulent times, found him reluctant, reticent, or even scary. There was a memorable exchange between Steve Kroft and Eastwood on *60 Minutes* in 1997, upon the release of *Midnight in the Garden of Good and Evil.* Eastwood and Ruiz's daughter, Morgan, had only recently been born, and Kroft suggested provocatively: "You've got a lot of kids."

Eastwood: Yeah. I have—I like kids a lot.

Kroft: How many do you have?

Eastwood: A few.

Kroft: Seven kids with five women, right?—not all of whom you were married to.

Eastwood: No.

Kroft: You would agree that this was somewhat unconventional?

Eastwood: Yes. It's uncon . . . unconventional, yeah.

Kroft: But how would you describe your relationship with those kids? Are you in touch with all of them? Do you know . . .

Eastwood: I'm in touch with all of them.

Kroft: When I ask the question about family, I have to tell you, that is a pretty awesome expression you have right now.

Eastwood: Wha . . .

Kroft: I don't think I've had anybody look as me like that before. It's a real Clint Eastwood look. It's intimidating. You let me know, 'Approach with caution.'

Eastwood: Well, 'cause I—you—they're—these are people that are—there are other people that are—other people that are involved there, and they're vulnerable people. I can protect myself, but they can't.

That was then, this is now. There will be no Clint Eastwood looks on this sensational day in the backyard, with the sun glistening off the Pacific below, and a pretty fair opening drive sailing from this elevated tee down to the welcoming fairway of the 515-yard first. "That's about where you'd like to be," says the host. "That'll be okay."

As he E-Z-Goes to his ball, Eastwood happily brings up the subject of Steve Kroft. "He's a good golfer," Eastwood says. "He was pretty excited about being out here. We played Cypress and he had never played there. He had a nice time."

Was Eastwood pleased with the *60 Minutes* segment?

"Oh, I thought it turned out okay," he says. "Steve Kroft's a nice guy. All of them were nice. They were out here for a while, talking to everyone I knew, talking to my mother. She liked them fine."

Eastwood's 87-year-old mother Ruth may stand as the most important figure in his life. His father was a stockbroker brought down by the Depression who went to work in and around Oakland as a gas-pumper/salesman/pipefitter/you-name-it. From his dad, young Eastwood got the ferocious work ethic. His mother was the artistic one. She loved jazz, and encouraged the boy as he learned to play piano and flugelhorn. Teenaged Clint fancied himself a black kid trapped in a white kid's body, and this conceit was solidified when he saw Charlie Parker play in Oakland in 1946. Eastwood has been a backroom jazzman ever since—right through the hard-labor years as a lumberjack; through the hard-bitten years in the Army; through the dicey years as an aspirant actor, before landing a role on *Rawhide;* through the breakout years of spaghetti westerns and Dirty Harry movies, into the whatever-you-want years of superstardom. In this last chapter, Eastwood can indulge himself by making a biopic of Parker, for instance, or by filling film scores with his own jazz compositions or with favorite songs by others.

Neither Eastwood's mother nor father had anything to do with his discovering golf. "When I was in the Army, a couple of us would go play at Pacific Grove," he says as he drives the cart to the second tee, having made birdie at Number One. "Fifty cents, you could play all day. I was no good, didn't know anything about the game. That was 50 years ago." He pauses, tees the ball, gives it a good spank.

He used to play with his buddies for half a buck, all the holes they could chew up. Now he's a walking golf empire. Just as ubiquitous as—if way, way quieter than—Jack Lemmon or Bill Murray at the Pro-Am, he has been chummy with Tour players for years. "I really like Ray Floyd, have had a lot of fun with Raymond," Eastwood says, after that solid drive at the 450-yard second. "He's a great guy." (There are a lot of "great guys" and "great gals" in Eastwood's world.) He has never left the sport in a half-century as a golfer, but it was only an occasional pursuit until his mature years, when an occupational hazard turned out to be great for his game. "I was doing a picture, *Pale Rider,* and the horse and I were riding through some rocks and he decided to roll over. It was one of those things. I broke my shoulder. I had been playing a lot of tennis, but when I started rehabbing I couldn't serve, so I said, 'I'll play more golf.' By the time the shoulder healed, tennis had lost out—I was crazy about golf."

His involvement was as a recreational player until two years ago when he started a line of golf wear. His is the antithesis of Tiger Woods's Nike gear: It's classical, even retro, and extremely clean; it's what you see Arnie Palmer wearing in those terrific black-and-white photos from the late 1950s. It is man's-man clothing, and like the new course, it is branded Tehama. An Indian word, this refers to a county that lies across the northern part of California's Central Valley—a land of milk, honey, sheep, olives, grain, tall trees, and one of Eastwood's many properties. It also refers to an extinct Native American tribe that lived thereabouts. That's a playful irony for you: The man who has extincted more Indians, fictive or not, than anyone since John Wayne pays tribute with golf garb and a greensward.

Eastwood has a marvelous sense of humor. Almost everything he says has a touch of fun about it, a bit of teasing—teasing of his guests or of himself. (His reply to the often-asked question about whether he is bothered by the age difference in his marriage: "If she dies, she dies.") On the golf course, the banter is light—seldom hilarious but always engaging. "This is one of my favorite holes," he says as he watches his approach to the second green fall short. "I guess 'cause I birdied it last time." His speech has a two-beat rhythm to it; he talks in semi-colons. He says a thing, then the famous voice drops subtly—a sixth of an octave—and he adds a little joke, or a bit of provocation.

"Time for the chipmaster to go to work," he says on the fringe at Number Two, then he pauses. "If the chipmaster can."

It's like an extra waggle in his thinking.

On Number Three: "When we started building the course, the Sierra Club and their friends were up here protesting, dancing around in the meadow"—pause—"I think they had a pretty nice time."

On Number Four: "The land pretty much looked like this before, with the native grasses and all"—pause—"we're basically watering the meadow."

On Number Five: "I've never had so much fun with the father thing, never enjoyed doing the father thing more"—pause—"and I've done it a few times."

You look at him closely as he stands over a 160-yard approach to the green, having waggled, having dropped that *I-know-that-you-know* line about his kids or about the tree-huggers. You're sure you see a half-smile on his lips. Then again, he seems to wear a perpetual half-smile. It belongs to his face like the scowl belongs to Harry Callahan's.

As for the voice itself, it is a tenor, you are surprised to realize (though never has a tenor so possessed the gravitas of a baritone). It was said of Louis Armstrong and Ella Fitzgerald that their voices blended perfectly, like Jack Daniel's and champagne. Eastwood's speaking voice, which is extraordinarily musical, stands at the intersection of Louis and Ella—it's got sand in it, and bubbles too. It's friendlier than Harry's.

And as for the squint, well, that's the one trademark item that is as indelible to the real Eastwood as it is to his movie characters. All day long, his eyes never open; you wonder he doesn't plow E-Z-Go into a tree. In lining up a putt, every golfer in the world squints like Clint Eastwood. But let it here be recorded: In lining up *his* putts, Clint Eastwood *really* squints like Clint Eastwood.

"I like everything about the game," he says as he briefly surveys the uphill par-three sixth. He takes his whack and flies the green. "I love playing around here, we have so many great courses. I love playing in Scotland." Eastwood may make a golf movie there one day, as he owns the rights to *Golf in the Kingdom*. "I think I've got the mystical stuff figured out," he says. "But it'd be a real easy film to do badly."

As he drives the cart up a winding path through the trees, he says, "The one thing I don't like is slow play. I didn't even play the Pro-Am last year, and I'm on the tournament board. The pro game has gotten *so* slow. I just can't stand it, taking six hours to play a round of golf."

There will be no problem with slow play up here at Tehama, it is suggested.

"That's true," Eastwood says, then pauses. "But we *will* have mulligans on this course."

He's a good golfer, plays to about a dozen, even if he's dismissive about his talent. He says, "I do that all the time" whenever a playing partner dips or duffs, but in fact, he doesn't do the bad things much. He's got a smooth swing that he forces himself to contain. "Stay within it," Hickman urges all afternoon. "Too fast," Eastwood says to himself when he hooks an approach. He adds constant commentary: "a real worm-burner" after a line drive or "I've patented that shot" after shanking one. "Okay, chipmaster's going to be put to the test here," he says as he prepares for his comebacker on Number Six.

"He had a great day chipping two days ago," Hickman says. "How many did you hole, Mr. Eastwood?"

"Oh, a couple," the chipmaster admits. He waggles, then pops up short. "No chipmaster today."

Suddenly, there's another cart on the course, and it heads this way. Frank Chirkinian, retired as a CBS exec and sporting a fabulous retiree's tan, is playing with a partner. Handshakes all around, a few nice words about absent friends—Lou Gerstner, guys like that—and then Chirkinian says, "Well, you've got a beautiful course here, Clint, absolutely beautiful." He drives off.

Will most of the members here be Hollywood folks? Eastwood is asked.

"No," he says. "All over. All kinds." Three hundred of Clint's best pals.

Eastwood has always been one of the more remote stars in the firmament. "Well," he says, "I live here, not L.A. I'm there a lot, but this is home. When I was in the service I came down to Carmel if I had half a day off, and I said, 'Boy, that's a place I'd like to live.' When I could, I did." He's been here for three decades and has employed the same philosophy—"When I could, I did"—over and over. "Back in 1951 I used to go to the bar down at Mission Ranch, and it was nice, just a dive with music and a dance floor. And then eventually it fell into disrepair, and so . . ." And so in 1986 Eastwood bought the expansive ranch that sits on Point Lobos and threw a vault of money at it. These days at Mission Ranch, you turn on the flame in your suite's fireplace with a light switch, and Eastwood admits with a smile, "The rooms don't cost five dollars anymore." Importantly, the bar they call the Little Barn "is just the same as what it was in 1951." There's music nightly, and Eastwood sometimes hangs out there with friends, a Tehama golf cap affording him scant disguise. (In script on the back of the cap: *Fac Diem Meiam,* which is Make My Day in Latin.) Eastwood hardly cares if he's recognized. He's in his clubhouse in his backyard with his buddies, so he's happy regardless.

He was Carmel's mayor in 1986 and 1987. He says of his tenure, "I phoned it in." Everyone else says this is nonsense. Eastwood simply won't buy into a compliment; he wasn't raised that way. If you say that *Play Misty for Me* (his first film as director, shot in Carmel), or *Unforgiven,* or his putt on the seventh green, was terrific, he answers,

"Turned out okay, I guess." He prides himself on being a thoroughly professional moviemaker, bringing his films in on time and under budget, or taking direction agreeably when he's acting. He talks of his "career," never of his artistry. "I take my career seriously, yeah," he says as he stands on the eighth tee, sizing up a 435-yard dogleg with a Sahara of sand, left.

Didn't you just wrap a project?

"Yeah," he says, squinting more tightly than normal. "It's done. I may look at it again. It'll be out in the spring. I could've hurried it and got it out for Christmas, but I don't really like to hurry anymore with the career. I don't have to." The movie, *True Crime,* starring him and his occasional golfing buddy, James Woods, marks the 18th time Eastwood has played both offense and defense, acting and directing. His Oscar came for directing (*Unforgiven* in 1992). His wherewithal to build Clint's Club derives from the acting, which by now includes lead roles in 50 pictures that have grossed a billion-and-a-half semolians. Leo DiCaprio is a very nice boy, but there is no bigger star—as in *star*—than Clint Eastwood.

His tee shot floats toward the traps and selects the middle one. "Sand?" Eastwood asks. "Yes," Hickman confirms. "I think so."

"Well," Eastwood says, "I need the practice."

He has a good lie in the bunker, and hits a nifty seven wood that nestles just before the green. "I'll take it," he says.

Did he mean to imply, just earlier, that the career means less to him than it used to?

"Oh no," he says as he rakes sand. Only in exiting the traps does he seem anywhere near 70; he climbs out stiffly. "I'm just not hurrying things anymore. And as I mentioned, there are other things I'm enjoying."

Where does music fit in, and golf?

"They fit in," he says as he pilots the cart. "I'd call them passions. They're fun. They're relaxing. I enjoy playing piano and composing, and I play golf maybe three times a week. I love it, but I don't *have* to play golf." In the winter, he skis. He flies his own helicopter over to Tahoe—"I love it up there in the clouds"—while aides drive a chase-car laden with skis and clubs. "It's good to have recreations," he says. "I don't over-analyze them." He jogs, he lifts. He has practiced transcendental meditation for three decades. He has never smoked, not even as No Name did he inhale, and he gorges on vitamins. There are a lot of surprises with Clint Eastwood, but he won't help you get all metaphysical about them. "I don't necessarily see similarities in the things I choose to do," he says. "Maybe rhythm. Golf, music—they have rhythm in common."

He likes a smooth rhythm. He seeks it in his swing. He might have made a movie about bop avatar Parker, but Eastwood's piano playing owes more to Errol Garner than it does to Bud Powell, and if you get him going on the very smooth singer Johnny Hartman, whose music Eastwood boosted in the *Bridges of Madison County*, well, you'll find the 8th hole behind you before the subject changes.

It is suggested that a lot of the rhythms in his life are flowing smoothly these days. "That's true," he allows. He is reminded that he used a particularly nifty metaphor with Steve Kroft. He told Kroft that he was on the back nine of life, and was playing a lot better. He might even be under par on the home holes, after a rugged front nine with a lot of triple-bogeys.

Had he figured that out before being interviewed for *60 Minutes*?

"I don't think I thought about it beforehand," he says. He smacks another good seven wood out of the rough, around the dogleg of the difficult, uphill ninth. He adds, "But you never know what you might've thought about before, really."

The chipmaster goes to work, and the puttmaster saves par by canning a downhill 15-footer.

The front nine of Tehama have been completed: nine sensational holes in one of God's great settings. The back nine are still under construction. Jay Morrish, the course architect, is on site today checking progress. Eastwood spots him at the turn, and drives over to visit. He makes certain to introduce everyone to everyone else.

After a bit of conversation about the course, Morrish says, "Heard about your hole-in-one yesterday."

"My first real one," says Eastwood again, then he pauses. "We played late and the bar was empty, so I didn't have to buy."

"You done for the day?"

"We're having fun," Eastwood says. "I think we'll play the par threes." These are Numbers Twelve and Seventeen, and that section of the course is ready for action. Eastwood has honors, and misses right on Twelve. "Guess there'll be no aces today," he says, squinting tightly. You think he is at the semicolon, but this time the bald statement is all there is. He chips on, then sinks a putt that he thought he'd misread. This pleases him more than any well-struck roller finding all cup. It's more fun this way.

He's right of the green again on Seventeen, if barely. "No aces today."

As he rides E-Z-Go down the short fairway, he says, "We came up here the other night, just Dina and me." This is in answer to no question, as questions have run out. "The little one was with us, sacked out in the car. The moon was full. It was so light out, you could've played golf. There wasn't a soul around, just Dina and me and a lot of little nocturnal things—possums, skunk, deer. The ocean. It was quite a night." Out in their backyard. On the home holes.

"Time for the chipmaster to go to work," he says, taking his stance. The ball is in the light rough. Clint Eastwood is in clover.

Chapter XVI

A Sort of Homecoming

Much Has Changed, Some's the Same, in Ireland—Fifteen Years On

The Backswing:

The founding editor of Travel + Leisure Golf, *Jim Gaines, called and asked, "You went where we wanted you to go. Where would you like to go?" I said I'd call him the next day, which I did. I said, "Jim, I'd love to go back to Ireland. And I'd love to take my family." He said fine, and in May 1999, he published this travelogue. By the way: I suggested some lame headline, best forgotten. The one above, which I'm now sticking with, was by Jim and his top-notch colleague Kate Meyers.*

Moving through Shannon Airport for the first time in 15 years, I sense immediately that Ireland has changed—perhaps even, as Yeats once had it, changed utterly. The people piling off our Aer Lingus flight are different than they once were, if similarly freckled and red-haired. They are younger, better dressed, possessing better luggage, traveling with babies. There are many more of them than there used to be; the plane was full. They are smiling, and so are the kin who wait in Baggage Claim to greet them. There is none of the slowness, the Irish sense of mourn that I remember.

Where there was once a single hire-car desk, maybe two, now there are a half-dozen, including all the ones you know. At ours, finally, there is something reminiscent. The young women are cheerful and friendly, and it all comes back, the best reason for traveling to Ireland: the Irish themselves, nicest people on the planet. "And how old is the wee one?" says Mary, tickling our baby beneath the chin. Everyone's named Mary here; Mary, John or a variation on John (Ian, Eaonn, Sean, and so forth).

"She's 11 months."

"Lovely. You call her?"

"Caroline."

"Lovely name. Lovely. Hello, wee Caroline. Now tell me, wee Caroline, why did you all give that nice Mr. Clinton so much trouble? We love him over here."

They do. He was just here, Bill Clinton was—traveling about, playing golf, playing the Irish-heritage card just like JFK and Reagan did with great success, and as Nixon, a descendant of Irish Quakers, tried to do, with results as sad as a Dublin drizzle. No one turned out when Nixon came over. Clinton, they love, whenever he comes over, whatever he does. They love him for his help in the North, of course, but they love him just as much for his smile, his naughtiness, the cut of his jib entire. They take a kind of pride in looking past his scandals. It makes them feel modern, cosmopolitan—European if not quite French. The Irish have a prime minister who steps out in Dublin with his mistress, they elect woman president after woman president and, just now, they are demanding that curbs on Viagra be lifted. Have the parish priests all boarded curraghs and made off to St. Brendan's isle? What's happened to the auld sod?

"This isn't the place I visited," I say to my wife as we bundle Caroline and Caroline's grandma out to the Ford hire-car. "Something's going on."

"That so?" Luci replies, then glimpses the glistening hills just beyond the airfield—shining wet on a dry day—her first sight of Ireland. "It certainly is a beautiful land."

"Ah," I say. "That's not changed, thank God." I help my mother-in-law into the back seat. "Come along now, Aged P."

And we're off, still on the wrong side of the road—that's not changed, either. We head north northwest, up the Dingle coast, perhaps the loveliest place on earth. "What a wind! Keep both hands on the wheel!" says the Aged P, an inveterate and strongly opinionated back-seat driver who, in this instance, offers sound advice. A gale is charging off the ocean, buffeting our little vehicle as it trundles up the winding road. When we stop at the stunning Cliffs of Moher for the requisite walk along the bluff, it is decided that the grandparent will stay with Caroline in the car because she would certainly be knocked off her feet by the gale, and perhaps would lose the baby to sea goblins below. As my wife and I struggle toward yonder tower—there is always yonder tower and yon castle ruin, in Ireland—we can't tell if we're being lashed by rain or ocean spray thrown violently up the 50-meter sandstone cliff.

"Is it always like this?" my wife shouts.

"Often is."

"And you're going to play golf in this?"

"Sure," I say gamely. For when you go to Ireland, you go expecting weather, particularly on the seaside links—the true Irish courses— and you go ready to play, come what may. Still and all, as I taste salt in the spray (it's not raining, this is the sea), I have an unspoken hope that the breeze blows a few knots more sedately tomorrow.

Tomorrow we play Lahinch, where I last teed up a decade and a-half ago. Back then, I played the grand old courses during a coast-hugging circuit of the island that ran a fortnight. We started at County Down north of Belfast, then went up to Portrush at the top, over to County Sligo (the locals call it Rosses Point), then down to Lahinch and Ballybunion, thence back to Dublin for a round at Portmarnock. We played ancient games in what seemed a very old land: worn, tattered, wispy-haired, tired. At the time, Ireland was a lament. Things were lousy with the British, of course, and every youth who had not yet fled into the Diaspora was unemployed. The golf courses were undeniably lovely, and the characters hanging about them left vivid memories. But images of a thousand tinkers camping by the roadside are equally sharp and indelible.

Loving Ireland as I did—loving the idea of the place, the people who lived in the place, the place itself—I didn't go back for a long while. It made me melancholy to think about it.

Then things started to happen. Elvis Costello (Declan McManus, thank you very much) and U2 happened, and the Chieftains recorded with the Rolling Stones. The Waterboys, Hothouse Flowers, the Cranberries, the Corrs happened, and Enya and all that Celtic New Ageyness; Clannad recorded the farfennuggen theme for the Volkswagen ads. Neil Jordan and *The Crying Game* happened, and all those other movies: *The Commitments, My Left Foot, In the Name of the Father.* "Riverdance" happened, and that weird boyo from Chicago, Michael Flatley—he happened. Frank McCourt conquered the world with his tales of Limerick poverty. And that's only culture: President Mary Robinson happened. Merciful heaven, a cease-fire happened, and was accompanied by an agreement that we still pray for nightly. So much happened and so fast, the Irish behaved as if dizzy. They bulldozed James Joyce's house in the Millbourne Road in Dublin, the one used as setting in *Portrait*, meanwhile proposing a nutty new construct in town: a 300-foot stainless steel pole to be built at the end of O'Connell Street in commemoration of the millennium. Cost: $5 million.

Five mill? So what? Overnight, money had no meaning. The European Community was happening, and it emptied pots of gold onto the island. Jobs were created; roads were fixed or built; second homes sprouted on the moors; Irish yuppies developed a taste for fine wines. *Wines!* The new economy was called "the Emerald Tiger," alternately "the Celtic Tiger." Many of the wine-sipping young'uns were employed in the computer trade, and another buzz phrase was born: "Eire—Europe's Internet Gateway."

"There's a reverse migration going on," my friend Mike Padden told me at Molly's one night. "The kids are staying home, and others are coming back." Mike goes over at least once a year, and seems to know what he's talking about. "Dublin's a hot town. Even the food's good."

Now this was an impossibility, surely. This was Mike talking through his flat cap. Then again, Guinness had invented a special can with a widget that keeps stout fresh during transatlantic shipping. So . . . mightn't anything at all be true about Ireland?

It was time to go see.

The trip would be about golf, of course. Why go, otherwise? What's that expression: All the best courses in Scotland are in Ireland? I'll buy that. "I'll do the planning, honey," I said, making Luci equal parts relieved and suspicious.

We would be traveling *en famille*, as they say in Cork, so I figured we shouldn't venture too far about this time—not the emerald necklace trip of 15 years ago. I came up with what I thought would be a nifty, Daddy-friendly, Mommy-accessible gameplan. Sticking to the southwest and south, Daddy would play two old links, for old time's sake, and two newish ones—so that he could compare old and new, while experiencing this "new Ireland," this kingdom in renaissance. I'd start at Lahinch this time, then do Ballybunion, then scoot down to that just-opened course in the south, Old Head, the one they're calling "the Irish Pebble," and then I'd play the design that Arnold Palmer drew for Tralee, which opened in 1984. Luci, Caroline, and the Aged P would, meanwhile, take in the haunting drama of the Burren, the astonishing beauty of the Dingle peninsula, the sea-village charm of Kinsale, and would come within a long six iron of the Waterford factory store. On our final night, we'd stay at Dromoland Castle, making everyone happy.

A nifty game plan. What had slipped my mind was that you can never not "venture too far about" in Ireland. Everyone tells you the place is "only the size of Maine" or "barely bigger than Indiana," but who ever drives all around Maine or Indiana, especially with a baby and an Aged P in the back seat? Moreover, wherever EC money has not yet been spilled across an Irish road, the road remains an Irish road, which is to say a one-car-wide, hedgerowed, twisting lane. You can't get there from here anywhere in Ireland, no matter where here is. So please do not consider the following account as any kind of sensible itinerary. Book your golf wherever and whenever you like, but plan for plenty of extra driving time between courses. Do not trust your map. Maps of Ireland are like the Irish themselves: They are friendly and inviting, but they're telling you only half the story.

We are headed north into the Burren, wind blowing the ghosts about but good. The Burren, from the Irish *boireann* meaning a rocky or stony place, is a fantastic bit of Ireland that sits above Limerick and below Galway, lying for the most part in County Clare. Terraced limestone hills paint a grey horizon line all about you in the Burren—you're on the moon. And then, in the valleys tucked beneath these hills, there are the greenest green fields, the most colorful flowers, the healthiest looking cows and sheep. Contented cows, sanguinary sheep. Five thousand years ago, the Irish who were here dug megalithic tombs and cairns throughout the region, and today remnants add to the great druidic chill of the place. The Aran Islands belong to the Burren, and if you consider for a moment the tight knit of a coarse-wooled Aran Islands sweater, you know what the Burren's about. You'll want to keep the peat fire burning in the Burren.

The fire is burning in the grate at Gregan's Castle when we arrive to check in. The smoldering turf bricks suffuse the inn with warmth and a sweet, sharp aroma. Gregan's, as well as the other places we'll be patronizing during our week, is certainly part of the new Ireland: Five-star hostelries and restaurants that charge five-star tariffs but deliver on the promise. If there were any of these in Ireland when last I was here, they were hiding under rocks. Dublin had a French restaurant, I remember, and one other place said to offer fare other than cheese and overcooked meat, but that was about it. Luci has a friend who used to travel regularly in Ireland back then, and would routinely order "salad"—just for kicks, just to see what it was. Sometimes it was a piece of lettuce, sometimes it was whatever random garnishes could be found. Once, it was a pickle.

Gregan's isn't really a castle, it's an extremely comfy country house. But it was built by a clan that really had a castle. When the Martyns of Galway married into the O'Loughlens of The Gregans in the early 1600s, they built and lived in a castle. During a rare peaceful period in the neighborhood, the clan constructed an elegant house, which is now Gregan's Castle. It is, today, owned and operated by descendants of the O'Loughlens. They are hosting neighbors and friends in the parlor as we arrive to check in. The son, Simon, leaves the tea and takes care of us. "Some folks from the parish," he explains unnecessarily. "A new stained-glass window was dedicated this morning at the old church in Ballyvaughan, and the congregation leaders have come up here for a bite." The Irish are always a phrase too effusive as they seek to help or explain. But when you're freshly off the plane from New York City, niceness is sweet tonic. Simon gives us a key and directions, and we're delighted to enter, at the end of inscrutable halls, the O'Loughlen Suite itself. We are agreed that it's the best accommodations we've ever settled into: spacious, high-ceilinged, bright, with a certain slant of white Irish light coming in over the Burren, twice-filtered by the flower bushes outside. If the golfing weather is raw, this will be a nice place to come home to.

The afternoon is spent upon the Burren. With Caroline in the knapsack, her mother and I go walking, as the Aged P holds down the parlor—with intermittent strolls across the hall to the Corkscrew Room, where she's already learned that she has a taste for Guinness.

"Glass or a pint, mum?"

"Oh, well, I think—what do you think? Oh, do you think I could?—one of those there, the large ones."

The family unit, meanwhile, peaks into Newtown Castle, a particularly handsome example of Generic Ruined Tower (Eire). In the lower chamber, there are bats on the ceiling, and a young woman who will take us on a brief tour of what was once an O'Loughlen stronghold. As it happens, she's an O'Loughlen herself, as are many of the folks hereabouts. The clan has always been immense in the Burren.

And the Burren has always been immense in the Irish imagination. It takes effort to envision the prehistoric hunters and gatherers who encamped here on the unfruitful plain, but less effort to conjure the Neolithic people whose eeriest remaining marks on the land are the many "passage graves": beautiful, decorated, labyrinthian works of carved stone, usually set on hilltops or in cemeteries—as awe-inspiring and inscrutable as Stonehenge. These tunnels, sometimes built with a solar orientation, were certainly a link to the gods—a place from which to transport the dead, or to pay homage. They represent a vivid first chapter in Ireland's remarkable religious history, and when imagined from the upper-chamber windows of Newtown Castle—you know they're out there, winding through the stone, harboring spirits—they send a shiver.

Later in the afternoon, from the highest nearby point, the summit of Cappanawalla mountain, a view of the castle and a handful of other remnant *fulachta fiadh* (Bronze Age cooking pits), *cahers* (stone forts) and monasteries brings the subsequent history of this region into relief. The Celtic tribes came, then the Christians, then the Vikings, then the Anglo-Saxons, variously converting and combating one another. Napoleon and his French never made it to the Burren, but the emperor had his designs, and Martello Tower at Finavarra, just north of Ballyvaughan village, stands as stoic testament to Irish readiness. Or to an Irish sense of worry.

Speaking of readiness, the Aged P is ready for a sumptuous dinner when we return from our ramble, and all of us are ready for sleep at an early hour. Next morning, Daddy's ready for golf, and so are John, Steve, Bob, Peter and Bobby. By casual prearrangement, friends of ours are traveling in southwestern Ireland just now. We'll meet up for golf, drinks, and dinner in the next several days. John and I have plans to play the four courses on Daddy's Itinerary, while the others will play Lahinch, Ballybunion and Old Head but not Tralee.

A note before passing: We called well ahead for our tee times, and still we had difficulty. That's a big difference from 15 years yon, and so are the tariffs. Last time I played Lahinch, the greens fees were $6. Ballybunion was about a ten-spot. And you could almost always walk on, easily slipping into the shuffle of local pensioners. Now those courses are nearly a hundred clams per go-round. And as dear as that might seem, securing the privilege to pay is dearer. It took us about a dozen fax exchanges with exceedingly regretful club secretaries to arrange suitable midweek, low-season dates and times.

Ah, but it was all worth it, I realize as I set eyes upon Lahinch once more. Rolling in and out of, up and over great gorsey mounds by the sea, Lahinch looks funny for a golf course—it's not the terrible beauty that Ballybunion is, but a funky, hairy, oddly lovable layout. It was designed—placed, rather—by Old Tom Morris in 1893, at the behest of locally billeted Scottish officers of the Black Watch regiment. Originally, Lahinch featured a host of the quirky, tricky holes such as were fashionable at the time. Alister Mackenzie did a redesign of "Ireland's St. Andrews" in 1928, after he'd built Cypress Point but before he'd done Augusta. He left the land alone—he proclaimed this the finest parcel of linksland he'd ever seen—while smoothing Old Tom's more eccentric edges. Today, only Numbers Five and Six are pure Morris, and we'll get to them in a moment.

Presently, we are in the first tee box, happy to see no goats. The Lahinch half-dozen are descendants of goats that belonged to caddy Tommy Walsh, and it is believed they have inherited their forebears' keen instincts in affairs meteorological. If Lahinch's goats are cowering by the clubhouse, rain's coming in; if they're out upon the course, the weather will be fine. How firmly do the locals believe the legend? Years back, when the barometer by the pro shop broke, a sign was taped to its face: SEE GOATS.

No goats, and I step to the plate. I hit a timid three iron right down the middle on the 385-yard, par-four first. I remember that Lahinch is not a long course (only 6,698 yards from the blues, in fact), and that the thing to do in Ireland is stay out of trouble if you can. Trees are no worry on a links, but pot bunkers and the surrounding hay are to be assiduously avoided. Especially the hay. Hay-to-hay-to-hay-to-hay holes are not uncommon: The gorse is so thick and blown down, you can scythe your way to the green without ever tasting fairway. John DeGarmo did that once, and wrote about it in his book *The Road to Ballybunion* (Longstreet Press, 2001): "As I struggled onto the green I said 'Phew!' in utter exasperation.

"To which my caddy responded, 'It's a tiring game, sir, when it's badly played.'"

And it's a fine line between wry and wise guy with an Irish caddy. Ours, this day at Lahinch, is Joe, a short, grizzled fellow of between 45 and 85. He's Joe to us, at least. He was introduced to us as Joe, and responds to it when we peer at a putt and ask, "Whaddya think, Joe?" But when other caddies give him a wave, or when the groundskeepers drive over to bum a smoke, they call him "Bob." Joe's little joke, I guess.

Joe seems disengaged on the opening holes, while John and I are enjoying ourselves mightily, and hitting the ball not too badly. There's a devilish aspect to an old links course, and I remember it now with dread: None of them really begin at Number One. The clubhouse is usually a wee bit further inland than most of the holes, and that makes all the difference. You limber up and gain a false sense of security as you head seaward, and then after a nice little par-three third, the wind picks up, the sound of the surf changes from a drone to a cadence and your swing blows away on the breeze. "Course starts here," Joe-Bob says as we gaze at an immense hill fronting the fourth tee box. A big, steady wind is in our face, and this mere 200-yard carry to a plateau seems impossible. "Take out everything you've got and hit it all you can," Joe-Bob advises. John and I follow instructions but it's no use. I sink a putt for a six and am more than happy.

Which brings me to Klondyke, my favorite par five in the world. Old Tom found this alley in the valley—a curvy, 482-yard lane that passes between grasping, greedy grass dunes—and Dr. MacKenzie wisely did nothing to alter its course. From the tee, you ask your caddy about a presumed or even prospective fairway, and Joe-Bob tells you, "It's out there." He points to the big-shouldered hills and says, "Hit that gap—you'll find the golf course." I try, and fail. On a hillside right, I have one of those level-with-your-head lies that aren't to be countenanced, but I give the ball enough of a nudge to send it skimming over the gorse and down onto the fairway.

Now I wait, obeying the bright red letters on my scorecard that announce: "SPECIAL WARNING RE KLONDYKE: 5th HOLE— The Committee of Lahinch Golf Club informs all players that they will not accept liability for accidents at the crossing of the 5th and 18th fairways." Yes, the crossing of the fairways. Golf balls fly every which way, and Joe-Bob confirms that people do get whacked. So we wait, then play through to our own green.

And things get stranger. Number Six, the Dell, is a blind par three. *A blind par three.* There's a tee that faces a hill and—Joe-Bob absolutely promises—a green on the other side. A white rock is moved to a new situation on the hill's rounded summit each morning. This indicates your line to the pin placement beyond. Your job is to hit the ball 155 yards and then not worry.

When you anxiously round the hill, you find a small gem of a green in a cathedral setting. There are dunes all around, and no wind in here. Suddenly, you can't hear the ocean. You putt out with a smile on your face.

Number Seven swings back out toward the ocean and your mind needs another adjustment, then Eight presents another series of big hills. "Last o' the Mohicans," Joe-Bob pledges, but you don't quite trust Joe-Bob. Nine proves him an honest man. It's a placid, slightly downhill 384-yard par four, and you're calm again as you take your waggle. You peer ahead and notice four kids—goat kids, real kids—scampering up the fairway. Their mom is grazing in the rough not 20 feet from you, and you stand off the ball to marvel as the family gathers and settles—at the very farthest reaches of the course.

So of course, it starts to rain. Poor excuse for goats, these are.

Expect rain every day you play in Ireland. Expect rain in every season. You can get a cold, wet day in July or a balmy day in December, but it's an odd day that doesn't have a spell of mist, drizzle, or worse. Sometimes the rain can be brutal, cutting, and cold. Most often, though, the rain is gentle. It's rainbow rain: It comes whispering in, and leaves the gorse glittering in the sun. It almost makes the damned gorse pretty.

We are in a lovely little shower at Lahinch as I launch a wedge on the 138-yard 11th toward another pin I do not see. I think I've pulled it too far left and onto a hill, but Joe-Bob offers "maybe." Indeed, the ball is ten feet from the pin, I learn as I approach. "Ah, the pookah's up there today," says Joe-Bob. You'll hit a lot of these pinball shots in Ireland, but there are not cheapies. The lay of the land is the lay of the land—you're playing true golf, and if you know how to bump-and-run, you'll have a ball. There are pookahs everywhere, particularly on the old courses.

And that's how I come to regard Lahinch as we finish: a great, still-old course. Nothing much appreciable has changed in 15 years.

Well, the town is livelier, I guess. Luci and her mother, along with John's wife Mary-Lynn and the kids—human kids, not real kids—meet us in the car park and announce that the shopping in town was "terrific." Lahinch is a Burren town, and never when I was here was there any shopping in a Burren town that was "terrific" or even "extant." Now, indeed, young people come to Lahinch to shop, and to Lisdoonvarna to listen to music. They dress up to eat at Gregan's Castle, or they fall in love, as our friends did, with the village of Doolin. Intimate restaurants—the mellifluously named Bruach Na Haille and the unfortunately named Lazy Lobster—serve up warmth and good food, and cozy pubs offer hot fiddlers and good Guinness. But then, of course, there is no bad Guinness. And there never was, not even back then.

Lahinch to Ballybunion is 67 miles. To which I might add, like hell.

The roads of County Clare are sweet and scenic and slow, and then you take a ferry, which is slower. Now you are in County Kerry, which is slower still. Only last decade, Kerry still had no phone service after 2 P.M. on Sunday afternoons. Kerry has come a ways since then, but only a ways.

As for me, I like all this . . . oddity. This is what I loved about Ireland then, and it's what I love now. That the people are happier than they were only puts a sheen on the situation. A more prosperous Ireland that is still slightly askew is my ideal. I think this is why I never felt Dublin was a necessity. Three-point-six million people live in this country and one-third of them are Dublin, so you feel obliged to go see it. But Dublin's a *city,* and that's not what I want out of Ireland. This is what I want: long, slow, beautiful drives—throw in a ferry ride across the Shannon, why not?—with one of the world's greatest golf courses waiting on the other side.

Tom Watson said so, about Ballybunion being so great. Fifteen years ago, the folks at Bally-B were quick to tell me that this was one of Watson's very favorite courses, and this morning they tell me the same.

But I barely hear them, for I am gazing around mystified, certain that I'm in the wrong place. I'm standing here in this massive, modern, cement clubhouse and I'm wondering: Where'd Ballybunion go? I remember a dark, dank room. I remember a stained snooker table. I remember the walls creaking and leaking. I remember thinking this was the worst clubhouse I'd ever seen at a world-class club, and the one I liked best.

Now . . . *this:* Albert Speer takes up golf! Bally-B's Bauhaus bunker. A monstrosity. An obscenity!

Progress.

Well, what're you going to do? You're going to pay your fare and shake hands with your caddy, a scruffy teen named Padraig. Then you're going to wait a good little while to tee off, for they're running backed-up on this Tuesday morning at Ballybunion.

With time to kill, I stroll over to Ballybunion's new course, the Cashen, designed by Robert Trent Jones Sr. in 1982 on what he called "the finest piece of linksland that I had ever seen." The golf writer Peter Dobereiner has called Jones's layout "the greatest links course in the world, and by a clear margin." But the locals aren't sure. A friend of mine who summers over here feels the new course is undeniably beautiful and reasonably fair, but that some of the tightness between its huge dunes seems manufactured. This could be sentimentalism, a knee-jerk preference for a time when laying out a golf course meant laying it out—meant *finding* it in the land—not building it. My friend likes Fenway Park, too.

Padraig, however, confirms that the Cashen Course is "terrible tight," and you wonder if the new links are a different species than the old, or just a further-evolved beast. You are looking forward to playing Old Head, and seeing what 1990s steam shovels can do.

But first, Ballybunion. "Hit when ready!" cries the starter, and I smile at something familiar. Ah, yes, the cemetery. Any kind of slice on the first at Ballybunion takes you not only out of bounds but into a stone-fenced, 300-year old country graveyard that's thick with Celtic crosses. Jack Nicklaus rattled the bones, I've been told, and this provides a measure of solace as I watch my drive sail high and right toward an exceedingly unplayable, altogether unpalatable lie. "Reload!" cries the starter, and I do as I am told.

Now that the clubhouse is behind me, everything seems the same, particularly the weather, which is ferocious. Christy O'Connor, Sr., once said of Ballybunion "Anyone who breaks par here is playing better than he is able," and I would extend the sentiment on a day such as this to: Anyone who breaks par on any given hole . . .

Ballybunion, like Lahinch, does not open fearsomely, the graveyard excepted. What it does is tease you. If the hole is long, like the 220-yard par-three third or the back-to-back par fives that follow, the greens will be welcoming, and you might save your par. If the hole is short, like the 364-yard par-four 6th, then the green will slope on all sides, impossible to hold.

At the 7th tee, Padraig announces, "The course begins here." It does, with even more sudden drama than Lahinch's opening salvo. The wind and rain are howling off the Atlantic, which is right *there,* down below, at the bottom of a cliff that has to be shored up each year, and that nevertheless erodes apace. Your job is to stay left, for all of Ireland is left, and as Henry Longhurst once observed, a slice with good carry will land on Long Island, U.S.A. But to go left is to go into the straw, which is now wet and heavy. The 7th is 432 yards, and my card says I escaped with a five, but remembering the experience, I figure I must have shaved. That's okay. President Clinton played the course only weeks before I did, and scoring standards at Bally-B surely must have been loosened.

The last holes of the front nine are appetizers. Eleven, Fifteen, Sixteen, and Seventeen all bring the cliffs and the sea back into play, even if sometimes only psychologically. I'm already flailing, soggy and sagging, when I reach the postcard perfect 131-yard par-three 14th, an inland respite from the *sturm und drang* out by the shore. So, of course, I seek out the only trap available—front left—and have one of those special Irish-pot-bunker experiences. I'm out, finally, and Padraig offers kindly, "That's truly bad form in the sand." He pauses, considering, and adds without rancor, "real shitty." I like a boy who's not sycophantic as he angles for his tip.

My card says I took a snowman at the 385 yard 17th, and I believe it. As I recall the scene, I am standing at the tee, spitting into the wind. I gaze through the storm, and there it is: the Vision of Killasheen. She is walking the eternal bridge that leads from Ballybunion out across the ocean, just as they said she would be. Any shopkeeper or *seanachie* in Ballybunion can tell you of the Vision of Killasheen.

Now, then: How can you play a hole of golf after seeing such a thing, particularly when you have the foreknowledge that the Vision means you'll be dead within seven years' time? Well, you can't. And I didn't, not really. Subsequent to that, I came limping in on 18, a short par four with a mammoth fairway bunker that adds little luster to one of the world's finest courses; Ballybunion deserves a more spectacular finish than 18, but that's a quibble.

To recap my round: I hit into a graveyard, see the Vision, and catch my death of cold all in an afternoon. So I hate Ballybunion, right? I don't. I love the place. I love its look, its feel, its raw emotive power. Ballybunion is where Finn MacCool would have played, were he a contemporary rather than ancient Irish chieftain (and were he considerably less mythical). If Lahinch is Leopold Bloom, a bit dotty but every man's friend, then Ballybunion is Molly—passionate, dramatic, a lot more dangerous, but no less lovable.

The drive from Ballybunion to the Mustard Seed at Echo Lodge in the village of Ballingarry, just south of Limerick, is 42 miles. To which I would append: like hell. But the slow going gives me a chance to take stock.

"A lot more foreigners than when I was here," I mention to John. "A lot more Americans, especially at Ballybunion." I know that statistics back me up: Fifteen years ago, Irish golf drew 60,000 visitors to the Republic annually, about 60 percent of them British, a fifth of them Yanks. With the coincidental booms in golf and Ireland, the yearly traffic is that number several times over, and your foursome might today include Japanese or German players just as quickly as Bostonians.

"It seemed Lahinch got a bit less of that influx than Bally-B," John offers.

"Yes, definitely. Lahinch still has its clubhouse, anyway. I'm sure they built that thing at Ballybunion for the world clientele. The boyos wouldn't have given a shite about replacing the old one." We had been in Ireland for a few days now, and were starting to say things like "shite" and "aye."

Our insolent caddy, Padraig, had, in fact, told me that there was much local lamentation over the passing of the old clubhouse, and the ever-increasing influx of tourists. "You can't move in town during summer," he'd said. "It's true everywhere in the country. We're overrun. We can't get on our own golf courses in the summer."

This is particularly too bad, because many in the new Irish generation finally have the wherewithal and will to play the game. As John and I pass a turn-off for Limerick, I think about what Frank McCourt told me about the game hereabouts, back when he was a boy. "We saw the courses of course, but it looked like a rich game to us," he said. "Of course, we were so very poor, everything looked rich. It might not have been that rich at all, but it looked Protestant to us. We couldn't play that game, we knew that, because you needed shoes. My brother Mike was a caddy—that's as close as a lot of Irish kids came to golf, at least in Limerick when I was a boy."

There's a fire by the roadside, and John asks, "What's that?"

"A tinker's camp," I answer. "First one I've seen this week." More than a century and a half ago, the Irish took to the roads when the potatoes withered, and still some of them haven't come in.

Only a few miles down the road is another beacon of the new prosperity, Echo Lodge, and only a few miles from there is the even more *cher* Adare Manor, where Bill Clinton recently dropped $500 a night (or someone did; you and I did). What shortly ago was seen as "junk" now fills local antiques stores in this "Vale" region to overflowing, and crafts shops, too, are thriving in the villages. Echo Lodge and its well-regarded restaurant, the Mustard Seed, promise "an oasis of good living in the heart of the Golden Vale," which might be true except now the oasis is a tinker's camp, while the good life is general. The vista of the surrounding valley from Echo Lodge is interrupted by a metal tower built for cellular-phone transmissions.

It is a serene place, Echo Lodge. A stately yellow house, it was built in 1884 as a convent, so it has traveled the full Irish road from deep blue sea to the devil. Today, Dan Mullane's eclectic, raffish taste in antiques and other ornamentation makes the place feel like an easy, effortless meeting of Soho and Vermont. As Luci and I load our bags into our spacious, second-floor room, I wonder what the nuns of old would make of the small dominatrix statuette on the mantle.

Dinner hour is certainly a hedonistic experience that the good sisters would scorn. It starts by the fire, with some smoky Irish whisky, neat, to warm the cockles. I've developed a taste for Tullamore Dew on this trip, which is good because I used to like Black Bush and that, of course, is from the North. What I don't understand about the Mustard Seed and some other places in the New Ireland is this: you can't get a Guinness. Why is there cache in *not* serving the world's finest stout? (And tell me no lies of Murphy's or Beamish, please.)

The food is superb and the best way to emphasize what a departure it is from old Irish cooking is to say, merely and succinctly, the vegetables are extraordinary. But then, the Mustard Seed is famous for its herb and vegetable gardens, which surround the house. Fresh vegetables. Cooked perfectly. Not to a turn. In Ireland. Hell is freezing.

And speaking of hell, it is the next A.M., very early, and John and I are driving south to Old Head, which is said to be 77 miles away—like hell. Proprietor Mullane was kind enough to rise himself and make us breakfast before the appointed hour, but still we are pretty quiet during the ride, not yet awake. The Waterboys' "Fisherman's Blues" comes on the radio, and I'm sad to realize it's now an oldie. The news is about five convicted killers being released by the North under the Good Friday agreement, along with late-breaking opinions in the Viagra controversy. The sports report says that next year the soccer league's premier division will use instant replay.

Halfway to Cork, we are stopped by cows crossing the highway. Farmers shoo them along with switches. This makes me sentimental. I'm reminded of what I used to call the SF. The SF represented the amount of time, during my earlier tour of Ireland, that I'd build into our itinerary each morning so as not to be late at the first tee. "The Sheep Factor," I explain to John, "would routinely add a half hour to an hour's trip. We'd hit a sheep block on the road about three times a day. That or a cow block."

On this trip, we have been slowed much more regularly by tour buses passing one another in opposite directions on the rural roads, getting locked up like rutting moose. Every tour bus you see in Ireland—and you see tour buses everywhere, all the time—has badly scraped sides. Some of the buses carry the Ladies Sodality or the Knights of Columbus from Spring Lake, New Jersey, but many more of them are now transporting cycling trips, nature tours, and golf-vacation groups. At least half of the foreign golfers we've met so far have been members of a bus tour.

The cows pass and we are on our way again to Old Head, where we will meet many, many more foreign golfers.

The rain stops—the rain starts and stops constantly—as we get south of Cork. This is not what we've heard would happen. We've heard that, down on Old Head, the wind will knock you down, the rain will drown you, and your body won't be found for three days because of the fog. But as we head from Cork to Kinsale, the sky clears, the sun shines, the breeze calms, and the birds chirp. It's not what we've heard, but we'll take it.

Another thing we've heard is that Old Head, if it is visible, is spectacular. That's the word used over and over again: spectacular. Breathtaking has been invoked, and awesome, but spectacular keeps coming up when we talk to those who have played the place since its opening in the autumn of 1997.

"Spectacular" is what we've heard and read, for Old Head has been cranking out PR material and FedExing it across the Atlantic with the vigor of Tiger's downswing. Fliers, histories, scorecards, aerial-view Christmas cards. Testimonial after testimonial comparing Old Head to Pebble Beach. The drumbeat raised by Old Head's management would have been suitable for the entrance of Bono at the Belfast Opera House, say, or the opening of a new Hooters in Miami. Coming from an Irish golf course, it seemed rather . . . much.

But you looked at that aerial view Christmas card of the pork-chop shaped peninsula with high sheer cliffs plummeting to the sea, and you whispered aloud the slogan, "'From the aeons of time—spectacular beyond belief.' Hmmm. Maybe so."

The cliff road winds onto an isthmus where there's yet another castle ruin—Dun Mac Padraig Castle, if you're keeping score—which seems to guard the entrance to the peninsula. It used to serve that very task, and today it does the same: A guard checks that we've got a tee time. If we hadn't one, we would be charged a fee to stroll upon the bluffs.

We drive toward the car park, and even before we get there, we know one thing for certain: Old Head is spectacular. It is impossibly beautiful as a piece of land, and all but inconceivable as a golf course. "How'd they pull this off?" is the first thing that comes to an American's mind. Well, it wasn't easy. The contrarian story is that the O'Connor brothers—developers, entrepreneurs, sharpies—got ahold of an erstwhile farm for $26 and a handful of beads, never 'fessing up that they intended to turn the 220 acres of National Monument and Ancient Royal Site into 7,100 yards of sensational golf (from the championship tees; 6,756 from the blues). The O'Connors, as might be imagined, see things differently. Patrick will tell me later, over drinks in New York City, that everything was on the square, and that the local castle-huggers and bird-watchers are just a bunch of Neanderthals who made his life a misery during several years of legal battling. "I won," O'Connor says, sipping his cocktail with a dram of satisfaction.

How are relations now with the locals?

"Don't need 'em."

Really?

"They don't play at Old Head—can't afford it—and it wasn't built for them anyway. It was built for the international market. We have an annual day for the Kinsale police and fire, things like that. Keeps 'em sweet. But that's about it."

The Irish are honest, you've got to love them for that. When O'Connor says the majority of his countrymen can't afford his course, he means it. Next year Old Head's fees will top out at $200 a round. And when he says he doesn't need the Kinsale trade, he's probably right again. Old Head is a course of such beauty, such uniqueness, such spectacularity that it will soon be on every international's life list, if it isn't already.

Which is not to say it is necessarily the best thing in Ireland.

I'll explain shortly.

Ronan is our caddy, and like Padraig—and as opposed to Joe-Bob—he'll be returning to school soon in the college town of Cork. He's a tall, affable fellow, a bit shy but very nice. "The first isn't much," he offers in the first tee box, and, really, it isn't—an uphill middle-distance par-four that's very pretty but . . .

And then, Number Two, a dogleg-left four, takes you out along the cliffs. *The cliffs.* The cliffs are what Old Head's all about. They filmed *Ryan's Daughter* over in Kerry—right in Tralee, in fact—but *this* is *Ryan's Daughter* golf. Even on a day so mild as the one we have at hand, this is Maureen-O'Hara-with-hair-blowing-aswoon-in-John-Wayne's-big-Irish-arms-in-*The-Quiet-Man* golf. It is not, properly speaking, links golf. It is certainly not links golf in the sense of Ballybunion or Lahinch. It is headlands golf, like Pebble Beach. The bulldozers came in and quite obviously pushed the peninsula's topsoil around. Not once today will John or I scrape sand.

But that's not a complaint, it's merely a semantic exercise. Call Old Head what you want, once you are out by the cliffs—as you will be on 9 holes of 18—it is gorgeous golf. The par-three third is, literally, a cliffhanger: It's the first of several holes that remind you of those phantasmagoric paintings, the ones where the green seems a half-mile above or below the tee. "The Old Head will give golfers an opportunity to play holes they could only dream of," course designer Ron Kirby has said, and it turns out he isn't bragging. Number Four stays hard by the bluffs, and after this three-hole sequence of 2-3-4 has left you gasping, Five and Six give you 900 yards of inland breathing space. These holes, too, are beautiful—but Old Head will forever be known for its cliffwalking.

"It is a pliss who's high and bending head looks fearfully on the confined deep," said Shakespeare upon visiting Old Head, and I figure he was standing in the 7th tee box, even as they were erecting a structure that is now known as "ruins of seventeenth century lighthouse." (Lots of ruins on this course: "seventeenth century lighthouse," "signal tower 1803–1804," "archeological site," which is an ancient monastery at the turn—no hot-dogs available.) Four of Old Head's five par-threes have the ocean in play, and that makes for a real treat during your go-round. On such a hole, you're not in trouble at the start—even though you're facing Armageddon—and if you strike it well, you can make a heroic shot. I didn't, at Seven, but that's not the point.

The back nine is even better. The par-five 12th desperately hugs the north side of the Old Head, and even if you're not willing to try the carry from the championship tee, go view the hole from there. You're hitting over a bird sanctuary and a crashing surf as, a mile distant, sailboats and fishing boats bob in the Atlantic. The 13th, a long par three, comes back from the northern point no less dramatically.

John is lighting it up today, which makes me feel good because John is a man of even temper. He never showed frustration during our outings at Lahinch and Ballybunion, and he deserves a day in the sun. I'm scoring much better than I did earlier, too, but I figure that in Ireland it all has to do with the weather. Today is calm, and swinging is easy. I par 12, birdie 13, and bogey 14, a 429-yard par four that travels up and inland. That's a sequence I couldn't have expected this trip, the way I'd been playing.

All of the touches at Old Head are lovely: the wildflowers they've planted, the brickwork in the tee boxes—the way it bleeds off the stonework of the monastery at the 10th tee. It's all beyond criticism, certainly, and almost beyond belief.

The Irish love their views from the tees—I remember this particularly from County Down, but it's true of Ballybunion and other courses—and Old Head has taken this adage to heart. (It's odd, how very *Irish* Old Head seems, even though it wasn't built for the Irish.) The view from the 15th tee is astonishing. And then, the view from the 16th is astonishing. These holes are so close to the cliff that the 15th is named Haulie's Leap—Haulie was a bulldozer driver who had to leap when his vehicle plunged down a collapsing bluff during construction of the course—and the 16th green has been drowned by surf thrown up during the winter, and is badly in need of repair.

The 17th is 628 yards from the blue tees, 650 from the back, but not as bad as all that on a calm day. It's a big hole, but not a patch on the 18th for drama. This 411-yard par-four starts at the signature lighthouse, carries over water, and climbs toward an elegant, low-slung clubhouse that Ballybunion meant to build. Again: Even if you're not feeling like a champion, walk back to the lighthouse and see that longer, 200-yard carry that's been built into the cliffside. Sensational.

So what is my problem?

That's the question I am asking myself as I sit in the lovely bar in the lovely clubhouse chewing the foam off a perfectly lovely Guinness.

The Old Head is John's favorite course of the one's we've played, maybe his favorite in the world. He has just told me so. The foursome of Steve, Bob, Peter and Bobby have just decided that, yes, this is their favorite too—drop-dead gorgeous, and all that—even if it seems a bit "Americanized, like a resort."

I, too, had a wonderful time: among the best times in my life on a golf course. But . . .

You see, what happened was this: At the third, a sweet, pretty colleen drove up in a bar cart.

At Lahinch and Ballybunion, they didn't even have real carts.

She drove up and said, in a lassie's lilting voice, "Would you like anything, sirs?"

She broke my heart.

It is, ultimately, a question of what you ask of Ireland. I don't ask Ireland to be poor or hidebound. I want Ireland to be prosperous, happy, and healthy. (I want it to be whole, too, but that's another question.) I want Ireland to be a place where, on my wife's birthday, I find myself in a village named Ballyvaughan and cannot buy her flowers because the nearest cut flowers are across the bay in Galway, but where I'm told, "You can pick those there," and the publican points out the window. I want Ireland to be a place where old caddies named Joe call themselves Bob—or vice versa—and young caddies named Padraig will tell you, twinkle in eye, that your sand game sucks. I want Ireland to be a land of fast play—hit the ball, trod on, hit it again, trod on. In Ireland, I want to be following a foursome that consists of John, Sean, Mary, and Maighread, not four Steves from Idaho. I want Ireland to be the last refuge of Sunday bags. I want Ireland to be a place where cows have the right of way. I want Ireland to be a land of Viagra and instant replay, if Ireland wants, but I'd like James Joyce's house back.

I want Ireland to be a place without cocktail carts.

I don't care if the Old Head sweaters are $300 or if the greens fees wind up being a thousand. I want the cocktail carts gone.

The new Ireland seems to be on the fence about a few of these things, and it'll be interesting to see which way it goes.

The distance from Old Head to the Ballymaloe House is 60 miles, but the claim comes with a postscript: like hell.

No matter the time or distance, the Ballymaloe (say it, Ballyma-LOO) is worth seeking out—or so we have heard. What else we have heard: This stunning stone country house in Shangarry, a fourteenth-century castle at its core, is ground zero for the Irish food . . .

What?

You can't call it a renaissance, for it was never there before. You can't call it a revival.

The Irish Food Thing.

Myrtle Allen is the Julia Child of the new Irish Food Thing, and her daughter-in-law, Darina Allen, is the Martha Stewart—she comes complete with TV show, cookbook line, cookery schools, spin-offs, the works. Myrtle is the dame of Ballymaloe House, and Darina the engine; Rory Allen runs the farmlands; Fern Allen runs the Art Gallery Cafe down in Cork. You get the picture.

That said, the Ballymaloe House is no post-modern, hyper-busy, out-of-my-way industrial complex. It is, rather, heaven. From the moment we weary, exhilarated golfers drive up the graveled lane, we know we are in paradise. The acreage spreads forth, and we say to ourselves, "Hail the New Ireland!" The cocktail cart is forgotten.

Everything seems high-ceilinged in Ireland, and the library of the Ballymaloe House seems particularly so. With Jack Yeats paintings on the wall, Caroline on my knee and a Tullamore in hand, I'm a contented lord. "Nice day today, John!"

"Fine day."

And dinner is finer, in fact, the finest. I never expected that this could possibly turn into a competition—The Best Dinner in Ireland Contest—but it has, and to beat Gregan's and the Mustard Seed, Ballymaloe must rise to the occasion.

It does so by, first, breaking its rules. "Dinner is more formal," the literature reads. "The children are in bed or out-doors for their last evening game. The food is always carefully chosen for its quality . . ." Which is to say, No Kids. A similar rule was in place at Gregan's and at the Mustard Seed—a rule that surely came with the new-ing of Ireland. All of these places are apologetic about the rule, and eager to line up baby-sitters. Better still, when you ask if you might "try" with the baby, all of them break their rules and answer, "Well, certainly, yes, of course. And what do we call the wee one?"

Mary, our waitress at Ballymaloe, loves Caroline—and Caroline loves Mary. They have a gay old time, while the adults have a grand time diving into local fowl and fish. To cut ahead, and skip our blissful night's sleep: We all have a joyous time at breakfast, too. The Ballymaloe does for the bare idea of an Irish Breakfast what Henry James did for ghost stories, what Monet did for haystack pictures. I could live many a day at the Ballymaloe, if they'd let me.

An off-day from the golf, now, and we trek to Kinsale. What to say of Kinsale, besides the fact that it is red hot, a prime beneficiary of recent good times? Let's first describe it. Kinsale is an Irish fishing village that has less to do with fishing than it used to, thanks to money. There's a good measure of Nantucket in Kinsale, a dash of Newport, seasoned with Catalina and Sausalito. It calls itself the gourmet capital of Ireland, and that's fair enough: any Irish town with more bistros than pubs has a right to make the claim. Kinsale is a charmer, and as Mommy, Daddy, Caroline, and the Aged P sit on the back patio of the Blue Haven, a chic restaurant housed in an eighteenth-century fish market building, enjoying Guinness and applesauce (Caroline's), we figure Kinsale is fine indeed, if not exactly what we had expected.

It's odd, the way this trip turned out. We didn't plan it, except to put the old links courses first, but we have traveled from then to now. The Burren is still the Burren, and Kinsale is ready for the new millennium. Ireland, in its recent good fortune, is a stew.

John and I have one more golf game to play, and by now we've learned our lesson, so we are up before dawn. I won't tell you how far it is from the Ballymaloe House to Tralee because I don't want you to try it, but I will tell you that if you do, you should add to the distance: like hell. And the drive back is in a rainstorm.

As mentioned earlier, Palmer built Tralee in the 1980s. But he didn't really build it, not all of it. When I was last in Ireland, or so my tattered old *Ireland Golf Guide* (Bord Failte, 1983) tells me, Tralee was a nine-hole town course. Palmer, it seems, massaged those nine holes that lay out by the sea, and added another nine to them. Overnight, Tralee was famous as a great new Irish links. I want to emphasize: It is that. But my rendering of Tralee must be impressionistic because of what happened that day on the course. My notebook blew away on 11. My scorecard is unreadable.

The synopsis is this: John and I drive west across southwestern Ireland; we play nine serene holes of sensational, scenic golf; the rain comes in; we play King Lear golf for about an hour and a half; we towel down with paper towels in the rustic men's locker room, while local lads talk in Irish about the weather (they still speak Irish in County Kerry); we drive east through the storm, stopping at (I'm sorry) McDonald's; we arrive back at Ballymaloe; we kiss our wives and children; we meet in the library for stouts and Cohibas (have to finish the Cubans before Shannon Airport); we breathe deeply; we go to bed, sleep soundly, rise and head north—no more golf in prospect.

Our last stop is Dromoland Castle, and on our final night in Ireland, we are reduced again to the family unit: me, Luci, Caroline, and the Aged P. Dromoland Castle is perhaps the world's very grandest airport hotel. Only 10 miles—really!—from Shannon, it is an honest-to-God, huge, wonderfully restored castle, a Relais & Chateaux special charging Relais & Chateaux rates. It is filled nightly with Americans either coming or going.

We check in, and everyone is exceedingly nice, as is required by their job and their heritage. When we get to our room, we receive a phone call advising us that the person in the snuggli—that would be Caroline—probably doesn't want to come to the dining room on a Friday night. This time, there seems little wiggle room. It is suggested politely that we might like the Fig Tree restaurant at the golf clubhouse, and to me this seems pure serendipity. I didn't even know Dromoland had a course (it does, a fine 18-hole parkland), and here we are presented with a restaurant in the clubhouse on closing night of the Ireland golf sojourn.

Everything's coming 'round. Dromoland Castle was the ancestral seat of the O'Briens, barons of Inchiquin, who were and are one of the few native Gaelic Irish families of royal blood, and direct descendants of Brian Boru, high king of Ireland in the tenth century. More significantly, to me at this moment, the O'Briens were the O'Loughlens' big rivals in Clare; it was the O'Briens who handed Newtown Castle over. Remember Newtown? With the bats on the ceiling, and the view of the Burren? An ancient, empty place, with the past whistling through. Tonight we will bed down in Dromoland, and we'll doze off to CNN. What would the O'Briens think? The O'Loughlens?

The Fig Tree restaurant looks marvelous: big wooden chandeliers, big beams, a display of old clubs and prints on the wall. The artwork depicts the life and times of Old Tom Morris, designer of Lahinch—whence we'd come. The waitress couldn't be happier to see wee Caroline and the Aged P (who joins me in ordering the Guinness stew; she's begun a stout addiction). We are happy here.

I choose to start with a Jameson's 18, and then another. My wife opens the door. "So how did it go yesterday?" Luci asks. "Tra-la-la?"

"Tralee," I say, and smile at the memory. "Tralee. It went very well. It was weird. It was the whole thing, the whole thing in a microcosm. We'd played nine beautiful holes that Arnold Palmer carved from a farmer's field."

"I know Arnold Palmer," offers the Aged P.

"Lovely stuff, those holes, with fairways to grab our drives. Arnold used these stone walls that were already in place to find his way, tee to green. Brilliant. Beautiful stuff."

I notice Mary Black is singing "Ireland" on the sound system.

"And then we make the turn." I see the Aged P glance up from her pint. "We get to the 10th hole," I explain more fully. "And the blue sky moves inland. Sweeping in off the ocean is this cloud bank that is thick and dark. We feel the rain.

"I can't tell you how quickly it turned. By the time, John and I thought of putting on our rain gear, we were soaked. Everyone in our foursome was changing gloves every hole. It's laughable how hard it was coming down. My ball on the 11th green sailed on the water. I was walking up to the green, and I saw it take wing with the wind, and sail across the puddle. It sailed toward the hole, so I let it go. I sank the putt. Next hole, when I'm putting, the cup is full of rainwater, and it's bubbling over the top as I'm trying to line up my attempt. Simply wild.

"You couldn't see. Well, you could see that the course was spectacular. The back nine at Tralee is amazing—up and down hills, into hollows and up to grassy peaks where you're exposed to the ocean. On the 13th, one of our partners took a mighty swing and the club went flying, end over end, into a pit 50 yards deep. He trudged down, found the thing, chipped on, made par.

"We couldn't talk to one another—the storm was out of *Captain's Courageous*. We played on. All these other golfers were fleeing up the hills to the clubhouse, but we played on.

"Then I realized it: These are the old holes. These were here back then. Sure, Arnie foozled with them, but this was the ancient game, and the gods of the ancient game had blown in, right at the turn, to send us a message."

"Is this like that Vision thing in Ballybunion again?" Luci asks reasonably.

"No," I say. "No, it's different. It's . . . Well, anyway, here we come, homeward bound, and we reach 18. It's dark now, truly dark, and the other three have quit—they're going to walk the hole. But I tee it up. It's a 422-yard uphill par four . . ."

"Is that good?" asks the Aged P. Caroline says, "gud!"

"Yes, it's fine. And the wind's right in my face, and the rain's streaming down, and I hit an iron low. I get to it, and whack again. Then once more. The balls are starting low, then getting stood straight up in the gale. I'm a wedge from the pin now—can barely see it in the dark—so I take out a seven iron, and try to kill it. It rises up, falls straight down, and settles by the pin. I walk up, striding like Finn MacCool, and sink the putt."

"Is he a golfer?" the Aged P asks reasonably.

"Not exactly."

What I don't mention is that, although wet and tired and cold, I had never felt better or more excited playing golf. I merely whisper to my family, "Irish golf, isn't it a grand thing altogether?"

My wife gets the gag, knows the answer, and she says,

"'Tis."

From the Veranda

Chapter XVII

The Mysterious Mr. Jones

*The Man Behind the Masters Was
Many Things, Including an Enigma*

The Backswing:

*This is one of those one-thing-leads-to-another stories. The New York Times
columnist Dave Anderson found the little mystery novel mentioned herein and wrote
about it. That led to Travel + Leisure Golf asking me to review it. I did so, and doing
so got me thinking about the mysteries within the mystery. So I wound up doing this
second look at Bobby Jones and Mike Veron for Attaché. This one ran in April 2001.*

When I was a kid, summers would inevitably involve balls to
be batted, swatted, caught, or kicked, and books to be read.
What downtime I took from sports, I spent reading (and yes, that
was the order of priority). I can recall passing Tolkiens back and forth
with my brother one teenage summer, hopping daily flights from
Massachusetts to Middle Earth. Junk like *The Babe Ruth Story* stood
alongside Hemingway and Fitzgerald on my vacation reading shelf.
And there was always an Agatha Christie or two, maybe a Georges
Simenon, a Ngaio Marsh, or a Dorothy L. Sayers.

My mother was the big-time mystery buff, and she handed down
the habit by leaving her 25-cent paperbacks lying around. The first
Christie I read was *The Murder of Roger Ackroyd,* and I was hooked

instantly. I became an immense fan of Hercule Poirot, Miss Marple, and that husband-wife team. What were their names? Dick and Jane? Nick and Nora? Tommy and Tuppence? Something.

There were hardly any sports mysteries out there—or none that I stumbled upon—but if there had been, I would have been one ecstatic little camper. Had *The Greatest Player Who Never Lived* been available when I was a boy, it might have made its way onto my All-Time Summer Reading Top Ten list, up there among *The Great Gatsby, White Fang, Ten Little Indians, The Catcher in the Rye* (not then available during the school year), *Fahrenheit 451,* and *Bobby Orr: My Game.*

As it is, *The Greatest Player Who Never Lived* was published only last year, which is when I came upon it. It's a fanciful little mystery by a fellow named J. Michael Veron. It concerns Beau Stedman, a golfing protégée of the great Bobby Jones, the storied but very real golf champion who is still, Tiger's efforts notwithstanding, the only person to win his sport's Grand Slam (Jones did it in 1930). As you golfer-readers know, Jones was co-founder of the Masters tournament at the Augusta National Golf Course in Georgia, a layout he co-designed with Alister MacKenzie and which opened in 1931. Anyway, this Beau Stedman, having been accused of murder, goes on the lam—and takes his golf game with him. With Jones serving as his behind-the-scenes promoter and matchmaker, Stedman, wearing aliases if not false mustaches, is able to post match-play wins over Francis Ouimet, Tommy Armour, Gene Sarazen, Walter Hagen, Jimmy Demaret, and others. Who ever suspected that Arnold Palmer turned pro because of an encounter with career amateur Beau Stedman? Who, before the publication of *The Greatest Player Who Never Lived,* that is.

Now, when I was a boy I never dreamed that I might just call up an author—Tolkien, Christie, Salinger, whomever—and discuss their books with them. But now I'm an adult, more or less, and I know all about 555-1212. There was something at the heart of Veron's book that intrigued me, and I thought I'd ask him about it.

Like any good sleuth, I followed a trail. It said on the cover that the book had been published by Sleeping Bear Press of Chelsea, Michigan, so I called out there. They told me that first-time novelist Mike Veron was in fact a lawyer, a partner at Scofield, Gerard, Veron, Singletary & Pohorelsky in Lake Charles, Louisiana. "Hmmmm," I said to myself. That made sense. That, in fact, was what I was interested in: the lawyer angle.

I called down to S, G, V, S & P, and the very pleasant barrister/author got on the line. It turned out that this Veron, 49, had degrees not from fancy-pants writing programs but from a couple of pretty fair law schools, Tulane and Harvard. He was indeed, first and very much foremost, a lawyer, having recently won a $51 million verdict in a soil contamination class action suit against Shell Oil, one of the largest jury awards in Louisiana history. "If that award stands up," he said, "well, I'll tell you, you have to sell a lot of books to make that kind of money."

Veron-the-lawyer's alter ego, Veron-the-author, was, like Beau Stedman's several aliases, born of the mother named Necessity. While in Baton Rouge to gather a deposition, Veron-the-lawyer was killing time in his hotel room when he came up with a notion that he simply couldn't shake until he had disgorged it. The way to do that was to write it—or, rather, dictate it to Marilyn Haile, his secretary at the firm. Ms. Haile eventually helped her boss understand the intricacies of word-processing software, and Veron-the-lawyer was on his way to being Veron-the-author.

The notion that had caused Veron sleeplessness in Baton Rouge was the very issue I was wondering about: Bobby Jones's law career. Veron's flight of fancy was that there were some long-buried files in Jones's old law office, and these files held the key to a golf mystery greater than how to stay dry on Augusta's 12th with the Sunday pin placement. What if Jones found himself personally involved not only in a young champion's career but in a murder case? This was Veron's notion.

How, Mr. Veron, did you come up with an idea like that? "Well, of course, I knew Bobby Jones had been a real lawyer," he said. "And

I had been a law clerk like the Charley Hunter character in the book. So I thought: What if you found these files and tried to solve this case years later? After that, the book had a life of it's own—it just sort of came out."

(As a brief aside: In the book, the Veron stand-in character, Hunter, is saddled with a 10-handicap, but is invested one day with the spirit of Jones, or perhaps Stedman, and shoots a lights-out 69 at Augusta National. Veron takes you through the magical round hole by hole, and that part of the book is a real treat. It would make for great reading this month, as you wait for the Masters broadcast to start on CBS.)

I thanked Mike Veron for his time and hung up the phone. I quickly realized my detective work was not done. I hadn't really learned any more about Bobby Jones as a lawyer than I had known before—only that he *was* a lawyer, as well as a great golfer.

I went back to the books, nonfiction this time.

Robert Tyre Jones, Jr., was a golfer, lawyer and others things, and in this, the month of his hallowed tournament, it is good to recall him. He was born in Atlanta on St. Patrick's Day, 1902, to a lawyer and his wife. His dad had been a star baseball player at the University of Georgia, and that game was Bobby's first love, too. By age nine, however, he had given himself wholly to golf. He was a prodigy of Tigeresque stupendousness. At age 10, he shot 90; at 11, he shot 80; at 12, he shot 70. At 14, he won a men's tournament, and got to the third round of the U.S. Amateur. At 21, he won the U.S. Open.

He was wondrous, but there was a snag. The gods, having granted him all the talent in the world (he never needed nor took a lesson), saddled him with a temperament ill suited for the game. So nervous would he get during a tournament, he couldn't keep down food beyond dry toast and tea. He had a terrible temper as a junior player, and many observers agreed with British pro George Duncan who opined that, because of a lack of control, "Jones will never be a champion." The 1921 U.S. Open champion, Jim Barnes, begged to differ: "Never mind that club throwing and the beatings he's taking. Defeat will make him great. He's not satisfied now with a pretty good shot. He has to be perfect. That's the way a good artist must feel."

Barnes was right about the artistry and prescient about Jones's ultimate triumph. In 1924, Jones decided the only way to stop from going mad was to inflict upon himself a new mindset: He determined to play for pars and come what may. He promptly won the U.S. Amateur and "the seven lean years" of Jones's career yielded to seven years of plenty. He would eventually win 13 major tournaments including, in 1930 at age 28, the game's slam: the British Amateur, the British Open, and the same titles on this side of the pond. Before he was 30, he would announce his retirement from golf, never having found a way to play without suffering unbearable stress.

If 1924 was the year of epiphany, it is surely not coincidental that his maturation on the links was twinned with his marriage to high school sweetheart, Mary Malone. Jones, though forever plagued by anxiety, is remembered today as a paragon of sportsmanship. That the erstwhile hothead won such a reputation is testament to how dramatic his transformation was, and to Mary Malone's influence.

Bobby Jones got sick: in 1947, he developed a spinal ailment that required surgery in 1948 and again in 1950. He went from a cane to a wheelchair. Wrote Herbert Warren Wind: "As a young man he was able to stand up to just about the best that life can offer, which isn't easy, and later he stood up with equal grace to just about the worst." Jones saw his last Masters in 1967 and died in 1971 at 69 years old.

He once said, "First come my wife and children. Next comes my profession—the law. Finally, and never a life in itself, comes golf."

This was still vexing me, this law thing. I knew about Mary Malone now, and certainly the golf. But the books I scanned were of scant help in re lawyering.

Torts and testaments were not how Jones, who died a wealthy man, made his biggest bucks. Shilling for Spalding and making instructional films and books built the larger part of his fortune—all the reference works agreed on this. Some books and encyclopedia entries said that, in fact, Jones never even practiced the law. Others said that, after getting bachelor's and master's degrees in engineering at Georgia Tech, then a second bachelor's at Harvard and a law degree from Emory, Jones joined his father's Atlanta firm in 1928. And they left it at that.

I called Mike Veron back. "I forgot to ask last time," I said. "What about Jones as a lawyer? Your book got me all curious about that. What's the deal?"

"I'm not really sure," the mystery writer said mysteriously. "I don't know what kind of law he practiced, or really much at all about it."

"David Owens in his good book on the Masters barely mentioned it," I said.

"The bios I looked at had next to nothing," Veron agreed. "I was able to learn only that Jones was serious about the law and worked at it as his full-time job."

"Why?" I asked simply, dimly, dumbly. "Why did he do that?"

"Well," said Veron, "Everyone knows that he stayed an amateur his whole career. Some seem to think that's strange, but in his day the concept of a career gentleman amateur golfer was still very strong. Professional golfers were, through lack of education or privilege, obliged to be professionals. Prize money was small, and they made a meager living. Anyone with a good family background or an education, such as Jones, found little to attract him in pro golf. It would demean him to turn pro.

"Besides, Jones, with his reputation, made much more in endorsements than a 'professional' made playing golf.

"I want to emphasize, though: Being a lawyer wasn't entirely image with Jones. He was serious about it, and worked at it some years in his father's firm. In the cold months when the 'pros' were down in Florida working at club jobs, Jones was in the law office."

This points to one of the more remarkable aspects of the remarkable Bobby Jones story: He played the game like a lawyer—Wednesday evenings, weekend mornings, no spring training—yet became the best in the world. "Exactly right," said Veron. "He hung up his clubs all winter long. Even after he became prominent nationally, he played about as much as I play." And Veron, though himself a multitalented fellow with a handicap of two, is no Bobby Jones.

Jones will figure prominently, again, in Veron's second golf mystery, *The Greatest Course That Never Was*. The novel (Broadway, 2002) concerns a heretofore-unknown—not even rumored—second layout at Augusta National. In the book, Jones is portrayed as quite a lawyer. Maybe he was in life, too. It's still a mystery.

Chapter XVIII

The Journey of Harry Bane

A Schoolboy Finds Playing with a Rare Cancer Is Par for the Course

The Backswing:

I spent my college years in the early 1970s at Dartmouth, and during that time came to know the school's sports information director, Jack DeGange. Jack and I have stayed in touch through the years, and he put me onto this story. I published this account in September 2003 as an open letter of sorts to my alma mater's admissions office. Well, Harry Bane wound up instead at Middlebury College—where he made all conference as a golfer his first year out.

It's September and back-to-school time, so let's tell a schoolboy's tale. It's about a lad now entering his senior year at Pingree School in Massachusetts, a fine fellow by the name of Harry Bane. He is fiercely eager now, if not so much to get back to the books (which he's not bad at), then certainly to the first tee. He has been denied that opportunity often enough in the past decade, and so he's fairly champing at the bit as he embarks upon the autumn golf campaign as captain of the Pingree team.

But let's not start with now, let's start at the beginning. Let's travel back to a much earlier school year.

It's 14 years ago. Harry is only four, and he is happily participating in a nursery school outing to Marblehead, just up Massachusetts's

North Shore from the family home in Swampscott. "I remember vividly being on this little merry-go-round," says Harry. "I jumped off it, and nailed my leg on a swing set. My teacher looks down and sees this huge bump on my leg. She figures I got it from whacking the swing set. So do I. My parents take me to Jim Higgins, who's our—what do you call it? the regular doctor?—yeah, he's our general practitioner. He isn't quite sure about it, and sends us to another doctor. 'Should be nothing,' he says. Another doctor. 'Should be nothing.' Another doctor. 'Should be nothing.' A specialist finally says, there's a one-in-a-million chance, but . . .

"And it turned out to be the one-in-a-million."

Actually, it was a one-in-a-billion chance. There have been, in world history, between 200 and 250 diagnosed cases of adamantinoma, Harry's being one of them. Adamantinoma is what's called a "benign-acting" cancer—not a good thing, certainly, but not the worst possible scenario. The cells in a benign-acting disease are low-level malignant but usually do not spread. In Harry's case, though chemotherapy was unnecessary, the cancer was slowly and surely eating away at the tibia in his lower right leg. There would be surgeries in the boy's future, and who knew what else.

Harry had advantages in fighting his disease. The three principal ones, even above the expert medical care at Boston's Dana-Farber Cancer Institute and the Rubin Institute for Advanced Orthopedics at Sinai Hospital in Baltimore, were his own remarkable disposition and the strength of his parents. Rich and Tami Bane resolved early that they would never show their nervousness in front of their son or his younger sister, Haley, although they realized the boy might one day lose his leg, and stood a very remote chance of having his cancer metastasize to his lungs or elsewhere. Harry, it seems, took a clue from their compassionate stoicism, and determined his life goals were, (A), to be as healthy as possible and, (B), to be as normal as possible. He was a boy who liked to play and so, darn it, he would play. He was a kid with a sense of humor, and he would keep that bright smile resolutely in place. "Yes, of course, you have your ups and downs," he says. "You get really, really high when you're on the recovery train. And there are the down points when the doctors have to sit you down and say, 'Another six months in the cast.' But if you're living with something like this, well, you just deal with it. There's nothing else to do but deal with it and move forward."

Before we turn to Harry as an athlete, which needs to be the subject matter in a golf column, let us briefly outline some of the things he has dealt with as Harry the patient. On November 21, 1993, when he was seven, doctors removed nearly five inches of bone from his tibia and replaced it with bone from a cadaver. On July 2, 1996, they replaced his fibula, the smaller part of two bones in the lower leg, with a metal plate. On October 4 of that same year, they grafted bone from Harry's hip onto his tibia to replace a cancer regrowth, which was removed, and on September 15, 1999, a similar operation was performed for the same reason. On December 18, 2000, they attached to his lower leg an external Ilazarov fixator, a leg-straightening device that was stabilized by 17 pins inserted along the tibia. "Right now, my leg looks great," Harry jokes, looking down. "Of course it has all these scars, and the holes from the pins."

As you might imagine, each medical procedure sent Harry to the sidelines—to the dugout, bench, or clubhouse—for a substantial period. And other setbacks were to come. But we'll get to all that, after we briefly sketch the career of the other Harry Bane: Harry the athlete, not Harry the patient.

"I wasn't going to let my leg keep me from playing," Harry says, "I just wasn't going to let that happen." His parents supported this thinking. When Harry had his first surgery at age seven, the doctors told them the boy might never be able to do sports again. Tami and Rich replied, "This kid's going to be your poster boy."

Lest you assume, because you are reading the *Attaché* "golf column," that Harry Bane chose golf because the relative slowness of our beloved pastime made golf the only sport available to someone in his condition, please consider that his other two games are baseball and basketball. He starred as a Little Leaguer, and at age 11 led

Swampscott to the state finals, missing a trip to the Little League World Series in Pennsylvania by one game. He was a feisty point guard for the St. John's Catholic Youth Organization basketball team, and made the town's traveling team.

And, yes, he was a golf phenom. The son of one of New England's top 30 women's amateur golfers and a dad who plays to a six, Harry had birdies in his genes, and lots of available instruction. He won his first junior club championship at Kernwood Country Club in Salem in 1998 and retained the title through 2001. The next year, he moved up to the adult division and reached the finals, losing 3-and-2 in a close 36-hole match. He registered five top five finishes and one win in six New England Professional Golfers' Association (NEPGA) events in the summer of 2001, and has starred at Pingree since his freshman year in 2000, when he was 5-0 before getting injured and having another surgery.

That's the thing: the setbacks, so far, have always been just over the next horizon. Harry picks himself up, dusts himself off, gets back in the game—then life knocks him back down.

And then Harry picks himself up again.

"There was one summer, I couldn't enter tournaments because I wasn't healthy enough to carry my own bag," he says. "Stuff like that is tough, and I couldn't wait until I could carry my bag again." When he arrived at Pingree in the fall of 2000, he had what was, essentially, a broken leg, and was wearing his metal fixator. But he didn't want favors and, more, "I didn't want to be the 'crippled kid,' so I went out with the broken leg to try to make the team and didn't mention anything to the coach. I did well enough, and asked the coach after seven holes if we were done. I was pretty sore. I came home that afternoon and my mom was happy that I'd done well, then asked if I had taken a cart. I said no, and she was . . . well, she called the coach and told him what was up." Pingree's coach lobbied the league to allow Harry the use of a cart, which was granted. Harry has taken a ride only when necessary, and much prefers to walk. "My parents have told me they'll help me get a cart, and I've thought about it," says Harry. "But the kids would say, 'He won because he had a cart.' I don't want that and, besides, if I'm healthy, I want to be normal like everybody else."

Harry's sophomore year at Pingree was sensational: 11–3, a scoring average of 37.2 for nine holes, Eastern Independent League All Star, third-place finish in the EIL championship. Then came hoops and soon would come baseball. "Three days before the first baseball game, I was playing basketball and I made a steal, planted my leg, and went in for a lay-up. The leg snapped in half. It was a huge mess, as you might imagine. I went into surgery that night and was in a cast till June 15. So much for that baseball season." At the time, Harry was simply growing too fast for his diseased leg, and all of the building, straightening, lengthening, and snapping was a consequence. But, goodness, could this kid bounce back. In July 2002, only a month out of the cast, he was part of Team USA, a junior squad playing a series of Ryder Cup-style matches on storied Scottish courses: St. Andrews, Gleneagles, Eyemouth, Gullane. "That was the best trip of my life," Harry says. "But about halfway through, I took off my brace and noticed a bubble starting to form on the top of my leg. My mom had come along for the trip, and we decided to wait till we got back home to deal with it. Honestly, it was the best trip of my life, and . . . "

Back in the States, the infection went away, then returned, and Harry and Tami spent New Year's Eve in Maryland enduring yet another surgery. The spring 2003 baseball season was another washout.

Now, according to Harry, "They say I'm one hundred percent healthy." He says it like a boy who has heard people say a lot of things, some of which have come true. He doesn't get angry at the uncertainty; it's part of who he is. He moves forward.

Because of his singular history, Harry Bane has become a celebrity in certain circles. He has counseled other, younger kids with difficulties, and is happy to do so. He gave motivational talks this past summer. He has received acclaim and even awards for his strength of character. In Chicago a couple of years ago, he bonded with Arizona Diamondbacks star pitcher Randy Johnson, who was giving him a citation, and the two now have a standing date to play golf. He talks regularly with Casey Martin, the pro golfer who successfully challenged the PGA Tour's rules and was granted use of a cart because of the condition of his withered leg. "Casey's been an inspiration," says Harry. "No, we don't talk about our legs. When I'm talking with him, we talk about golf, life, whatever. That's one person I can talk to about something other than my leg."

Schoolboy Harry Bane is 6'2", 185 pounds, plays golf to a 1.4 index (meaning he's a 1 or 2 handicap), drives the ball 285 yards, has a deft short game, and, well, if he improves his putting from 10-feet-and-in, is a force to be reckoned with. He is healthy now, and hopes he is tomorrow. "I've learned that hoping is all you can do." He hopes to go to Dartmouth, his dad's school: "My SATs are solid. I'm a B-plus, which isn't really Dartmouth, but maybe with the golf and, well, the whole story . . ."

The whole story.

It's quite a story, and if Dartmouth becomes a chapter in it, then Dartmouth is fortunate. If Dartmouth passes, then some other institution will be fortunate.

Whoever gets to know Harry Bane is and will be fortunate.

Chapter XIX

Questing After the Holy Featherie

The Strange and Fevered World of Golf Collectibles

The Backswing:

Within golf, there are subset communities. There are, for instance, the Community of Golfers, we who play the game. There's the Fraternity of Golf Fans—those who follow the game on TV or in the sports pages. There are golf-literature devotees. There are golf-history nuts. There are the course baggers. There are associations of Donald Ross disciples. In August 1997, I ventured into the community of those who treasure golfiana. I should note: I returned unbitten by the bug, which has proved healthful for my marriage.

I gaze at the design touches in the corner of the bedroom and, just for a moment, it makes me melancholy. They're pretty enough, and I do like the aesthetic that's at play. There on the wall hangs the old Jack Kramer racquet (that seems the right way to spell it: archaically), its gut sprung, it's decals peeled, its wood bowed, its lamination cracked. And protruding from the toleware bucket are the clubs, their hickory shafts leading down to the dinged and still-dirty heads of what I know to be a six-iron, a seven, an eight, and a nine. I know this for a fact because I used to swing these very clubs. Not Francis Ouimet, not Bobby Jones. Me. When I was a kid, my mom bought me a pick-up set of clubs, and though the low irons were made of metal, the high ones were wood-stemmed and leather-gripped.

So, then, our little display: It is pleasing enough to the eye and heart. My wife thinks it's Ralphiesque. But to my mind and memory it says youth. Your youth, kid. Long, long ago, when sticks were made of *stick* and titanium, not to mention Tiger, wasn't even a gleam in golfdom's eye.

My self-centered mourn lasts, as mentioned, just for a moment. Then I start to appreciate the tools for what they also are: remembrances of tennis and golf when tennis and golf were games I came to love.

Ahhhh, now—that's better.

The ability that this . . . this *junk* has to conjure pure emotion is an uncanny attribute indeed; for sundry and I'm sure complex reasons, few things can warm the soul or coax a smile like sporting stuff from years long past. A tattered baseball card, a worn pigskin, a dog-chewed cap, an old mitt: These things taste, to some of us, like good, warm tea on a winter's night.

The recent news has been about the rise, then dip, then rise, and continued rise of baseball memorabilia. What did that famous Honus Wagner cigarette card go for last time 'round? A half mill? More? *My kingdom for a Honus!* And let's not talk about the McGwire auction.

More quietly (of course more quietly, for ours is the quietest of games), there has been increased activity in the golf-collectibles market as well. "The boom in golf collecting has been as big as the boom in the game itself," says Sarah Fabian-Baddiel, author of an authoritative book on collecting and proprietor of the Golfiana Gallery at Grays in the Mews antiques market in London. As Fabian-Baddiel notes in *Miller's Golf Memorabilia* (1994), "No golf artefact is too trivial to collect—from the most essential equipment, such as clubs and golf balls, to buttons with golfing motifs." There is value beyond the sentimental in old scorecards, spikes and spoons, mashies, mammoth niblicks and mustard pots, badges, baffies and bags, putters, posters and pencils, tees, trophies and goofy-looking Toby jugs (the kind my wife would heave at me, were I to bring one home). Sotheby's and Christie's are not above auctioning golfabilia these days, and the

Golf Collectors' Society, founded by two low-handicap "lovers of the Gayme" in Lafayette Hill, Pennsylvania, in 1970, has grown to a far-flung membership of 2,400. A guy from Finland belongs, and pays 50 dollars a year American for the privilege.

I wanted to learn more about golf collecting, so I went in search of these Golf Collectors. They took a bit of tracking. The Society doesn't really have a clubhouse; it's headquartered wherever the top dogs are headquartered—Lafayette Hill in one generation; Shawnee Mission, Kansas, in the next; and now Dayton, Ohio. There lives the current Society Administrator Karen Kuhl, wife of Society Newsletter Editor Tom Kuhl and daughter of society co-founding father Robert Kuntz. It was 27 years ago that Kuntz and his pal Joseph S.F. Murdoch put their John Hancocks to a charter that asserted in part, "The purpose, if indeed there need be a purpose, is to serve as a means of getting collectors together . . . To establish friendships between those who share common interests." They mailed their warm-and-fuzzy declaration of principles to 67 collectors throughout the world and heard back from 25 of them. A membership directory was begun, as were annual gatherings of the faithful. At each of these confabs, the members would repair after seminars to a local 18 for that year's Hickory Hacker Tournament, wherein contestants were encouraged to don plus-fours and swing their vintage clubs. The word of such fun doings was spread via the society's *Bulletin,* which became, eventually, a quarterly. Growth was unabated, and nowadays the newsletter runs to 20 or more pages per issue, and includes not only features—"A Case for American Clubs," "Golf Course Ghosts"—but book reviews, cartoons, announcements of upcoming auctions and regional meetings, "Collector Profiles" and dozens of classified ads— "wants Nicoll Recorder 1 iron and 5 (mashie iron); Burke (brass) Grand Prize putters G-2 and G-4; 1930 Walker Cup memorabilia"; "w/s adjustable irons, putters; pre-1940 toys, games; pre 1940 full/ empty golf boxes; Schoenhut toy clubs." Et cetera.

I asked Karen Kuhl if there was a Holy Grail of golf collecting, some kind of fairways-and-greens version of the Honus Wagner card. Kuhl didn't know about a Honus, but said that, yes, there were items especially coveted. "A very early featherie ball by a very good maker in very good condition would be a prize," she said. "If clubs are your interest, a very early eighteenth-century long-nosed club would be the thing. There are a lot of book collectors in our society, and the early, early Scottish books are quite sought-after." I told her I collected P. G. Wodehouse and had acquired all of his golf books in the effort. She said that was nice. (I've subsequently learned that my 75-year-old copy of *The Clicking of Cuthbert* (Herbert Jenkins, 1922) could easily fetch a hundred dollars. Yes, true, this is naught compared with the $30,000 you could reap for your copy of the first known golfing book, *The Goff: An Heroi-Comical Poem in Three Cantos* (by T. Mathison, 1743), or even the $2,500 you might get for a fine-condition copy of the limited first edition of *The Golf Book of East Lothian* by the Rev. John Kerr (T&A Constable, 1896). But, surely, it's *something*. And being by Wodehouse, it's *readable* to boot.)

Books, it turns out, are at the top of the leader board of valuable golf collectibles. Balls and sticks aren't far off the pace. When one considers that King James VI of Scotland appointed William Mayne as his Royal Clubmaker in 1603, and subsequently in 1608—now as James I of England—he asked James Melville to custom-make his golf balls, it becomes evident that there is a lot of equipment out there to collect. Until the mid-nineteenth century, the game was played with balls stuffed with feathers and five or six wooden clubs. Those leather-covered balls and those long-nosed clubs can fetch up to $10,000 apiece in today's market. (A marked ball made by Allan Robertson, a master of featheries from St. Andrews, Scotland, can command twice that princely price.) First-generation irons (made by British blacksmiths circa 1850) can cost more than $500, and a gutta percha ball painted red rather than white (for use in the snow!) can set you back nearly $5,000. But please realize: Nothing is not worth collecting. Corporate-logo golf balls are avidly sought by some, golf cigarette cards by others. There is a lot of golf-motif flatware out there, and don't forget those Toby jugs. Paintings by Thomas Hodge go for thousands, as do watercolors by Harry Rountree; *Saturday Evening Post* golf cover art goes for hundreds. A rare Snoopy Christmas ornament from the 1960s has quintupled in value.

I asked Karen Kuhl if there were good places to go for just a whiff of golfiana, without paying such freight. She said that yes, indeed, there were not just one or two Cooperstowns of golf, but several. St. Andrews is, of course, Mecca. But in North America, there are wonderful exhibits at the American Golf Hall of Fame at the Foxburg (Pennsylvania) Country Club; at the James River Country Club in Newport News, Virginia (a brassie used by Bobby Jones in all his national championship wins from 1925 through 1930 is on display); in the Ouimet Room of the Massachusetts Golf Association in Weston; at the United States Golf Association Golf House in Far Hills, New Jersey (8,000 books and artifacts); and at the Toronto Royal Canadian Golf Museum. The Ralph Miller Golf Library and Museum in City of Industry, California, a suburb of Los Angeles, has 6,000 golf books. At the PGA World Golf Hall of Fame in Palm Beach Gardens, Florida, Karen Bednarski is overseeing an upgrading that promises great things. "You could collect golf museums," I suggested, and Kuhl agreed that you could.

Or . . . golf courses, I started figuring. Why not take a trip to the Balsams in the White Mountains of New Hampshire and work south, playing nothing but Donald Ross layouts? Keep all your Trent Jones scorecards, and your Nicklauses. By personalizing your collecting in this way, you'll gain added value—sentimental value

Which, at the end of the day, is a value that, I will argue, is of great value indeed. For in learning about golf collecting and collectibles, I learned for a cert a couple of things about the clubs in my bedroom display. I learned the facts about them, yes: that they were probably made before or in the early 1930s (as by then high-carbon steel was giving the shaft to hickory sticks). So by the time mom paid her 50 cents for them, these clubs were already a quarter century old or even older. I also learned that they are undistinguished clubs in poor to fair condition and are worth, today, just about what mom paid for them—adjusting for inflation.

I learned, in short, that they were valueless . . . except to me. Because I alone remember the rotten places those clubs took me to—the ponds, the roughs, the out-of-bounds cow pastures. I alone remember heavy-dew mornings, setting out with those sticks, hoping for sevens in full anticipation of snowmen or worse. I alone remember coming to love the game, even as I played with those forlorn six-through-nine irons.

I learned something about myself. As a collector, I'm a duffer. I've never bid for the Honus Wagner card, not only because I don't have that kind of dough—which I don't, in spades—but also because I never saw the man play. There has to be memory in memorabilia for me, and when I gaze upon the corner display and recall that singularly lucky lofted eight iron when I was 10, maybe 11—struck at Trull Brook in Tewksbury, Massachusetts, on a mid-week morning—the one that cleared the branch and bounded onto the green, surprising the cup and, even more, me . . . That's when I figure I've already got collectibles enough.

Though in my travels I did see a pretty nifty Toby jug shaped like a golf bag. If I could get it by Luci . . .

Chapter XX

Nodding at Windmills

*Miniature Golf Is the Don Quixote
of Sports: Fun, Silly, Quirky, Goofy,
Entertaining, Beloved*

The Backswing:

Not long ago I returned home from work to learn that Wendy, our nanny, had taken the kids to a miniature golf course a few towns over. "How'd you like it, gang?!" After a few accusations of sibling cheating were leveled, the three of them declared that they had liked it fine. Wendy's helping us to raise them right.

When I looked into mini golf in 2000 for Attaché, *I found it to be such a maxi topic we had to split the piece and run it in over two months, August and September.*

Not long ago the fine British golfer Laura Davies observed, as she was not winning the Ladies Professional Golf Association event in Mobile, Alabama, that the Magnolia Grove greens resembled those of a miniature golf course. I, for one, didn't know how to take that. Did she mean the greens were fun and fascinating? That the greens provided no end of enjoyment? The greens were tricky? The greens were a little goofy? You could bounce the ball off their edges?

There were windmills?

I missed Laura's point entirely. I presented her testimony to a friend who is more knowledgeable than I in the perplexities of golf and he explained, "She didn't like the greens. She was quite undone by the greens."

Oh.

Now, I'll tell you: I just can't understand anyone saying a discouraging word about miniature golf. Miniature golf is an altogether charming and disarming pastime. It is a game that is nearly as rich in lore, legend, and style (if not substance) as the great game of golf (jumbo size) itself.

Allow me to prove my point.

Miniature golf was not invented at St. Andrews and, in fact, there is nothing royal nor ancient about it. As you might guess, it's an American game. It was born in Pinehurst, North Carolina, but was not the brainchild of Pinehurst's great man, Donald Ross. In 1916, one James Barber hired one Edward H. Wiswell to design a miniaturized golf course on the Barber estate, and the story goes that when Barber looked upon Wiswell's creation, he said not, "It is good," but, rather, "This'll do." The course, which had greens and grass bunkers but no windmills or waterwheels, was quickly dubbed Thistle Dhu.

Barber's links was a strictly personal folly, and so although real golf was public on the Scottish moors before it was private, miniature golf was private until it went public. In 1926, a couple of New Yorkers named Drake Delanoy and John N. Ledbetter built a miniature golf course on the roof of a skyscraper near Wall Street, hoping to catch the lunchtime trade (their progenitor layout would be followed by 150 other Delanoy/Ledbetter courses on 150 other NYC rooftops). And that same year at the Fairyland Inn in Tennessee, miniature golf as we know it—with humps and bumps, gnomes and elves, fairies, and other flights of fancy—came into being. Frieda Carter, who ran the inn with her husband Garnet, was an avid and imaginative designer; she had already fashioned 10 cottages at the 700-acre resort into "Mother Goose Village." When she built her whimsical golf course and gave it the suitable name Tom Thumb Golf, she started a craze, what Karal Ann Marling in *The Colossus of Roads* called "the very last of the goofy fads of the twenties" (University of Minnesota Press, 1984).

Now, quickly, let me file an aside under the heading Credit Where Due. Marling's has not been my primary resource for this account. If there can be such a thing as a seminal book about a silly trifle, then Abbeville Press's succinctly titled and lavishly illustrated 1986 volume, *Miniature Golf,* is it. John Margolies took the pictures and Nina Garfinkel and Maria Reidelbach wrote the narrative. Much of what I relate here I learned from Mmes. Garfinkel and Reidelbach, who stand collectively as the Gibbons of the rise, fall, and resurrection of miniature golf.

As to the fall: It was precipitous, and was brought on by various factors.

By the end of 1930, 30,000 courses, representing an investment of some $300,000,000 had been laid across the United States. (Many were of the trademarked Tom Thumb kind, and the Carters were millionaires.) Four million Americans were playing every day, and tangential effects of this boom were everywhere. Movie receipts dropped by a fourth, and the song "I've Gone Goofy Over Miniature Golf" climbed the charts. Even the United States Golf Association responded, declaring: "The Association considers Tom Thumb golf courses as coming within the rules of golf and governed by them. Any golfer accepting cash prizes violates his amateur status. Anybody giving lessons for pay becomes a professional." When the Caliente course opened in California, 45,000 fans lined up. When Mary Pickford's course opened, four lanes of cars stretched back a mile. "There is millions got a putter in their hand when they ought to have a shovel," said humorist Will Rogers. "Half of America is bent over. In two more generations, our children will grow upwards as far as the hips, then they will turn off at right angles and with their arms hanging down where we started from. Darwin was right."

Maybe so, but Rogers was wrong. Only one generation on, moss was growing on the mini-golf greens and the "Madness of 1930" was as dimly remembered as the Dow before the Crash.

What happened?

Well, first, the sideshow got showier, which might have been amusing in the short-term but didn't bode well for long-term vitality. Vaudevillians entertained at a Texas mini-golf marathon that lasted 39 hours. The Singer Midgets played a Tom Thumb course in Pasadena and drew a huge crowd. New obstacles went beyond loop-de-loops and crocodiles to include roulette wheels and dice. Unsavory stuff.

Mini-golf's foes cast it as the nefarious, nocturnal pursuit of pathetic addicts—obviously something that had to be shut down, a la saloons. What Garfinkel and Reidelbach colorfully call "Lilliput legislation" took the form of early-closing laws: 1 A.M. in some places, 11 P.M. in more puritanical precincts. The Tom Thumb Association fought the putt-putt temperance movement, but the drums were beating. In New York, the mob was linked to mini-golf, which leads you to wonder: Whose reputation was being sullied? (Would Tony Soprano be caught dead, so to speak, packing a putter?) Blue noses said blue laws should apply to Sunday mini-golfing, and suddenly Tom Thumb was tarred, feathered, and being driven out of every town in this great land. A sad end for a storybook character.

By the time the country was focused on World War II, miniature golf was a memory. By war's end, it was as dead as flagpole sitting and marathon dancing.

And then the baby boomers started bursting with babies, and what had always been golf's only true family pastime—no wives excluded, bring the kids, too!—was reborn.

If anything, the *nouvelle vogue* of mini-golf was even more family friendly, with funneled cups allowing Li'l Suzie to score an ace at the other end of the barrel. Each course was different than the last; there were no massive franchises this time around. There was no nuttiness, as attended mini-golf's first flourishing. Rather, there was a nice, wholesome, sun-dappled spread of pastel castles and dragons and hit-the-ball-in-the-clown's-nose-on-18-and-win-a-free-game throughout the land.

I grew up on this brand of mini-golf, never having known the previous one. I loved it to the point where, as a kid, I would choose an hour at the putt-putt over an hour at the driving range any day. My brother and I played early and often. We played in Hampton, New Hampshire, and on Cape Cod. We played in our backyard. One summer, we built a mini-golf course there, an occasionally cratered Huck Finn layout that held our attention for a whole half-week that August.

Who's to say we weren't budding Jim Bryans?

(And who is Jim Bryan?)

Jim Bryan is the Donald Ross—excuse me, the Frieda Carter—of postwar mini-golf. The president of Golf Projects of America, a firm in Arlington, Virgina, he has designed more than 150 colorful courses and is largely responsible for what's known as the Myrtle Beach Style in mini-golf. Bryan, in the business since 1953, builds fantastic, sophisticated courses that are, as he once told *Sports Illustrated,* "integrated, harmonized, unified. I want the flower beds the same shape as the lake, the lake the same shape as the hole and the hole the same shape as the course. The parts belong to the whole." We have come a long way since E. H. Wiswell sketched 18 holes around J. Barber's summer house.

Today, miniature golf—the industry, the institution, the game, the thing itself—is doing fine, enjoying a Baby Boomer's baby boom growth spurt, if not a frenzy like that of its earliest years. The Miniature Golf Association of America has more than 10,000 members now, who play on more than 2,000 courses. The MGAA stages national championships each year in Boca Raton, Florida. The winner goes on to the world championships but usually fares poorly. This is because miniature golf has gained exalted status abroad. In Japan and in Denmark, the game is more than just a game, and mini-golfers are considered true athletes, great sportsmen. They are paid to play. They are paid to shill products, and in the new millennium, can there be any greater proof of stature and esteem?

The closest thing America has to a pro circuit is the Putt-Putt tour, which is actually just a handful of events but which features purses with real money inside: $130,000, including $50,000 to the winner of the Professional Putters Association National Championship. As opposed to the MGAA events, which are held on a variety of courses, Putt-Putt golf is played on Putt-Putt layouts, which are as rigorously stylized as the cookie-cutter Tom Thumb courses ever were. Putt-Putt Golf Courses of America, based in Fayetteville, North Carolina, has a menu of 108 holes that it has deemed proper, and from these, a franchisee chooses 18 and builds a course.

Putt-Putt golf was born in 1954 and, like miniature golf itself, it has seen glory days (the 1970s, when Putt-Putt's championship was televised). And it has seen somber depths, particularly in the 1980s, when as Mike Brown, 1996 national champ who once won a Putt-Putt tournament by 14 strokes—the P-P near-equivalent of Tiger's performance in the centennial Open at Pebble—admitted in a *Maximum Golf* article, "It became uncool. It's still uncool, but in the '80s it was *totally* uncool."

I played a Putt-Putt course in Oklahoma once, and I was cool to the game. The putting surface was super smooth, but the stark, geometric designs of the holes, with hazard-blocks in the shape of triangles or rectangles, didn't inspire me. Yes, I could appreciate how you might improve at the game as you never could improve if windmills were involved. I could see how, with practice, a golfer might become skilled at Putt-Putt as at billiards, a pastime to which it has often been compared. But who had that kind of time to waste on miniature golf? I could waste that kind of time on real golf.

Putt-Putt, the MGAA, and the Jim Bryan mini-golf factory are only three modern phenomena in the expanding miniature golf universe. There are others, and you really never know what you're going to come across next. In 1993 in New York City, I played a course that existed in a netherworld between rec-room and art gallery when an exhibit called "Putt-Modernism" was mounted by the Artists Space gallery at the South Street Seaport. The kitschy course had heaps of attitude, and I got a kick out of putting toward a rotating rabbit covered in Cheez Doodles, then toward a big clown that looked just like Jesse Helms.

"Putt-Modernism" was a one-off, and after it trotted through Cleveland, New Orleans, Buffalo, and Salt Lake City, the exhibition dismounted. Grass-course mini-golf, however, is here to stay.

Real golf has ever been grass-course, of course, and interestingly, so was miniature golf: Freida's original Tom Thumb course in Tennessee was purely natural, save the elves and dwarves. Sooner rather than later, it became apparent to her that heavy traffic was death to the layout, and an artificial surface was substituted. Now, three-fourths of a century later, a return-to-the-grass-roots movement is afoot.

Most of the real-grass mini courses are real in another way too: They seek to approximate the big-course experience, demanding draws and fades, approaches and lags. There are no obstacles on these courses unless you consider humps, sand traps, and undulating greens to be obstacles. At the two grass courses in Kill Devil Hills on North Carolina's Outer Banks, a golfer never faces anything less than a par three, and often as high as a five, for a regulation go-round of 72 on each course. The grasses are Bermuda and rye, just like the many neighboring 7,000-yard layouts. Photographed from above, many grass-course courses could pass for real golf layouts as seen from the blimp. At ground level, they are fascinating—and fun.

Or at least that's what I felt after I played a couple of them. I returned from my experiences wondering: What would a big league golf-course architect think about these minimalist but extremely high concept designs? I decided to go back to Dr. Michael J. Hurdzan, author of the definitive *Golf Course Architecture: Design, Restoration and Construction* (Sleeping Bear Press, 1996) and past president of the American Society of Golf Course Architects [the same Michael Hurdzan we heard from in Chapter XII, "Laying Out the Layouts"]. Dr. Hurdzan was erudite, as always; well-informed, as always; respectful, as always. "First and foremost they are fun and good for golf," he said. "Anytime the industry can put a golf club in a person's hand, even a putter, it helps the game grow.

"Natural grass miniature golf courses are best suited to southern climates where more wear-resistant Bermuda grass, or overseed

Bermuda, can be used for the turf," he continued. "Cool-season grasses will work, but they have many more maintenance problems and a facility has to be prepared for a major pest problem. It will need a licensed pesticide application on staff or call, such as a golf-course superintendent. Otherwise, the turf could be wiped out overnight . . ."

Dr. Hurdzan, we're interested not so much in maintenance but in style and . . .

"The use of windmills and clowns is definitely on the decline, for they are not needed," he said, emphasizing that the new courses represent an entirely new challenge. "My son, who is a single-digit-handicap 18-year-old, enjoys playing a three-story-high miniature golf course at the mega-mall in Minneapolis, at a greens fee comparable to a 9-hole rate at some municipal golf courses." Hurdzan, who has designed a couple of artificial-turf mini-courses, said he would like to build a natural layout: "I would borrow the Tour 18 idea and build 18 holes that were reminiscent of famous golf holes like the postage-stamp Numbers Ten and Eleven from Augusta National, or Number Eighteen at TPC Sawgrass. With the right choice of holes it could be very interesting for golf addicts and lots of fun for kids or casual golfers who couldn't care less about those places, but would enjoy the design."

His is a course that I would like to play. But, for now, it exists only in his mind.

As I mentioned, I have played two other replica-real courses, and have enjoyed the experience. The first was a lush layout with wide fairways (stop laughing) at the stunning Atlantis resort on Nassau in the Bahamas. It was a Tom Fazio design, in fact, and was just like Atlantis itself: fantastic, over-the-top, approaching unbelievability.

The other was at Walt Disney World. This was not natural-grass, it was turf, but it had the bends in the fairways and the tricky greens and the sand. I now dwell on it because Disney World is, as you might imagine, the perfect place to wind up if you want to glimpse the past, present, and possible future of—well, of anything.

Disney World has three miniature golf courses. First I played Winter Summerland, which is brand new but centered around the old conceit: choose a leitmotif and stick with it. In this case, Disney senses that it is fun and ironic—and it is—to have Santa and the elves all over the lot in hot, sunny Florida. This is a sweet little course, directly descended from the original Tom Thumb idea. Play it and you'd swear you were five years old again, being enchanted by your first brush with miniature golf.

The Gardens Course at Fantasia Gardens, with dancing hippos, leaping fountains, marching broomsticks, music, interactive obstacles, and tee times until 11 P.M., is more sophisticated but still a classic, stunt-filled putt-putt course.

And then there's Fairways. It has a par of 62 and a length of 1,445 feet. I'll quickly take you through it:

After falling off devilish mounds into a left-side trap on Number One and taking a 6 on the 91-foot par three third, I realize the pars that the designers have ascribed are not frivolous. Okay: anyone can hit a ball 91 feet with a putter. But when the architects say, "take three swings," they mean it. Set yourself up with a smart tee shot, next find the green, and finally sink the thing. I par the par-four fourth, which is a dogleg left with bends and bumps.

The fifth is straight but a monster at 101 feet (a par 4). Did I say straight? Ha! They bury small pimples in these things that send your ball scurrying, and you take a five. On Number Six, I play the boulder and the ball comes back at me; I take a bogey 4. I slip between three protecting traps on Number Seven for a par three (I'm no longer trying for the green off the tee, even on par-threes). On Number Eight, I enjoy what I think is a great drive, splitting the boulders, but my ball rolls off the green toward me as if on the 12th at Augusta. It's a 60-foot par three and I take a four. I par Number Nine, a mini (61-foot) dogleg with waste areas around the green.

We make the turn: Number Ten is a large dogleg right with traps draped head to toe. I play the bend nicely and face only a lofted wedge (sort of), which I slide into the bunker. I putt directly across the domed green—Donald Ross mini-golf!—and go trap to trap en route to a six. Eleven proves there are no straight putts (a bogey five) and Twelve proves that, when water's in play, the hole can be easy if you stay dry (a birdie three). I par the par-three dogleg 13th by riding the spine of a humpbacked fairway, and birdie the par-three, multi-trapped 14th by driving an astonishing 72 feet to the green and sinking the putt. I bogey the 15th, 16th, and 17th—all par threes—but they're no-luck bogeys, and on the heels of my recent hot streak, I am feeling confident about my game. The finishing hole is the longest on the course, a punishing 103 feet, but I hit a beautiful drive between the rocks. It runs out of steam before falling off into the greenside traps: perfect. I've never had an eagle in my life and . . .

I still don't, after I lip my putt and tap in for a bird.

I finish exhilarated, as if I had just played golf. Which, I guess, I have.

So there it is, under one roof at Disney World, miniature golf yesterday, today, and tomorrow. Long may putt-putt prosper. May mini prove as immortal as Mickey and Minnie themselves.

Chapter XXI

The Eternal Handicap

Everything New Is Old Again for
Noblemen and Sandbaggers

The Backswing:

It's an irony of our sport that a brilliant device employed to make things fair and square—to make things nice—leads, when abused, to nothing but hard feelings, even sundered friendships. It's a second irony that the abusers are pumping up a number, when the ongoing goal of any athlete should be to lower it. Perhaps I should have called this one, which was published in May 2001, The Ironic Handicap.

If the way that you play your game has a handicap in football or foosball, baseball, basketball, boxing, bocce, hockey, handball, hunting, hurling, tennis, table tennis, paddle tennis, wrestling, rugby, roulette, swimming, sailing, squash, ski-jumping, bobsleigh, badminton, bridge, lacrosse, lawn-bowling, luge, checkers, Chinese checkers or chess, then you lose. If your game has a handicap in golf, you might win.

I love our game.

And so do you. And you have never really questioned where the handicap came from or by whom it was bestowed. (You're like me!) You just took it for granted and said, "thank you, thank you, thank you" as you prostrated yourself at the 19th hole, having won a fiver with a tap-in for a seven (which counted as a five) on the 18th. You kissed the unseen feet of the Golf God of the Handicap, the uber-shaman who came up with the notion of making things equal, of rendering life square. Yes, you kissed his feet.

I was wondering recently just who he was. After delving into it, I still couldn't suss him out. It appears there is no Albert Einstein or Thomas Edison of the handicap. Seems that a long-bygone forebear of Mikey MacMulligan came up with the handicap on some forlorn Scottish links on an unexceptional afternoon that is now lost in the mists of time. "Aye, laddie, an' if ye spot me a stroke on the incomin' side, then eye'll buy ye two drams, should ye beat me." I'm presuming Mikey's forebear drank free.

I surmise it is some anonymous gre', gre', gre', gre' grandpa of Mikey's because the United States Golf Association, which lays claim to the handicap in United States (and lays claim to whatever else it can), does not claim that it invented the handicap, only that it institutionalized it for Americans in 1912. So someone else must have come up with it, which surely bugs the USGA no end.

What started me thinking about the handicap was a report issued earlier this year by statisticians at the University of North Carolina at Chapel Hill (UNC) and published in the journal *Chance.* The Tar Heel numbers-crunchers claimed they had figured out why the USGA handicap system doesn't always work so well—why a preponderance of matches are won by the better player, no matter the stroke allowance. The researchers said that by analyzing scores of nearly 200 golfers, they had determined that bad players are less consistent than good players, and therefore their handicaps are less representative of how they'll play on a given day. The report got a lot of play in golf magazines and even in the *New York Times.* It was greeted as a revelation.

I read about it and said to myself, "No *kidding,* Sherlock. I could have told you that! I'll bet that's been known forever!"

I went to the books and, as expected, learned that the notion of handicapping as a flawed system is nothing new. Consider how similar to UNC's conclusions were these from a 1971 computer analysis of 200 *thousand* golfers done by a Boston University mathematics professor for *Golf Digest:* Because of duffer inconsistency, handicaps for poor players in two-ball (one-on-one) matches should be increased by 27 percent, in fourball matches (two against two) by 7 percent.

I went further back, much further back. I found an old—like really olde—article about the handicap written by the estimable Horace G. Hutchinson for inclusion in his 1890 volume entitled simply, succinctly, serenely, serendipitously, *Golf* (Longmans, Green). Mr. Hutchinson wrote, "One of the best features in the game of golf is the ease and accuracy with which players of very different calibers can be put upon an equality by the giving and receiving of odds." He went on to explain why golf was uniquely suited to handicapping, a summary that perfectly and blithely expressed the glory of the handicap: "Each man plays his own ball, without any interference from his antagonist; 2. The game is played by installments, so to speak; by holes, on each of which, if need be, a stroke may be given, and the result of which is not carried on to affect the score of the next hole."

He also wrote, shortly later, of the imperfectness of handicapping, a practice that proved "the paradox that there is nothing so misleading as facts, except figures. The man who receives a stroke a hole from a scratch player in match play will require probably somewhere about half as many more in score play. The reason is obvious. The better player is, almost always, by far more steady. It is very unlikely that he will exceed by more than one or two, at any hole in the round, the average fair number of strokes at which he might expect to do that hole. The inferior player, on the contrary, is equally unlikely to get through the round without exceeding his normal number at one or two holes by three, four, five or even more strokes."

So then: The bedrock of the North Carolina Illumination, now bolstered empirically, was laid 120 years ago. At least.

I was much entertained by Mr. Hutchinson's essay and would like to share with you a few more fillips from the early days of handicapping. Here's additional proof that everything new is very, very old:

In the 1970s and 1980s, the USGA continually tweaked its handicap system to account for not only yardage but slope, topography, rough, bunkers, size of greens, altitude, bar-carts, bird life—everything!—and issued course ratings that could then be used in a mathematical equation to find a player's "true" handicap for the mythical course of Perfect Flats, index 113 (the national average). Essentially: You'd get more or fewer strokes if you were playing Shinnecock Hills or Lower Crestfallen, depending on the index of that course, your personal handicap, and the index of your home club, all stirred together in a mathematical equation. Very scientific. Very helpful.

As it turns out, very ancient. Hutchinson recommended in 1880 that every club's handicap committee should include in its books "remarks on weather, disposition, and condition of the course, or what not," so as to better adjudge what handicaps should be allowed. In other words, figure in all conditions and fudge the numbers accordingly.

Everyone, from UNC wonks to USGA regulators, is always toying with little fixes for handicapping or whole new ways of handicapping. Fred Klein wrote in the *Wall Street Journal* in 1991 of one Thomas E. Brennan, a Michigan law school founder and president, who, in seeking an improved form of mediation for annual Father's Day matches with his three sons, invented RunningStrokes, a format under which a player gets one handicap stroke on a given hole for every stroke by which he or she was over par on the previous hole. You score five on a par four, you have a one-stroke handicap against your opponent on the following par three. As you might imagine, RunningStrokes applies only in match play, under the rules of which the player who has won a hole can concede a putt to the vanquished, thus preventing a savvy sandbagger from knocking the ball around the green, building up a bigger advantage for the next hole.

Well, I figured: If amateurs like Brennan were foozling with new handicap systems in 1991, imagine what they were doing back when Hutchinson was waggling a mashie, back when handicapping was a nascent notion. There must have been all sorts of schemes presenting themselves as the New Big Thing, or the Best System of Them All.

Sure enough. Hutchinson reported without prejudice that "less recognized means have occasionally been tried. A gentleman at St. Andrews once made a match to play level with a brother golfer who was a far stronger player than himself, on the understanding only that he should be allowed to say 'Booh!' as his opponent was about to strike the ball, thrice during the match. History goes on to relate how, making the most of this concession, he continually stole up behind his opponent (open-mouthed, menacing him, as it were, with a 'booh!') with such disconcerting effect, that the receiver of the three 'boohs!' won the match, actually without having used any of his 'boohs!' at all.

"On another occasion the same two gentlemen made a match on the following terms: that the stronger was to play with not less than eight clubs, and that the weaker was to have the advantage of naming, on each occasion, which of the eight the other was to use. Visions of compelling his opponent to take his driver on the stones and metal of the railway, and his iron niblick on the putting green, enchanted the brain of the recipient of these strange odds . . ."

I mentioned "sandbaggers" earlier, and for any gentle readers who are innocent of golf, I should explain: a sandbagger is one who would seek to inflate his handicap for future advantage by turning in only his worst scorecards, thus securing a larger allowance of strokes next time out. He is one of handicapping's "characters," a cast that includes the 19th Hole Handicapper (the antithesis of a sandbagger, he will fib to get his number low so that he can nonchalantly toss a single figure across the table in the saloon, eliciting a "wow") and the Honest One (who records only the truth, working assiduously to reduce his handicap even if there's a crucial Club Championship looming).

Were there such noblemen and rogues in Hutchinson's day?

Certainly you have caught the drift of this account and can chorus the answer: "Sure there were!"

Let's make that, "Sure . . . but." Hutchinson harbored a "hope" that "conscious fraud" was "very rare in competitions confined to amateurs." So perhaps nineteenth century Scotland had fewer cheats in cleats than twenty-first century America (and we are shocked, *shocked*). Nevertheless, H. G. wrote, "The despair of handicappers are those players who, from some paltry vanity or sort of delight at the satisfaction of seeing the scoring-card which has caused so much vexation floating in atoms down the breeze, habitually decline to record their score. Every instance of this immoral habit should be noted against them, together with every instance of their grumbling at their handicap, and a stroke deducted from their odds for each offence—at least, this is a useful menace to hold before their eyes. If put into literal execution, some pretty heavily handicapped gentlemen would soon find themselves in the position of scratch." And would, no doubt, feel hard done by.

Two points, then, in conclusion: Clearly nothing is new under the golfing sun, even on the serene fairways of the University of North Carolina at Chapel Hill. And, as the wise Mr. Hutchinson observed, "Taking one consideration with another, a handicapper's life is not a happy one."

True in his time. True in ours.

Chapter XXII

Fine Feathered Friends

Golf for the Avian Inclined

The Backswing:

Yes, of course: I was tempted to call this chapter "Seeking Birdies," but some things in life are just too easy. This story was suggested to me in 2001 by Cathy Wolf, a fine editor who was then at the United States Golf Association's now-late-and-lamented Golf Journal, which ran the piece that September. A footnote before proceeding: I would aver, based on nothing but our amiable conversations, that Ben Crenshaw must be one of the finest people in the game.

Ben Crenshaw was sizing up his approach to the 12th green during the Tournament Players Club tournament at Sawgrass when he spotted the osprey. "It was swooping along, and it had just caught its fish," Crenshaw says, the memory etched vividly. "And then here comes the bald eagle after him. That osprey, he had eyes in the back of his head. He was trying to get away but the eagle hit him. The osprey dropped the fish and the eagle swooped and caught if before it hit the water. The osprey flew off, the eagle swooped up. There were maybe forty of us there—players, caddies, fans. I'll never forget that day, we were all just stunned silent." Crenshaw, heart racing, considered a shorter club.

It was a life-list moment for any dedicated birder, and Crenshaw, as it happens, is as dedicated as they come, having fallen for birdies of all kinds as a young boy in Texas. "This state is just blessed, what with having two flyways," he says. "Spectacular birds all year long. I think I was nine years old when I started studying birds, buying little models and painting them. Then I got my guide on the birds of Texas. I had taken up golf just a bit earlier, at seven, and found the two were pretty compatible. I've been at them both ever since."

Crenshaw is something of a poster boy for a jock subgenus that might be called *niblickus avorem*: the golfer/birder. The golfer/birder loves his golf and loves his birding and treats those two affections just the same. He never goes to the course without the notion that this might be his lucky day, a string of pars in prospect or, perhaps, a phalarope in flight. He is very serious about his games, seeking out courses that are best for birds, keeping twin scorecards, one filled with all-too-common sticks and snowmen, the other with scarce species. To those who think that dividing one's concentration as one stalks the elusive par would prove a handicap, the golfer/birder answers, "Nonsense." Golf courses are, by and large, wet, wild, and wonderful. To go to a wet, wild, and wonderful place and *not* to bird is, in the estimation of the golfer/birder, the very definition of wasteful enterprise.

"Golf is a game played in nature, and by blocking out the sounds and sights of nature and turning golf into 'work'—well, then, where's the fun?" asks Ron Dodson, a golfer/birder who is president of Audubon International in New York (which, it should be quickly pointed out, is in no way affiliated with the National Audubon Society, a distinct environmental organization). "Golfing and birding at the same time is not difficult. In a typical four-hour round one spends more time between shots than actually taking shots. So I think if more golfers would stop thinking so much about their last divot and start looking around the course and enjoying the sights and sounds of nature, including birds, they would be better off for it."

Golfer/birders such as Dodson are, if not necessarily legion, at least semi-legion, and if not necessarily well organized, at least kind of organized. They converse with one another on the web about sightings. Via Google, for instance, you can monitor the species list at the Stanford Golf Course in California: "Sept. 16, 2000: Phil Kelly reports seeing wild turkeys on the 12th and 13th fairways, bringing the species count up to 75 . . . Nov. 1, 2000: Bill Kirk reports seeing an American bittern in a tree next to the 7th hole . . . Nov. 4, 2000: Rob Colwell reports three new species from his own golf course bird list. New additions to the list from Rob's report are the golden eagle, northern rough-winged swallow, and common merganser. With Rob's additions, the golf course species list moves to 79 . . . May 15, 2001: Bill Kirk along with his son John report seeing Forster's terns in flight over the golf course. Along with Bill's earlier contribution of the American bittern, this makes the Kirk family the reigning Kings of the Accidentals. (Accidentals are species spotted in locations far from their native habitats.)"

Golfer/birders even have their own competitions. "For the last several years Audubon International has hosted a North American Birdwatching Open," says Jean Mackay, Dodson's colleague at AI, where she is manager of educational services. "It's a friendly competition where the golf courses enrolled in our Cooperative Sanctuary Program see how many birds they see in a 24-hour period." This year, the Eagles Landing Golf Course, a 210-acre layout in Berlin, Maryland, which has given over about a third of its land to wildlife habitat, won the Open. Under AI's format—which, it is pleasant to report, is never Shotgun—Eagles Landing beat 71 other courses with 95 species identified. Twenty-nine of the courses identified more than 50 species each, and only 14 courses found fewer than 30. Mourning doves were sighted on all courses, but only one cited the clapper rail. (Besides the rail, six other federally Threatened or Endangered Species were seen, including the bald eagle, the sandhill crane, and the loggerhead shrike.) The top five courses were in Maryland, Louisiana, Illinois, West Virginia, and Michigan. The results of the Open confirm, if confirmation were needed, that golf courses are great places for birding, and that great-birding golf courses are everywhere.

Golf/birding, structured as it might seem when one visits the web or the Open, is not nearly as hallowed as golf itself, not least because, as Dodson points out, "Birding is not really an ancient activity. It's basically this century." It seems golf/birding is traceable in the United States to the 1920s. At that time, W. L. McAtee was contributing regular articles to the USGA's *Bulletin of the Green Section* on such topics as "Golf Courses as Bird Havens, and Their Improvement for This Purpose" and "Friendly Birds on the Golf Course." A brief excerpt from "Birds as an Adjunct to the Golf Course": "If added interest can be awakened in and added support given to the harboring of desirable birds on golf courses, the benefits to be derived therefrom should be far-reaching, affecting not only the greenkeeper [*sic*] and the golf club patron, but all who are in love with nature."

McAtee can be seen as the Henry David Thoreau of golf/birding, a pioneering naturalist ahead of his time. As with the bard of Walden, McAtee had few immediate followers. If anything, affairs for golfer/birders slumped throughout much of the twentieth century, reaching a nadir in the 1960s. For birds and wildlife generally, as Rachel Carson revealed in her 1962 classic *Silent Spring* (Houghton-Mifflin), various poisons in the post-war air and water made prospects dire indeed. And in golf, beyond its willful contribution of pesticides, there was a trend in new construction toward wide-open fairways—so called highway golf that allowed for faster traffic on the boomingly popular public courses. As Crenshaw points out, "It's an irony that the birder will be luckier the more trouble he's in. In the rough or even worse, that's where the birds are. They're in the woods, on the fringes of the course." It is suggested in passing that perhaps this is why Gentle Ben prospered so at the Masters, where Augusta's massive, welcoming fairways and lack of rough kept him safely away from his beloved birds and therefore free of distraction. Crenshaw considers a moment, then offers, "Maybe so, maybe so."

For all sorts of good reasons, contemporary designers have forsaken highway golf architecture and, together with the Clean

Water, Clean Air, and Endangered Species Acts, have spurred a golden era for the golfer/birder. Contours, varied terrain, naturalness, and water are prized in modern design, and this is good for birds. "In the last ten years or so there have been many courses built in which environmentally sensitive areas have been included in the design and the birds have flocked," says Bill Provan, who birds and golfs near his home in Napa, California. "Some golfers don't like these areas because if balls go in there, they can't retrieve them. But for guys like me, these new courses are heaven sent."

Before trodding forth, a pause at the turn with Provan. If Crenshaw is the Bobby Jones of golfer/birders, then Provan can be seen as the Bobby Jones of birder/golfers (*avis niblickus*). He has been golfing and birding with gusto for decades, and today his statistics include a handicap of 19 and a life list of birds that stands at 284, 14 of which he first espied on golf courses. Some of his best birding is done when he's officiating in local USGA events or simply spectating at a tournament. "I saw a Mississippi kite, which I'd never seen, at the U.S. Open in Tulsa earlier this year. It was feeding right amongst the golfers." Provan has anecdotage in his bag, and he has lore: "In Westchester, Tom Kite killed a purple martin with a short iron on a par 3 hole. To Tom's bad luck, the ball fell into the water. Cost him two strokes. Of course, it was worse for the bird." Provan can more readily recall a sensational birding moment on a golf course than he can a fine chip or sterling putt. "I was working a tournament out here once, and I went out at about 6 A.M. There was an American bittern in the middle of the fairway. Such a thing is very unusual—they're usually in the reeds, and when they are, they are very careful to disguise themselves. I'm watching this bittern, and he's right out in the open but senses me. I can see him hunching his wings like, trying to camouflage himself in the middle of the fairway. It was fun to watch.

"I like watching crows on golf courses. Crows are brilliant. They can tell a divot, and they'll turn over a divot to eat the insects underneath. That's a smart bird."

Provan never goes to the course without his binoculars; they are as important to him as his sand wedge. "Most of my playing partners are totally unaware of what's going on around them, but I hear all of it," he says. "And I'll tell you, when I take out my binoculars, the other guys always get excited and want to see." Provan is resolutely of the opinion that there is no such thing as a bad birding course. "A few are really superior," he says. "Almost any course in Florida with water on it will be spectacular. Seaside courses are great. Out here at Spyglass and Poppy Hills we get shorebirds and terns as well as the songbirds that are inland. Desert courses can be wonderful: entirely different species. And as I say, with all the new efforts toward naturalness, things are getting even better."

These efforts have often been coerced by local planning boards, environmental agencies, and state and federal laws. Other times, they have been more mildly encouraged by conservation groups, the most active of which with the golfing community is Audubon International. "Our USGA-sponsored Sanctuary program just celebrated its tenth anniversary," says Dodson. "Essentially, it's an environmental education program that is aimed at encouraging golf course managers, golfers, and golf officials to merge environmental stewardship with course management. The process to become a Certified Audubon Cooperative Sanctuary Course starts with a plan as to what they hope to accomplish in regard to water quality and quantity, wildlife and habitat management, pest management. Once their results are documented to Audubon's satisfaction, they're certified, and we help them promote their achievements. We think this is not only good for the environment, it's good for golf."

Birding and golfing, then: two of a feather? Flocking happily together? Birds and golfers, kin under the skin?

Not always. There have been several other sad bird/man encounters than Kite's, and there have been controversies. One extraordinary, pathos-charged incident that occurred years ago at the U.S. military base on Guam was caught on tape during the filming of a PBS documentary. A serviceman hooked a drive at the Naval installation's course. As he was walking up the fairway in anticipation of his second shot, an aptly named gooney bird, possessed of the mothering instinct, proceeded to nest on the ball. The golfer saw this happen, and when he reached his lie, where the bird was a-layin', he gently nudged the gooney with his club. Then he gave the ball a mighty whack. The confused and horrified albatross, now watching from the bleachers as a vicious stranger sent her newly adopted egg aloft, issued a squawk that could be heard in Hawaii.

Then there was the contretemps over CBS TV toying cavalierly with the hearts and minds of bird-lovers. Last summer, viewers who tuned in to the Buick Open from Flint, Michigan, were gently serenaded by a canyon wren. Later in the season, while watching the PGA Championship from Louisville, they heard the sweet song of the white-throated sparrow. Problem was, the wren is a stay-at-home westerner, and the sparrow summers far north of Kentucky. CBS 'fessed up to using new-agey recordings of birds to enhance its telecasts, while caring not a whit about matching a species with its proper range. Paul Green, executive director of the American Birding Association, likened the network's duplicity to "dropping in palm trees to decorate the Arctic Circle." He was not alone in his criticism, as bird watchers nationwide put CBS on notice that they would be listening—hard—come Masters time. In April, CBS's chastened producers behaved themselves. Ken Hollings, also an officer of the Birding Association, happily reported hearing a tufted titmouse, a Carolina wren, an eastern towhee, and some blue jays: "absolutely birds that would be on that golf course somewhere."

One golf/birding issue is of potentially more serious consequence than birds-on-tape soundtracks. As Mackay of Audubon International admits, "The major threat to birds on a golf course is exposure to pesticides. While many commonly used products may be safe for birds when used properly, others do pose risks—sometimes through direct exposure and sometimes through sublethal effects. I occasionally hear about poor management practices harming birds: a superintendent uses the wrong chemical or too much of a chemical to treat pond algae, a fish kill results, the next day a dead eagle or osprey is on the fairway."

Someone was bound to mention the deadly P-word, and Mackay finally delivers us at a complicated question: How can a sport that spreads about substances notoriously harmful to birds cast itself as an avian-friendly enterprise? Responses from golfers assume two tacks. First: We've learned much through the years, and the pesticide problem isn't nearly what it used to be. Second: The other guy's worse; the stuff in your garage is more damaging than the regulated chemicals that a golf course employs. "When I talk to our club superintendent about pesticides his comeback is, 'We use a lot fewer pesticides on our course than a homeowner uses on his lawn,'" says Provan. Adds Crenshaw, "The pesticide issue has been exhaustively studied by people in golf, and the golf-course business has done a tremendous job changing what its practices were thirty years ago. It's getting better—that's the bottom line."

Better, perhaps, but hardly perfect, emphasizes Donal C. O'Brien Jr., chairman of the board of the National Audubon Society. His is not, it should again be pointed out, Dodson and Mackay's Audubon organization. His is the one we usually think of as *the* Audubon Society, the one that has, after ad infinitum inquiries, felt compelled to issue a statement stressing, "The NAS is in no way connected with the 'Audubon Cooperative Sanctuary Program' . . . a product of Audubon International which is . . . a completely separate entity . . . On occasion, Audubon chapters work with local golf courses to help them adopt green practices, but no National Audubon entity has ever helped build a golf course and we never certify golf courses as sanctuaries. Frequently, our chapters protest the building of golf courses in environmentally sensitive areas."

Just so, says O'Brien during an interview. "Are golf courses good places for birds? To the extent that golf courses are open spaces for habitat, you might say yes. But to the extent that they're being poisoned by insecticides, then obviously no. I'm also chairman of the Council of Environmental Quality in Connecticut, and the number two concern of the council, behind open space, is insecticide use on golf courses, schoolyards, and people's backyards. A year ago the conservationists got up against the Trout Valley development plan in Weston, which was going to have all these homes around a course. The conservationists prevailed. If you're talking about a golf course with trophy homes around it, that's a no-brainer as far as I'm concerned. Don't do it.

"But even with the so-called natural courses, the situation is complicated. There are three kinds of bird habitat: nesting, migratory, and wintering. Golf courses might be fine for migratory and wintering, but when you put in a course, you often destroy nesting habitat. You're not going to preserve it by holding a little donut of reeds around a pond. You need large tracts of wetlands and undisturbed wild for nesting.

"Look, we're not anti-golf. I used to golf, and I can tell you: I'd rather have a golf course than a shopping center any day. But let's take this issue as an opportunity for people who are involved in golf to work more closely with conservationists to do things right."

Which is what the folks at the *other* Audubon say they are dedicated to doing. "Ron Dodson and his group are making things better for everyone—the birds and the golfers, both," says Ben Crenshaw.

Well, not quite for everyone. Not, for instance, for Frank Zarnowski.

Let's let Bil Gilbert, the esteemed naturalist and writer from Fairfield, Pennsylvania, tell this last tale—a tale that vividly points up the differences between a golfer and a golfer/birder and illustrates why the latter might be a superior, or at least more fortunate, fellow. "When I go out golfing, I like to watch the crows," says Gilbert, who is co-founder of the American Society of Crows and Ravens, which has grown to more than a thousand members in its two decades. "Where I live, we have about 60 courses in a 30-mile radius, and most of them have fine crows. I like to go to Piney Apple, a mountain course over in Wenksville. They have two ravens there who've grown so bold they've started grabbing balls that are still moving.

"Anyway," Gilbert continues, "a few years ago I introduced my friend Zarnowski, who teaches economics over at Mount St. Mary's, to golf. Well, I created a monster. Frank became a fanatic, playing four and five times a week, filing his cards on his computer, all that stuff. He played ferociously. For Frank, golf meant two things: playing often and playing fast and serious.

"We still played together, but I started to drive him crazy. I like watching things as I go 'round, watching for crows, taking my time. He was always fuming. 'C'mon, Bil! C'mon!'

"One day, we're playing at Piney and we're on the tee and I say as Frank's waggling, 'Slow down. I think there are crows in that tree.' Frank says, 'The hell with the crows!' Then he drives. The crows must have heard him because, sure enough, one of them comes down and moves his ball. Backwards. I'm thinking to myself, 'Look at that!' Frank, he's exploding. It made my round, and it ruined his."

That, finally, is the thing about golf/birding. No matter the number of bogeys, no matter the whiffs in the bunker, no matter the rub of the green . . . The golfer/birder never has a bad day.

Chapter XXIII

Playing Solitaire

Some Days It's Good to Go Out as a Onesome

The Backswing:

Do you ever play alone? I wondered, as I wrote this piece, how many folks do—and how many relish it as much as I do. I love to play with friends, of course, but if I'm at the course on a Sunday evening at 5:30, and see a teenager going out on Number One with his canvas bag, striving to stretch the weekend, I think to myself: Would that I were with him! But then, it wouldn't be quite so fine, for either of us.

In the way that November is a month of the heart and June is a month of the libido, February is a month of the soul. It is a time of introspection and inner flames; hearths and homes; book-reading and nook-cleaning. It is an intense month. It can be a lonely month. Some years, when it stretches itself to 29 days, it threatens to break us.

Sometimes in February, there is a thaw, a change in the literal weather and in the tonal climate of the month. This surprises us, and prompts us to throw ourselves impulsively into un-February things— into bright March-like rambles, or even blooming Aprilesque flights. We put on our spring jackets and venture out-of-doors. We pump up the tires and take a brisk bike ride. We hike in the woods. We golf.

I have golfed in February in Massachusetts, and it is a soul-stirring experience. This was back in the days when the spikes on my shoes were metal, and I remember changing back into my sneakers when the click-click-click of cleats on frozen ground told me that no purchase was available with the Footjoys. The shadows were long on the course as the sun was still traveling its winter, worm-burner pattern. The forest was thin, occasional pines in their fir coats adding a profound hunter green amid skeletal birches, maples, oaks. A few crows, no other birds. There was a sting in the hands when the ball was hit thin, and less flight time with even a well-struck shot. But, oh, that magnificent, laughably long roll when your drive landed on a bald, hardpan fairway.

The times I have played in February, save those on Florida vacations or Arizona business junkets, I have played alone. It's tough to scare up a game, on a nonce, in February. Having said that, I quickly add: This was a good thing. The February-ness of the situation only accentuated the solitariness of the enterprise and, at the end of the equation, produced a deep, introspective, darned-moving experience. Those rounds were unlike any I've played, and in memory rank among my favorites.

That's all I'm going to say about February golf, but I'd like to take a few more swings at solitary golf. I'm here to defend it as a pastime. Some days, it's good to play solitaire.

Make no mistake, the act of playing alone does need defense. The great golf writer and sometime novelist John Updike put the standard opinion succinctly when he wrote, in his essay entitled "The Camaraderie of Golf," "Solitary golf is barren fun . . . Golf is a game of the mind and soul as much as of the muscles and, without companionship, as pointless as a one-man philosophical symposium." Though I agree with the sagacious middle-handicapper from Beverly Farms on most things—that bit about mind and soul, for instance—I part company over playing alone. I think the license to trod forth solo, whacking Titleists while waxing poetic, rhapsodic, or indeed philosophic, is one of the true and unique charms of our sport. Tennis against a backboard is a mundane and monotonous thing; its value is strictly as a means to improve your stroke. And you can't catch your own passes or shag your own flies. But a golfing onesome is just as valid as a foursome, because it's all about the player and the course, anyway. A solitary go-round, properly approached—approached with the care you reserve for that 160-yard six-iron draw from light rough to the tiered green, pin back—can be as sublime a sporting experience as the 4:10, last-of-the-day ski run through glades on the western slope, the February sunset turning the mountains to flame, warming you in its fire.

As I say: properly approached. I have, over time, established rules for my golfing solitaire. Used to be, I was either haphazard or impatient when playing alone. I remember those rounds as unsatisfactory, moth-eaten affairs. I would hurry a shot if the green was clear, shank it; drop a second ball, skull it; drop a third, scalf it; drop a fourth . . . I wasn't paying attention to what I was doing. It wasn't that my mind was elsewhere—on the deer browsing just beyond the sand trap, say, or on the heron strafing the water hazard—but that my mind was nowhere. I was, in those moments, the very quintessence of scatterbrained, and that's no state to be in when you're wielding a golf club. After a round of six-score swipes, most of them poor, I would trudge toward the car park reflecting that the day's golf hadn't been worth the time or the money.

Then, one day, I went out upon the college course in Hanover, New Hampshire. It was a grey afternoon in early spring, and the club was only just opened for the season. There was no traffic ahead as I teed the ball on One, a dead-ahead par four. I sidearmed a four iron to the center of the fairway; it landed a middling distance out. I took a desultory practice swing with my seven iron, then swung easy but nevertheless hit a slight pull. Providence was a bank to the left of the green. The ball smacked into the summit, surveyed the scene, thought things over and then, hesitantly, trepidly, decided to go for a slide. Slowly at first, then faster—*wheeeee!*—then slower again, it scooted to the green and curled to the cup. It stopped there, and I had a tap-in birdie. I chipped in from the fringe on the par-three second and decided, against any previous habit in solo golf, to keep score. Had I not built a snowman on the par-five 18th, I would have broken 85 on the shortish, hilly course. That's a good score, for me.

The round probably took me 2 hours, 15 minutes, but I remember it as being thoroughly unhurried. The next time I played solo, I again kept a card, and again enjoyed myself. I reengineered my approach to solo golf as rigorously as David Leadbetter would reengineer . . . well, everything about my game. I laid down rules (or, rather, began following the rules): no mulligans, no rolling the ball over, five minutes search for a lost ball (and then add the penalty stroke), pull the pin for putts. I decided that if I wanted to play two or three shots in sequence to a target 60 yards away, I would do it on the range. In fact, I sometimes put in a loosening-up range session before a solo round, something I had never done in my impetuous youth. It's perfectly okay for the touring pros to drop balls and take extra swings during their Tuesday and Wednesday practice rounds; they're figuring out the course, they're doing their jobs. And also, they get to play every day. I get to play infrequently, and so when I'm going 18, the session should, I figure, represent a real 18-hole experience.

There came another turn in my travels as a golfing loner. I was in Ireland on a magazine assignment. Yes, I'll rub it in: My assignment was to play golf. This day, back in the early 1980s, I was to play the links at Lahinch, and by the time I arrived in that wonderful town on the coast of Clare, it was getting late in the day. I realized I couldn't play a proper round, yet I had to develop an impression of the famous course before moving on to Ballybunion the next morning. I checked in, changed my shoes, proceeded to the first tee, and threw a short drive into the fairway—quite like that opening salvo in Hanover.

I didn't scurry but I didn't tarry, and I didn't keep score. I don't think I played well or poorly that day. What I do remember is what I needed to remember: that whimsical blind par three (the green was on the other side of a hill; a stone atop the hill gave you your direction), gorse as high as an elephant's eye, a pot bunker deep as Beckett, casual sand on the holes closest to the beach, par-fours that meandered through hay-colored hills, a white-capped sea, those sheep on the course, a flat-capped villager out for a stroll on the back nine with his hound, the whistling wind, applicable verse from Yeats's *The Stolen Child* (sorry, I've forgotten it), a sunset behind the Aran Islands, good stout. As you might surmise, it was one of my most sublime afternoons of golf.

But I was left without a score and without any impression of my shotmaking. I couldn't recall a single swing. Was this golf?

It was, and that's when I refined my approach to solo golf a second and final time. Ever since that day, I have gone forth alone in two very distinct ways, with two very different intentions.

- **With Card**—Play by the Rules of Golf

  Keep meticulous score, as if there's a Nassau riding. Head-down golf. At least one practice swing per shot. Mark all putts beyond two feet; no not-obvious gimmes. Think like a golfer, think about golf. Stalk rare birdies.

  I have played rewarding with-card rounds throughout the Northeast, in the Southwestern desert, in California, Florida and, perhaps interestingly, on Mainland China (at night, under lights).

- **Without Card**—Play by the Rules of Golf

  With exceptions (let lost balls go without a search; leave the pin in if preferred). Drink it all in. Head-up golf. Practice swings as necessary. No need to mark putts. Don't start hurrying. Three-footers are good. Think like Thoreau, were he a golfer. Stalk rare birdies.

I have played rewarding without-card rounds in Scotland, on the San Juan Islands of Washington State, in Yellowknife in Canada's Northwest Territories, on a public course a mile from my house in glorious autumn, and on the Gold Coast of Queensland, Australia.

Once, the two styles of solitaire blended in a single round, and this happened recently. Last November, I was playing at the marvelous, welcoming Cranberry Valley course in Harwich on Cape Cod, Massachusetts. I teed off at 1:45, thinking nothing of it, and played as if to score for about two hours. At that point, I was finishing up on the 14th and the sun was lining up its final putt of the day. I checked the map on my card. If I skipped the 15th and 16th, out-and-back par fours, I could walk through yonder pines, play the par-three 17th and, then, the home hole, a par five. I put the card away for the day and set out on this revised itinerary.

My long-ago self reared its ugly head on the short hole and I swept through a half dozen lousy shots to get to the 18th. In that tee box, I bent to put in my tee, then straightened. There, just above the treetops, was rising the most massive, most orange harvest moon I had ever seen. You don't often have to clear your eyes before swinging, but I needed to. My blood rushing from the sheer beauty of the place and moment, I duck-hooked a drive to the ladies tee. I walked to the shot with my head in the sky, that glorious moon a-risin'. It was getting truly dark. I looked at the far away dogleg and said, what the heck. I pulled out my seven wood and shot toward the pines that defined the curve. The ball sailed up and over. Miraculously, even in the gloaming, I found that shot on the other side. It had landed in light rough. I chipped on and two-putted, having pulled the pin. I turned and stood on the green for five full minutes, looking at the moon.

Were I scoring, that was par. But by then, I wasn't scoring.

Chapter XXIV

Chi Chi's Kids

In Clearwater, Florida,
Golf Is Changing Children's Lives—
Maybe Even Saving Them

The Backswing:

I'd like to hide some specifics in this story if I may. It was written a few years ago, and I can tell you that it was true at the time, and is true today; I've checked, and Chi Chi's school is still doing very good works. But I'm going to change the names of the people in the family that is most closely in focus here, as well as those of a couple of other folks. Why? Because I can't find them all to update this account, and because theirs were lives in the balance; there's no way to know if things turned out well or poorly. They might not want to be reminded of this hopeful time. But please trust me: This was true at the time—just as true as the names are false—and it remains true today.

The pretty, new name of the development off Drew Street is Jasmine Courts, but once you're inside it, the new name hides nothing. There are bunkerlike, low-slung brick buildings tight on either side of roads that are begging for repair; there is broken glass; there are unkempt yards, graffiti, trashed cars, kids just hanging out. This place earned its reputation when it was known as Conden Gardens—the South Bronx of Clearwater, Florida. The name change hasn't changed much.

Now, stick with us. This is a golf story. Promise.

Inside Unit XYZ in the early evening, life, if not altogether better, is certainly cleaner. Efforts have been made at decoration; an old couch in the living room has been carefully covered. There is a quotient of domesticity in XYZ that is unusual for Jasmine Courts. A girl named Mary Grace, who will be five tomorrow, bounds from the small kitchen where she was eating her supper. She greets her older sister and brother, Caroline, 14, and Jack, 12, who have returned from their day and, just now, shrugged off their backpacks. It's evident that Mary Grace is particularly close to her brother, with whom she snuggles on the couch.

"Take your shoes off," says Jack. "Shoes off on the couch." Mary Grace burrows in tighter, ignoring her brother.

Make that, her half-brother. Caroline and Jack are, like their mother, Lucille Smith, white. Mary Grace's father was black and the girl looks black, a fact that causes no end of difficulty for this family in Jasmine Courts. Most other kids in the development are one minority or another, but there aren't a lot of mixed families, and this one suffers ridicule and worse. Mary Grace gets chased into the house constantly. Just last week, the windows of the Smiths' van were shattered by thrown golf balls, and now cardboard is taped over cracks.

"Golf balls!" says Lucille as she sits in a decrepit chair, talking about her hard life and her good kids. "Can you believe it—golf balls!"

She's making an ironic point, for golf looms as a very large and very positive force in this family on the verge. "Without the golf," Lucille says, "I don't know where my kids would be."

The Smith family's misfortune started in Colorado when Caroline and Jack's dad was still present in their lives. "These kids don't have contact with their fathers per se," says Lucille, tears coming to her eyes. "Their fathers have not been there for them. I don't know if I want to mention this but, well, in Colorado when Caroline was five, Jack just two, we ended up in a spouse-abuse shelter. These kids lived in a shelter there, and then another house that we were living in here in Florida, just when I started nursing school, the house got condemned, and we landed in a homeless shelter." She sighs, and wipes a tear. She looks at Caroline. "What these kids have been through. Now we're here, subsidized housing, and this is not the safest environment. I see a lot of violence and abuse here. I've had to call the police many times. I want to get into nursing and get out of here as soon as I can. I need to get my kids into a safe, reliable environment.

"Really, I look back, I don't know what I would have done without Chi Chi's. It has been the backbone of this family."

Jack and Caroline, clearly fine children, listen as their mother talks. There's no rolling of eyes, no groaning, no "Mom, please, *don't.*"

Lucille pauses after mentioning Chi Chi's, and Jack takes the opportunity to whisper to Mary Grace, "Shoes off of the couch." Mary Grace smiles and continues to ignore him.

When we say Chi Chi's, we're speaking not of fast-food Mexican but of "the golf." And when we say "the golf" in relation to the troubled kids of Pinellas County, Florida, we're speaking of the Chi Chi Rodriguez Youth Foundation (CCRYF). This is an organization that helps all of us get past our suspicions regarding marquee sports stars and their foundations, which we have come to look askance at, thinking them just so many photo ops and tax shelters. Chi Chi's, which has won more humanitarian awards than you can swing a six iron at, reaches out and leads us from the depths of our cynicism, and it does more than that for needful kids. Visit Lucille Smith's home and you realize that something vital, real and necessary is going on. Chi Chi's lives in Unit XYZ.

The foundation's driving force was not, it turns out, Juan Chi Chi Rodriguez, nor was the epiphanic incident that led to the foundation's founding anything that happened to Chi Chi. Four decades ago in Scotland, a 13-year-old boy named Bill Hayes, an American whose father was stationed abroad, was sexually assaulted and thrown in a well by older boys. He screamed for help and was saved. Young Hayes, shaking with fear more than rage, did not commit himself to getting even but, rather, to how he might change the world one day: make it a better place for kids.

Hayes, as it happens, was a fine golfer—he'd mastered the game at Gleneagles during his dad's Scottish posting. Back in the States, Hayes became a club pro and was eying Q School when a neck injury quashed his Tour dreams. He enrolled at the University of Tampa to study education, paying for the degree by counseling at Clearwater's Pinellas County Juvenile Detention Center. In 1979, he took kids from the center to watch a practice round of a Senior Tour event in Largo. The children followed local favorite Chi Chi, and afterwards introduced themselves. Chi Chi, in turn, followed Hayes and company back to the center for a talk. At night's end, Chi Chi asked Hayes, "What can we do for these kids?" Hayes had an idea.

To some it seemed a cockamamie notion, a theory without rhyme or reason. Hayes felt that kids in distress, almost all of them poor, some of them wholly neglected, some with undeniable criminal tendencies, might be lifted up by golf, the country club game. Chi Chi, who grew up poor in Rio Piedras, Puerto Rico, and who, as an eight-year-old caddy, began finding his salvation by practicing with a tin can and a tree branch, bought into Hayes's belief that golf could bolster self-sufficiency and self-confidence, could foster honesty, and could be played by boys and girls who were tall or short, fat or skinny, smart or less so, fast or slow. It could give all these kids something to grab ahold of.

What grew from those theoretical seeds is nothing short of astonishing. The foundation was, for years, an after-school program at a pitch-and-putt course rented for a dollar from the county. Counselors and tutors helped with studies and behavior modification, while volunteers from the neighborhood helped with the golf. Chi Chi brought the spotlight and big-name co-sponsors like Jack Nicklaus— Chi Chi and Jack came up with the Chi Chi and the Bear benefit tournament—and the foundation's programs grew. Seven years ago, the CCRYF became a bona fide school when it started offering full-day classes in grade five and, a year later, grade six. "At first a lot of folks including some educators were pretty skeptical about that," says Susan Stackpole-Kelley, grant director of the foundation. "But with what's being accomplished here, the criticism's died down."

Rodriquez and Hayes have talked many times about the foundation and it should be noted: Chi Chi, for a celebrity, is remarkably hands-on, and doesn't speak about "my kids" only in sound bites. When he says, "The smiles on their faces are worth more to me than winning a golf tournament," you needn't add a grain of salt. But to appreciate what is really going on in Pinellas County, it is best to look past the figureheads to the daily experience of the children.

Which, this day, begins hard by the pro shop at the Chi Chi Rodriguez Golf Club, a fine public 18—par 69, two-tiered fairways, firm greens, water in play on 12 holes—off McMullen Booth Road. The school—the Modesta-Robbins Partnership School, the only public school in the world residing on a golf course—hides here in two classrooms in the main building. While senior citizens are limbering up their putting strokes on a practice green two hundred feet away, 38 kids are inside, taking swipes at the three R's.

In Miss Jenny's sixth-grade class, adolescents grouped in units of four or five are working with rulers, compasses, clay, and straw, building models of earthquake-safe buildings. Stackpole-Kelley—who does a little bit of everything at the foundation, including the coordination of school tours—explains various premises as she walks around the room. "All the kids in the school and in the after-school program are at-risk kids," she says. "The criteria we use to select them are poverty, trouble at school, trouble at home, broken homes, trouble with the law. Such kids are on the verge of dropping out altogether, and we try to help them refocus and establish new goals. Our curriculum is motivation-oriented. We serve about 450 inner city children between ages 5 and 17 each year.

"All of the kids in the school here were not achieving at their grade level, but now our students exceed the state and county averages on the Comprehensive Achievement Tests.

"Ours is a public school that has been constructed with privately generated dollars—82 percent of our funds come from greens fees! With a teacher and a teacher's assistant in each class, we're able to achieve a nine-and-a-half-to-one teacher-to-student ratio. This is a real school, but when the kids aren't reading Harry Potter or building these models, they're out on the laboratory—which is the golf course. They learn about animals and plants out there with the groundskeepers. They learn organic gardening from Mr. Jones, our horticulturist. They learn how to handle money by selling cookies and lemonade at the turn."

Stackpole-Kelley pauses at one table. "You look nice, Ellen," she says to a girl in a denim skirt and print blouse. "Very nice."

Having moved on, Stackpole-Kelley explains to her guest: "Those clothes are new. A few of the girls have been doing good work and I told them if they kept it up, I'd take them clothes shopping. The foundation tries to help in any way that might build self-esteem, and, besides, I love to shop!" She asks another girl to show her fingernails. "Great!" she says. "One more week." If the girl can control her chronic nail-biting until next Wednesday, Stackpole-Kelley will treat her to a manicure.

Mr. Barry's fifth-grade class next door has just finished a reading session and is available for free-form discussion about how life is different at this new school.

"When we get all out homework done for two weeks we get pizza."

"They teach us better manners."

"We get to read Tiger Woods books."

"The teachers help us with our future and stuff."

"On Fridays the people who did their homework get to go to Glen Oaks and play the whole course."

"Mr. Barry—we have a good teacher teaching us right now, Mr. Barry."

The students are willing to continue the conversation even though school is out in two minutes. Later, as he watches the buses roll, Barry, an "achievement-specialist" qualified to deal with special-needs children, explains why the kids are in no hurry to leave: "This is better than home for most of them. By being here or at the after-hours programs at the golf courses, they're not just in an empty house. They don't have to deal with any lack of support. We teach citizenship and treating others well, and, frankly, sometimes these things don't apply at home. They can't even survive at home, practicing such things.

"It's getting better with this class. The first few months in any dropout-prevention program, the kids just don't smile. Now they're starting to realize why they're here and that people are trying to help them."

The people include not only administrators and teachers but also volunteers. Over at The Lodge, which is the foundation's headquarters-cum-clubhouse at the big course, other kids are arriving by bus from schools throughout the county for afternoon programs. Volunteers, many of them retirees in the community, arrive as well, ready to tutor in math or science, help the kids bake cookies, take photographs, search for wildlife or improve their golf.

Caroline Smith is here, as she is most days after finishing her classes at Clearwater High, where she's in the ninth grade. She has been a Chi Chi's Kid (as all the full-day and afternoon students are called) for five years. "My karate instructor was a volunteer here and he recommended it to my mom," she says. "From the first, this was like a home away from home for me. My friends here are my family." Lucille Smith, who works during the day and takes her nursing courses at night at St. Petersburg Junior College, can focus on tasks at hand knowing Caroline and Jack are at the foundation.

Which is not to say the foundation is only a baby-sitter. Everything the kids are engaged in is geared to building self-esteem or changing their attitudes about learning and life itself. Caroline conducts a tour of The Lodge, which has rooms for play, study, ballet, photography, cooking, computer work, and quiet time—a room that is a retreat. She proudly shows the files of the girls' golf team members. "I'm pretty good at putting," she says. "They say I look okay on the driving range, but I have trouble sometimes off the tee." Once a Chi Chi's Kid has bought into the program—once he has shifted his vision, and believes in new possibilities—the dream becomes a golf scholarship to college.

Everyone at the foundation plays golf, nearly every day. At The Lodge, three volunteers are trying to round up the girls, whose tee time is in five minutes. The group makes it, barely, tumbling out of carts at the first tee and attacking with nary a practice swing. These 12-year-olds have nice, large, rounded swings that send balls 150 yards down the middle, or left and right into the straw. There is no temper displayed. There is keen concentration. There is politeness, and an appreciation for the teachers who are surprisingly firm in their instruction. You see what Hayes was getting at when he felt that golf could be what these kids need.

It was what Brian Moody needed. A painfully shy boy from a broken home, he arrived at Chi Chi's when he was five and never left. "I've basically been here fourteen years," he says quietly. "After school every day, and in the summers I'd be here from eight in the morning till dark." On this day, he has watched the girls tee off, and is now walking back to the pro shop where he works after attending freshman-year classes at the University of South Florida. Last year, Brian was a first-team All City golfer at Clearwater High and he plays to a one, but "I'm not playing in college because I have to work." He is asked, simply, what the foundation has meant to him. "Everything, I guess," he says. "Up until eighth grade I didn't know where I was headed, and then with the tutors in math I was getting all the way up to calculus." He was, meantime, mastering the sport and gaining confidence. In the Chi Chi's Kids yearbook from last year, there's an entire page of pictures of Brian—as a towhead with Chi Chi, as an adolescent receiving a trophy, as a proud young man posing in his high school prom tuxedo—and the words: "Congratulations Grad! It must happen *in* us before it can happen *to* us."

Dedication and inspiration are not foolproof panaceas, and as Caroline and Stackpole-Kelley head over to Glen Oaks to pick up Jack, Stackpole-Kelley says frankly: "We have disappointments. We have kids who can't break out, who give into peer pressure and go back to the streets. One of our girls was a success story: She got a scholarship to Talladega Junior College and the coach stood behind her as she had troubles there. Everyone was pulling for her. Well, she just got pregnant, and now we just don't know what's next." Caroline—and all the kids—see the realities daily and make their choices; there is no naïveté at the foundation.

Stackpole-Kelley pulls her beater of a convertible into the small parking lot of Glen Oaks, the par-three layout where Chi Chi's program was born. This is the course that Bill Hayes persuaded the city to hand over to the foundation for $1 a year. He soon thereafter left his job at the correctional institute to become a teacher at Clearwater Comprehensive School, and there he first recruited troubled kids for golf. He took them each day after school to Glen Oaks, dressed them in donated golf clothes, got them haircuts, got them tutors, taught them swing mechanics and sportsmanship, and watched them blossom.

Life's no different at Glen Oaks these days, only busier. Now the staff here numbers 30, and mentors include not only adults but alumni of the program; Caroline, even now, is volunteering to help in the weekly golf program for kids with mental retardation. A brick building near the practice green has been converted to Chi Chi's Flower Factory. ("I painted this one," says Caroline proudly, indicating an azalea on the flower shop's flagrantly colorful wall mural.) At the Flower Factory, Chi Chi's Kids raise vegetables and other plants, which are then sold retail or to other Clearwater nurseries, the proceeds to benefit the foundation and a local assisted-living program.

Jack Smith is at the course and has been for most of the afternoon. Like any freckle-faced younger brother, he blatantly ignores his sister in public, who ignores him in turn, schmoozing instead with her girlfriends.

229

It's a facade. If any kids in Clearwater know what they're up against—and have been for some time, and will be for a time to come—and realize that they have to support one another, that they simply must hang together, then these kids are Jack and Caroline Smith. "We play together," Jack admits. "We used to play together more before she joined the older kids at the big course. But we played together a lot here last year. I beat her, most days." Jack usually gets in nine holes after school, and shoots "a 30 or a 29," which is, of course, only two or three over par. His driving is his strength, he feels. His hero is David Duval. Jack hopes to be a pro golfer one day.

But whatever eventuates, golf has been good to him already: "On a regular day, if I'm down or something about school or home, I get here and they'll cheer me up. I know if I'm coming here, I'll get cheered up." As he gives a tour of Glen Oaks, he exhibits the same pride his sister displayed at the big course.

Then it's time to go home. Stackpole-Kelley drives the Smiths to Jasmine Courts and drops them off at Unit XYZ. Lucille has time for a chat, and then says farewell at the door. She is standing on an old welcome mat that does what it can to keep the living room carpet clean. The mat has crossed golf clubs on it, and it's a safe bet this is the only golf welcome mat in Jasmine Courts.

Lucille has her hand on Mary Grace's head. "She'll be a Chi Chi's Kid soon," she says. There are two ways of looking at that. It's too bad she'll need to be. But also, and more: She's a very lucky kid.

Chapter XXV

Ode to Golf

Eighteen Stanzas Make a Round

The Backswing:
As mentioned earlier in the book, when you're a monthly golf columnist, you eventually try out all the forms available to you: reportage, memoir, commentary, sketch, satire, profile, travelogue, even rehash. Then comes the off-season month when you reach back to the old college humor magazine staple: The Mock Epic Poem. Mea culpa, mea maxima culpa—I culpaed thusly in Attaché *in November 2002.*

Why we love the game is manifold,
    From Tiger's today to legends of old,
The Allan Robertsons and Morrises, Tom,
Mashing featheries hither and yon,
Setting standards, starting traditions
Of fairest play and swing precision
That descend to now, extend from here,
To a great beyond for our game so dear,
Where lie nothing but fairways and greens,
Where lie nothing but fairways and greens.

Was it Dutch *kolven*? French *jeu de mail*?
First landed in Scotland with a hail:
"Come try this game, come take this stick,
See yonder ball, come take a lick!"
"Och, aye, t'is fun!" the laddies cried
When prehistoric gowf they tried.
Espying their moors, envisaged there
Flags a-flutter o'er links so fair,
A sweep of nothing but fairways and greens,
A sweep of nothing but fairways and greens.

Balfing and scalfing to and fro,
To the courses Scotties go.
King James says, "Nae, gowf's a distraction!
Play nae more, or I take action!"
The Scots say, "Tosh! Y' leave us be!"
Mary (Queen of)—even she
Takes up the cudgel called a club,
She wields it like Beelzebub,
And bellows, "Nothing but fairways and greens!"
She bellows, "Nothing but fairways and greens!"

Why we love the game is manifold,
Not least, the lore and legend told
Since time 'memorial down to present,
Revolvin' 'round queen and peasant—
And pros—the early pros! They perfected the swing.
They hit from their toes. Old Tom was the thing!
Young Tom was e'en better, his ball flying true,
Finding nae heather nor watery blue,
Finding nae naught but fairways and greens,
Finding nae naught but fairways and greens.

ODE TO GOLF

Scot crossed the pond with stick and ball,
A rulebook, and a passion withal
About the game he'd come to cherish,
He sold it with a spicy relish.
The Yank forsook his tennis racquet
And took up golf, for in fact it
Was a game above most other.
Baseball and its pastime brother,
Football, lost to fairways and greens.
E'en football lost to fairways and greens.

Scotty Don Ross set out a-designin'
Course after course, and then refinin'
His doglegs and his crown-ed greens,
Heroic tees o'erlooking such scenes
Of pastoral splendor as Sport had nae known,
Blending art and athletics, setting a tone
Sublime in the wide open air: this was golf,
Our newest sweetheart, Maine to the Gulf.
Americans flocked to the fairways and greens,
Americans flocked to the fairways and greens.

One day at the Club young Francis Ouimet
Put on a show we would never forget.
He beat the great Vardon and the great Ray
At the game they'd invented over their way.
Ouimet won America's title that day,
And his countrymen's hearts with the grace of his play.
A romance bloomed into riotous craze
As Ouimet led his game to golden days.
For golf, it was nothing but fairways and greens,
For golf, it was nothing but fairways and greens.

Stars came out. The great Bobby Jones!
Master of masters, and make no bones
About it: He won the Grand Slam,
The big four of his day, and thank you ma'am:
All in a calendar year, to boot.
Taking naught from Tiger, the point is moot
As to whose Slam is better, Jones' or Woods'.
Bobby's was clean, and the proof's in the pudd.
Was he the best ever on fairways and greens?
Best ever to challenge the fairways and greens?

Well, I'm sure we shall never see
A poem as lovely as Sam Snead's
Swing, which was a thing of beauty pure,
An arc of triumph on the Tour,
Throughout the '30s, '40s, '50s. More
Was our shock when Slammin' Sam yelled "Fore!"
Out of bounds? Not a chance! Sammy's the man
T'will bounce off a tree if it possibly can.
For Sam hit nothing but fairways and greens,
For Sam hit nothing but fairways and greens.

They say that ours is a gentleman's game,
And that is true, though all the same,
There have been temper tantrums thrown.
And clubs, balls and epithets sown
Across the greensward and into the ponds,
And out-of-bounds onto neighboring lawns.
The cause of outburst is always the same—
The eternal comeuppance of our fickle game—
A lack of connection with fairways and greens,
A lack of communion with fairways and greens.

ODE TO GOLF

Ben Hogan himself would glower and steam.
When the going got rough, sometimes it would seem
He was 'bout to blow as high as the sky.
But he wouldn't, which can't be said for the guy
Named Bolt, who would horribly storm and thunder
When into the gorse his fade would blunder.
If Tommy was playing and not playing s'well,
His visage resembled the Hound of . . . well,
Tommy could empty the fairways and greens,
Post haste, fans hied from the fairways and greens.

But sportsmanship was the normal rule
Taught on Day One in Golfing School,
And was it e'er better taken to heart
Than by the lad whose career did start
With fit and rage, but whose Dad did say,
"Arnold, that isn't the way that we play."?
Young Palmer listened, and channeled his fury
Into a swing that led to a story:
An Army of fans marching up t'ward the greens.
Arnie's Army storming fairways and greens.

Before Tiger, t'was Walrus, and Bear—Oh my!
A golden one, lofting wedges high
Into the sky, whence settled on green,
And trickled back at a pace serene
To nestle by cup, perhaps to drop in—
Clunk!—a birdie, saying Nicklaus had been
There and gone, now prowling in search of
An eagle, the Urbird Ursa did love
To stalk amid the fairways and greens,
To stalk amid the fairways and greens.

Meanwhile up at the ladies' tees,
The Zaharias Babe brought par to its knees,
Then handed off to Whitworth and Wright,
And Bradley and Lopez and others who might
Have given the lads a run for their money
In a friendly Nassau at the club on a sunny
Sunday morning, if there were ladies' times
Before noon, let's say, or Monday at nine.
Not all is fair on the fairways and greens.
Not all is fair on the fairways and greens.

Yes, the gals weren't dealt square, nor were the blacks
Or other minorities, matter of fact.
But then in the '60s things started to change
And not only down at the public range.
Sifford broke through, Elder did too.
Peete was a third, and if that was too few,
The Tiger whose distance no layout could tame
Was preparing to give a new face to the game.
An upheaval awaited the fairways and greens,
A New Age was dawning on fairways and greens.

From Cal-i-forn-i-ay came the young master,
Lean and lithe, an astonishing blaster
Who drove like Daly, putted like Faxon,
Chipped like Phil, he had a knack on
The course as had never been seen.
The Bear predicted six jackets green
Would be worn one day by the kid named Woods.
Who's already proved he's truly the goods.
He might be the best on the fairways and greens,
Best ever—perhaps—on the fairways and greens.

And so we proceed in the new millennium
With solid-core balls and sticks titanium.
But not everybody is up-to-date.
Muirfield and Augusta are more than late
As regards our women, who can whack the ball,
But not on those courses till barriers fall.
As they should! say I. At Hootie I hoot:
"Open your doors, you stodgy old coot!
Let ladies onto your fairways and greens!
Let ladies onto your fairways and greens!"

Why we love our game is manifold,
From Tiger's today to legends of old,
From 6 A.M. shotguns to playing at sunset,
From real-dough wagers to a wee li'l fun bet,
From Sunday bags or a helpful caddy,
To happy mixed foursomes, lass and laddie
Trodding forth with a second couple,
Finding that golf turns nature supple,
Falling in love with the fairways and greens,
Falling in love on the fairways and greens.

So that's eighteen, let's have one more!
The 19th awaits, libations galore!
T'is yonder bar, where fibbers gather
And work themselves to a frightful lather
'Bout the sand save on Sixteen, the five on Four;
They divide up their loot as they tally the score.
They drain their glasses, then head for home,
Leaving the course to the dusk and gloam.
Fairwell till the morrow, dear fairways and greens,
Fairwell till the morrow, dear fairways and greens . . .

Afterword

At the 19th Hole

There are times when you get lucky in this life. One of those times, for me, came just about 25 years ago when I was playing the grand Dunluce Links Course at Royal Portrush, in the far north of Northern Ireland.

A quarter century later, I remember the rain—the feel and smell of it, the acute slant of it as it blew in off the ocean. But we were in town for only a day, and if we wanted to play Portrush, this was the chance. Needless to say, we played.

I've saved the scorecard. Apparently I survived Fred Daly's (the tight fourth hole) without undue scarring (a six), and White Rocks (the fifth, with its green high on the cliff) with something shy of a snowman (barely shy). Nevertheless, I do recall feeling battered by the time we reached the turn. There was recompense in the scenery, to be sure, what with the spectacular Giant's Causeway rocks stretching into the sea, and the broad sweep of this linksland where Vikings from Norway once battled the Irish of Dunluce on harsh days just such as this. That was undeniably inspiring, but I was one soggy and bedraggled puppy as I trudged from the ninth green.

Then I got lucky. There was a wee wood hut painted green, hard by the tenth tee. It had a corrugated roof and a corrugated old barman inside; he wore his oil-cloth coat buttoned up snug, for his hut was unheated, the only energy supplied by a gas lamp, his own good humor, and what was in the bottles. There were only bottles, no food or snacks. There were soft drinks and beers and gins and whisky—one whisky, Bushmills, from the famous distillery on the outskirts of town. "You'll want a Hot Irish today," the barman said with emphasis. We gave him no argument.

Into each glass, he poured an informal measure of Bushmills, a teaspoon of brown sugar and a short shot of hot water from a Thermos. He added cloves, stirred gently, and handed over the concoction.

It was a toddy of sorts, the kind of good, warm drink that lives at the intersection of Restorative and Medicinal. It did wonders for this boy's spirit, if not for his golf. I see here that I took a six at Number Fourteen, Calamity Corner, the 213-yard par three, and I must have picked up my ball on Number Fifteen, Purgatory, which I remember as Hell. But I also recall, and vividly, feeling very bold in that tenth tee box, spitting into the gale like an ancient chieftain, drawing forth my club like a mighty sword, taking no practice swing.

That was a good drink, that Hot Irish.

Now then, how lucky was I? This lucky: The "Tenth Hut" at Portrush is open only during competitions (which means every Saturday), and competitions are open only to club members. I was fortunate enough, back then, to be in the company of a member, who had me pose as a member. The short of it: I snuck on.

But you needn't travel to Northern Ireland to feel the magic medicine of a Hot Irish. Bushmills, once a rarity in the States, is now generally available. When the wind blows and the cold rain falls at your local links, guide your 19th Hole barman through the procedures above. See if you don't feel lucky indeed.

Fairways and greens, fair reader!

Me . . . I'm still away.

THE END